OUR FAITHFUL GOD

OUR FAITHFUL GOD:

ANSWERS TO PRAYER

COLLECTED AND EDITED

BY

JAMES H. SMITH,

Editor of "Pray and Trust."

SCRIPTURE TESTIMONY EDITION

WALKING TOGETHER PRESS
ESTES PARK · JENTA MANGORO

Published in 2024 by
Walking Together Press
Estes Park, Colorado USA
Jenta Mangoro, Jos, Plateau Nigeria
walkingtogether.press

ISBN: 978-1-961568-28-0

Cover design by D. Thaine Norris
Typeset in Adobe Garamond Pro by Peter Kurdor

1

ABOUT THE SCRIPTURE TESTIMONY EDITION

"**O**UR FAITHFUL God: Answers to Prayers" is a powerful and inspiring collection of testimonies that demonstrate the power of prayer in the lives of ordinary people. This nineteenth century classic, which is being republished for a new generation of readers, showcases the diverse ways in which God answers prayer and provides guidance, grace, and blessings both in everyday situations and in times of great need. From stories of unsaved loved ones finding salvation, to preachers receiving the strength and courage to share the gospel, to individuals witnessing the provision of basic needs and even Christmas presents for children, this book is a testament to the unwavering faithfulness and kindness of God.

Through these heartfelt accounts, we are reminded of the incredible ways in which God works in our lives and are encouraged to deepen our own prayer practices and relationship with the Divine. Whether you are seeking guidance, comfort, or simply a reminder of God's love and presence in your life, you'll find this book a timeless and invaluable companion.

Data science reveals trends and patterns in information. The *Scripture Testimony Index* is an extensive research project using artificial intelligence and data science to develop a New-Testament-driven subject index across a large body of missionary biographies and personal narratives. As the story enthusiasts at Walking Together Press study these books programmatically; beautiful, bright threads emerge—threads of prayer, provision, deliverance, specific leading, healing, transformation, revival, and miraculous conversion. The end result is an index of thousands of short story excerpts organized by subject and Bible verse that empirically demonstrate the truth of the Scriptures, and which is freely available on our website at walkingtogether.life. Another result of this research was the discovery of dozens of great books that are long out of print and in danger of being forgotten. The *Scripture Testimony Collection* is a set of such books that we enthusiastically recommend, to the degree that we are making the effort to republish them.

Walking Together Press has enhanced this classic title, *Our Faithful God: Answers to Prayer*, by identifying and marking ninety portions of the narrative that illustrate specific Biblical topics and verses. An extensive *Scripture Testimony Index* has also been added containing short summaries of how each Scriptural topic is illustrated, making locating specific stories easy. Furthermore, this title is one of many in the *Scripture Testimony Collection*.

INTRODUCTION.

THE FOLLOWING pages are a record of God's faithfulness to His promises. The Answers to Prayer have been gathered from reliable sources, and are well fitted to strengthen the faith of believers. If one of the answers were read each day it would give help in many a time of weakness, and lift the load from many a burdened heart. It would teach us how real is the life of faith, and would make the throne of grace a familiar place to us. Those who have held daily and hourly intercourse with the Lord have been the saintliest and most Christ-like of men. They have lived above the world and its ways, and have caught the pilgrim spirit which looks for a far brighter and better home than this. They have learned to be fervent in the holy art of supplication, for it is the importunate pleader who gains his case in the court of heaven. Half-hearted men who are indifferent whether they succeed or not come off poorly in that high place. The gifts or the prizes of grace are not given to the slothful or indolent. The mere dreaming or wishing for spiritual blessings does not bring them. If we are to succeed in the holy art of opening the treasuries of heaven and drawing out of their illimitable stores, we must throw our whole heart into the work, and set ourselves to our task as earnestly and as systematically as tradesmen or merchants push their temporal affairs. Whatever our theory may be as to the province and power of prayer, we know from observation and experience that it is the diligent, and they alone, who bear rule in spiritual matters. The men who prevail with God are those who ask and seek and knock, and who, when convinced that their requests are according to God's will and for His glory, never give in, but continue, if need be, year after year, in fervent supplication until the gates swing open, and they receive full measure to their petitions.

This importunity ever springs from a deep sense of our need. Unless we are conscious of our own inability, we will never become successful suppliants at the throne of grace. The proud, the self-satisfied, the self-righteous ones God knows afar off. They never get within the precincts of the holy place where He dispenses His rich spiritual blessings. They ask but it is either in a self-righteous way, or in a manner which has neither heart nor soul in it, and they are sent empty away. But when we have made the discovery of our own worthlessness and sinfulness, when we have tested our hearts and our conduct by the Word of God, when we have yielded our lives to Christ and allowed His Spirit to search us, and let His light flow into our souls and reveal to us what lies there; when we pass through such experiences, we are willing to take the lowly place of humility and contrition. Sitting there in our poverty of soul, we turn our eyes to Him who alone can enrich us, and begin to pray with a fervency begotten of a sense of our need.

Our temporal affairs and the every-day incidents of life should give us many an errand to the mercy-seat. Our affairs get tangled, and we are unable to unravel them, business complications arise, our domestic or personal concerns take unexpected turns, and to meet and deal with them we need a wisdom we do not have. We fall into mistakes from which a little foresight and prudence would have saved us; but these we do not have, and we begin to find that as was yesterday so will to-morrow be. We know there is One who can help us, and we remember the promise—"If any of you lack wisdom, let him ask of God, who giveth to all men liberally and upbraideth not, and it shall be given him." If wisdom to guide us in all our affairs can be had for the asking, why should we not plead the promise? If in a humble spirit we approach our God, confessing our ignorance and errors, our inability to plan or even to think aright, and urge the fulfilment of His promise to illumine our minds with heavenly wisdom, to guide us by His counsel, and to teach us the way in which we ought to go, He will hear and answer our petitions.

In our service for the Lord one of our greatest needs is heavenly wisdom. Without it our work becomes a piece of mere routine—a lifeless thing. There is no warmth, no fervour, no inspiration about it. Spiritual triumphs are not looked for, and unbelief has closed the door against any signal display of God's converting grace. But when we feel our own spiritual impotence and stand helpless before the task of winning souls and building them up in the faith, we turn to our God, for in no other have we any hope. The overwhelming need of God's Spirit, if we are to carry on God's work, sends us to our knees. A man can receive nothing except it be given him from heaven, and if the convicting power is ever to be felt in our meetings, it must come from above. It is not very difficult for some speakers to gather the people together, to rouse enthusiasm, and to produce a deep impression on an audience; but if men are to be saved, if hearts and lives are to be changed, we must wait upon God in earnest, importunate prayer. There is no other way. If we search into the lives of successful workers, and if we study great revival seasons, we shall find that it was in answer to prayer that the blessing came.

May the reading of these pages lead many to prove in their own experience how faithful God is to His promises. To Him be all the glory.

CONTENTS

I. PRAYER FOR TEMPORAL NEEDS

A CHRISTIAN WORKER'S TESTIMONY.

I.-*In and Out of Business.*

"FOR YEARS I engaged in visitation work at the jail, hospital, and penitentiary, as my business admitted; then my business failed through a divergence of the

SCRIPTURE TESTIMONY
God will provide for our daily needs
MATTHEW 6:11

course of trade, and nearly all my time was given to the Lord's work. We would have starved had not a gentleman handed me, through another, a monthly payment. I did not know, and never asked, the gentleman's name who acted thus generously; but after some time the allowance stopped through heavy losses sustained by him in business. What was I to do? Just go on as if the payments were to be continued. What! and not know certainly whence support for my family was to come? Yes, that was what I did. It was a new experience, but the promise of God had become so real to me, and "I simply trusted in His Word." In May we were almost in want, but one evening a letter was handed in containing an anonymous note, which said:

"Two friends, the one sitting in a prayer meeting, the other sitting in church, have become impressed by the Spirit of God that you are in

1

need, and therefore beg your acceptance of the enclosed two bills"—fifty dollars each.

Next day I met a man poorer than myself, and I gave him one of the bills, so satisfied was I that the Lord had sent them that I might have the privilege of helping him, and that the Lord would make it good to me. Then in the end of June a friend said to me, "You are run down; you must take a rest. Go to the salt water and recruit. I am authorised by a gentleman to tell you to go, and he will bear the expense." I said it was very kind, but my wife needed rest more than I. "She is to go with you; take any outgoing steamer visiting the North Atlantic coast, and rest in some village by the sea for a few weeks; here is money for expenses."

II.-An Elim Abroad.

But that was not all, for the first evening after landing on the rocky coast of Cape Breton, walking in the outskirts of the little town, we stood admiring a cottage. The lawn, trees, flowers, and plants reminded us of England. The door opened, and an old lady came out carrying a large bunch of roses. We, of course, walked on, but she overtook us, and looked so kindly at us, as much as to say, "I see you are strangers," that I spoke, and lo! we were friends for eternity, introduced in this informal way to each other, as it were, by the Lord Himself. We took a meal nearly every day with them. They drove us in their carriage and sailed us on the bay in their boat, and introduced us to other Christian families, so we look back upon our sojourn by the sea somewhat as the Israelites may have looked upon Elim with its fountains and its shade.

III. A Timely Legacy.

SCRIPTURE TESTIMONY
God provides exactly what is needed
2 CORINTHIANS 8:15 · PHILIPPIANS 4:19

Let me tell another instance of our Heavenly Father's thoughtful care:—Said my wife to me on one occasion, "Here are the bills for the winter's coal, the taxes, the bread, milk, and groceries for the last month; where is the money to come from to pay them?" I had to confess I did not know, but the Lord did, and I was leaning on Him. (Is. xxvi. 3, 4.) It was a crisis in the experience of faith, and drove me literally up into the mountain, time and again, after the example set in Mark i. 35; vi. 46; and Luke vi. 12, &c. One day a long letter came from a beloved brother in New York, saying:—"For some days I have been led to pray for your temporal circumstances; let me know how it fares with you." I at once wrote him an answer in the line of the 130th Psalm, and went into the city to post his letter, when I met a lawyer, who informed me a man to whom I had ministered the Gospel in the hospital had died, and by his will, after leaving a donation to the hospital, made me his legatee and executor— all he possessed was in the bank, and would be paid at once. I sang the last verse of Hymn 302 (Moody and Sankey), where the way-worn traveller is described as "shouting loud hosannas, deliverance has come!" This poor man, whom the Lord had made the channel of His bounty to me, I had buried the week before in our beautiful cemetery. It was a curious funeral; people, as they rushed along, intent on business, stopped a minute to look—a hearse, one carriage, and one occupant. He was a lonely man, without kith or kin in the wide world, and had come to our city to die of that terrible disease, cancer. For five months he was dying daily; and being reserved and reticent, no one had the least idea he was possessed of anything, still less of his feelings towards me. The little legacy just served to meet the bills my wife had mentioned, including the rent falling due—that, and nothing more; but that was all I asked for.

J. LOWSON.

BLIND AGGIE'S TESTIMONY.

We take the following from the Memoir of blind Aggie Graham, who died in 1889. A few years previous to her decease, Aggie's slippers had become worn out. One of them

SCRIPTURE TESTIMONY
God answers prayer
LUKE 18:7 · JOHN 15:7 · ACTS 12:5 · JAMES 5:15

was almost minus the sole, and the other had to be tied on the foot to keep it together and make it retain the semblance of a slipper. Her poor feet also had sad need of respectable covering as well as protection, for her stockings had long before seen their best days. When so reduced Agnes carried her need to God in a very definite manner. She was not left long to suffer from want. An English lady who was staying at the Crieff Hydropathic called to have a little talk. Visitors on knocking were usually invited at once to "Just come in, please." Before asking the present one to enter, Agnes seated herself on her chair, drew near a hassock, placed her feet on it, and carefully concealed them with her gown. During conversation, which became very interesting, Agnes forgot all about her disreputable-looking slippers, and having shifted her position on the chair, they came peeping out from beneath the gown. The lady, who was well acquainted with Agnes, quickly noticed them, and fairly caught her. It happened that the lady had a new pair of cloth boots which did not fit, and she was just considering what should be done with them. She thought they would do for the betrayed feet, and said she would send them, along with a pair of stockings. In thanking her benefactress, Agnes demurely said—"Weel, ye see, mem, the Lord kent a' aboot ma puir feet an' your ill-fittin' buits, an' jist sent you here tae fin' oot what tae dae wi' them, for I hed laid ma need o' a pair afore Him. Praise the dear Lord, and thank you kindly."

The night before the terrible Tay Bridge disaster, Agnes had accidentally burned the slippers she was then wearing, and had no money to replace them with new ones. It was winter, and the need therefore was urgent. A neighbour happening to look in on her just then discovered what had occurred, and said mockingly, "Ye'll seek anither pair frae the Lord, I daursay." "Ay will I," instantly returned Agnes, and she did. Shortly afterwards a parcel from Edinburgh, sent by a Crieff lady who was residing there temporarily, was handed in, and found to contain the very articles required and prayed for—a pair of comfortable slippers. The lady knew nothing of the burning accident. Agnes took care to let her jeering neighbour know how the Lord heard and answered prayer.

A few years before her decease she had a bad attack of an inflammatory nature, which created a burning thirst, and she thought a drink of buttermilk would give her relief. Not knowing where or how to get any she cast her need upon God, who has said, "Delight thyself in the Lord, and He shall give thee the desires of thine heart." A townswoman, who kept cows and made a little butter occasionally, had been recently converted. She had heard of the blind Christian woman; and while at the churn one day, she recollected having been told that this woman was partial to butter-milk, and resolved to send her girl along with a small quantity. On receiving the milk and a kind message, Agnes said—"Praise the dear Lord, it's th' vera thing I hae been praying for. Tell yer mither sae, ma dear, an' thank her and you for being sae kind." From that time Agnes had no lack so long as she desired butter-milk.

DEBTS PAID.

Prolonged ill-health is a trial to every one, but especially to the poor, for it brings many other troubles with it. Loss of work and privation often follow in its train: but the

SCRIPTURE TESTIMONY
God will provide for our daily needs
MATTHEW 6:11

Lord never leaves His people, and sends relief from many quarters in answer to their cry. A man who had worked hard to support himself and an invalid wife became very ill. Their money was soon exhausted, they had little food, and the rent was due. They were Christians, and turned to the Lord for help, pleading that He would not suffer them to want. Shortly afterwards the landlord came in, as they thought, to give them notice to leave the house, for they could not pay him the money, and had no immediate prospect of relief unless God sent it. But the man's heart was so touched by their distress that instead of demanding his rent he handed them five shillings, and some time after he again called and gave them other five shillings. Their hearts were greatly cheered by this token of the Lord's goodness, but their ill-health continued, and as wages were not coming in the money was soon done. Again they cried to God, and again He helped them. A friend mentioned their case to the grocer with whom they dealt; he said they would get whatever they required, and he cheerfully supplied them until health returned, and they were able to pay all their debts. It was a trying experience, but they can now look back with devout thankfulness, and praise Him who drew near in their time of trouble and glorified Himself in their deliverance.

ABUNDANCE OF RAIN.

In Ho-nan, China, a very marked answer to prayer,at a time when drought was threatening famine, produced a profound impression. The natives had exhausted their idolatrous resources, and challenged a native Christian. Mr Slimmon and the native went out to his village home on a burning day, and a meeting was commenced under a cloudless sky. The native brother visited the houses all round, and collected the people together, telling them that they were now going to see what the true God could do. A curious throng they were, and, Mr Slimmon having thoroughly secured their attention, became eager listeners to the preaching that preceded the prayer. After prayer, he was again speaking to them, when the clouds rapidly collected, and soon the people began to run away to escape a drenching, which our brethren, who had a long journey before them, were unable to do.—*China's Millions.*

THE DUST-BIN.

SCRIPTURE TESTIMONY
God communicating during prayer
ACTS 11:5 · ACTS 13:2-3

A friend lately related the following interesting answer to prayer. He said: "One morning, before rising from the breakfast table, a letter was handed me containing a subscription of two £1 notes for a Mission in which I am interested. I had just read the note, and laid it and the money on the table, when I was called away to another room, and without thinking further of the letter and its contents, I left the house for my work. Late the same evening it flashed across my mind that I had seen nothing of the missive since the time I laid it down. The house was searched and researched, but all to no purpose. There was One at least who knew just where it was, and to Him I carried my burden. Kneeling down in my own room, I asked the Lord to lead me to the discovery of the stray notes. True to His word, He directed my mind to the dust-bin, a considerable way from the house, and there, though it was covered with snow to a considerable depth, I began my search. First I found the envelope, then the letter, in another place one of the notes, and lastly, the second £1 note came to view. They had all been gathered up as waste paper in the morning, and thrown where they were found; but now, in answer to prayer, they were in my possession."

D. A.

COULD NOT GET REST.

An evangelist was at one time sorely in need of money. He spent his life in seeking to bring men to a knowledge of the truth, and it was his joy to preach the gospel of grace to lost sinners. He urged men to put their trust in the Lord, for He would never fail nor forsake them. The Lord, however, tries His servants, and sometimes calls upon them to practise what they preach. One morning the Evangelist's money was done, and there was not food in the house for his wife and family of six children. He could not beg, and he would rather starve than go into debt. He knew his Lord was rich, and could supply all his need. His promises to believers in times of trouble were many, and faith could now plead these, and wait patiently for their fulfilment. The day wore on, without appearance of help, but at eleven o'clock at night there was a knock at the door. It was opened, and a friend entered, who said he had been greatly troubled all day, and could not get rest until he should come and give them some money, and he handed them £2.

THE WIDOW'S STAY.

A woman in a country district was bereaved of her husband, and was left with a large family without means of support. She was a Chris-tian, and knew that the Lord was a

> SCRIPTURE TESTIMONY
>
> *God will provide for our daily needs*
>
> MATTHEW 6:11

very present help in trouble. She carried all her cares and sorrows to Him, and prayed for help and guidance. There was a vacancy in a school for a teacher which she thought she might fill, and so earn a livelihood for herself and family. To become eligible for the situation, she had to pass an examination in a city about fifty miles distant. She had only a few pence, and did not know how she could get there and back, and support herself while away from home. She did not wish to ask help, and her only hope was in God. She left her house with one of her young children in her arms and set out for the city. On the way she called at a shop, which was kept by a woman whom she knew, but who did not make any profession of religion whatever. They entered into conversation, and the woman astonished her by saying, "I was wondering if you would not be the better of a pound or two, for I have some lying by me which I am not using." The widow opened her purse and let the woman see threepence halfpenny—all the money that she had for her long journey. Her purse was soon well filled, and, with a heart full of gratitude to God who had in such a remarkable manner provided for her, she paid her fare and was soon in the city. She passed the examination, got the situation, and brought up her family respectably. She has had many trials of her faith since then, but she still lives to testify to the goodness of her God. He has been with her in all her troubles, and she delights to speak of His kindness to her.

THE FATHER OF THE FATHERLESS.

One Sabbath in the autumn of a recent year a poor widow lay dying. She had a family of five children, all under eleven years, and the struggle to keep them in food and clothes must have been a hard one, but now the feeble hands would not work any more, and the prospect was dark indeed. Who would befriend them, and where would they find a home? The widow knew her God; He had been her help in the past; He had never failed nor forsaken her, and she could commit her children to His care ere she passed away. Her minister was full of sympathy for the little ones; at the Sabbath afternoon service he prayed very earnestly for them, and asked the Lord to raise up friends for them in this time of need. The prayers of that dying mother and her minister were speedily answered. By the following Tuesday eight persons had offered to take the children into their homes and adopt them. They were given to the five who had first offered, are now members of happy homes, and some of them worship in the church where the prayer was offered which brought such a gracious answer.

The widow has sometimes to pass through much trouble and dark days, but the Lord knows how keen the trial is, and claims a special right to uphold her cause, and to watch over herself and her children. "A Father of the fatherless and a Judge of the widow is God in His holy habitation." That word of the Lord has been a tower of strength to many a fainting and well-nigh despairing soul.

D. M'L.

HOW THE SUPPER CAME.
I.

About eighty years ago there lived in the town of Alnwick, in Northumberland, a very good man, named John Brown. His worldly property consisted of a horse and cart, and he made his living by driving coals from the pit's mouth. Business became at one time so very bad that John's family was reduced to a state of utter want. His cottage stood on the edge of a wood, and consisted of but one apartment, so he used to make the wood his prayer-closet. On a particular evening he went out to pray to his Father in heaven for food for his children; but so much was he carried above all his earthly troubles, and so much did he enjoy communion with the Lord, that he was half-way home before it occurred to him that he had forgotten to pray for bread. He found his door on the latch, neither lire nor light in the room, but by the light of the moon he saw two large white packages on the table. On examination he found two baskets covered with white towels. In one there were two loaves, and in the other two joints of cooked meat. He was much astonished, and awoke his wife, who had fallen asleep with the children to keep them from crying. She could not tell him anything about the provisions. John would not allow them to be touched till he had consulted his minister, who said he might use them, as they were sent by his Heavenly Father, whoever had been the instrument. With great economy and care this provision served them for a short time, till John's trade had improved. The baskets and towels were carefully put past, but no one ever called for them. John and his wife both died, the minister and his wife died; but still the matter remained a mystery.

II.

Four or five years afterwards, the minister's son, who was following in his father's footsteps, was attending the University in Edinburgh. A lady friend asked him to spend the evening with a family where there was an old lady visitor. After partaking of tea, they drew round the fire, and the subject of conversation was "extraordinary answers to prayer." Among other things the minister related the above facts. The old lady smiled, and said—"I think I can throw some light on that subject." Of course they were all anxious to hear, and she said she was at that time housekeeper to a farmer. He was a bachelor, very rich, but niggardly. The neighbouring farmers passed his house to and from market, and they often chaffed him by proposing to take dinner with him, so he thought he would get the better of them for once. He told his housekeeper to make ready a special dinner, although he wished them to think it was the ordinary fare of the house, and she did so. As the neighbours returned from market that day, he was waiting for their usual joke of wishing to dine with him, but no one spoke of it. As they did not, he was on the point of inviting them into the house when a sudden thunderstorm came on. They put spurs to their horses, and were off before he could say a word. When he came into the house and saw the preparations that had been made, he rang the bell, and ordered up the housekeeper. He told her to pack two baskets, and send them to that old hypocrite, John Brown, for he was sure he would need them, as his family was starving. The housekeeper was glad to get the order, and executed it at once. Almost immediately afterwards the bell was again rung to countermand the order. The housekeeper replied that by that time the boy would be at Brown's house. The farmer then said that she was never to send for the baskets and towels, and John Brown was never to be told from whom they came.

A. H.

HOW THE LORD CARETH FOR HIS OWN WORK.

SCRIPTURE TESTIMONY
God's work will not lack God's supply
PHILIPPIANS 4:19

Miss Abbot, of the American Board of Missions, Bombay, writes:—"One year opened under a heavy cloud, our numbers were depleted, our resources reduced, and need everywhere confronted us. Later, in September, we were again afflicted and tried, by the going home of Miss

Lyman for a period of rest and cure. The financial and physical burden seemed too heavy for us to bear. Yet now we do most thankfully affirm that we have tried, tested, and proved two of the Lord's promises, 'As thy day so shall thy strength be,' and 'Seek ye first the kingdom of God and His righteousness, and all these things shall be added unto you.' We took up our heavy financial burden in connection with the school, with the prayer in our hearts, 'Lord, if this is Thy work, bless it; if what we are attempting is not in accordance with Thy will, then speedily show it to us.' The answer came in the shape of about twelve hundred rupees—and we went on rejoicing. The boys in the dormitory were suffering from want of clothes; the need was very great—there came a day when it was imperative. This matter was laid before the Lord. In two hours a lady—a stranger from America —called on us. She saw our work, and as she was leaving she put a note in my hands for the boys—it was one for fifty rupees. Another instance from the many:—There was another great need; there seemed no possible way to meet it. At a social meeting a friend said, 'How are you getting on? What do you need? How much is it in rupees?' The answer being given, he added, 'Very well, send round your messenger to-morrow to my office; a few of us will provide the amount.' And so it has proved again and again, that the Lord careth for His own work. We have not had all we wished for; we have prayed and waited for labourers to come and fill the place of those whom we have greatly missed, but no one has! The why and the wherefore of this denial we leave to Him who knoweth all things."

"HAS HE SENT YOU?"

Over forty years ago an elder went one Saturday evening to consult a friend about a business matter. He left late at night for his own house, was seized with cholera, and died

> SCRIPTURE TESTIMONY
>
> *God using an inner voice to communicate*
>
> JOHN 14:26 · ACTS 10:19-20 · ACTS 11:12

next morning. A short time afterwards, his friend's daughter, Miss M., was much impressed with the thought that she must go and help some one who was in distress. She seemed to hear the Lord bidding her go and give a cup of cold water to a disciple. She was quite ready to do her Lord's will, but she did not know of any one who needed relief. She therefore prayed, asking the Lord to direct her to whom she was to go. The name of the widow came before her mind, but she was perplexed, as it was believed the elder had left a considerable sum of money. She went to her father's store, filled a basket with provisions, and prayed that the Lord would lead the widow to open her mind to her if she was in want. She knocked at the door, and when the widow saw her she burst into tears, and, with uplifted hands, cried, "Has He sent you?" Miss M. entered, and found that, after paying the funeral expenses and debts, the money was all gone, and there was not any food in the house for the children. She gladly opened her basket and relieved their wants. She was full of praise to the Lord, who that day had used her in ministering to His sorrowing and afflicted ones.

Shortly after the above incident, the widow obtained a lodger, and her affairs seemed to brighten. Miss M. left home on a visit to a lady friend, and one day told her the widow's sad story. The lady was greatly troubled about it, so much so that she could not sleep. Next morning she gave Miss M. £1, and said she was so anxious about the woman she could not rest until she had given her something. Miss M. returned to town, and went to see the widow and gave her the money. She found her on her knees in prayer, crying to the Lord for help, for her lodger had died of cholera. When she saw Miss M. she said, "It is the Lord again." She was an old disciple in the school of grace, and knew how to watch for the working of His hand. He had again brought her into deep water, and when she had no one to help she cried to Him, and He answered her in the hour of need.

AT BREAK OF DAY.

A working man was for a considerable time out of employment. He sought work in many directions, but always failed to get it. His faith was sorely tried, but he continued to wait on the Lord, pleading that He would open a place for him. One morning he awoke early, and became deeply impressed by the thought that he should apply at a certain large work. He told his wife, but she tried to dissuade him from going out so early. He was lying down again, but the impression returned that he must go to the place at once. He rose and left the house. He went direct towards the work, and on the way met the manager, who engaged him on the spot. He still cherishes feelings of thankfulness for this answer to his prayers in a time of trouble.

TRAVELLING EXPENSES PAID.

Mr W. D. Rudland says:—"The China Inland Mission was begun and is carried on by prayer. Each member, on being received, is told that he is to look to the Lord to supply his needs, and not to the Mission. Mr Hudson Taylor said to me when accepted for China—'The Mission might become bankrupt, but the Lord never could; difficulties might occur which would hinder funds being sent inland, but the Lord would be inland.' These remarks came with great force to me. I had been some months in London, and my stock of savings was exhausted. I was to pay a farewell visit to my mother some 200 miles distant, but I had not a penny to buy a stamp for a letter to say I was coming, and of course I had not money for my railway fare. I had only to mention my need and friends would have supplied it at once; but we were to look to the Lord in China, and if I could not look to Him now at home with friends around me, what would I do, perhaps alone, in a heathen land? I went and pleaded with God as perhaps I had never done before. Two days passed; I expected money by letter, but it did not come. It was Saturday, and I was at the usual prayer meeting. After the meeting Mr Taylor asked me to carry his bag to the station as he was to spend Sunday in the west end. I gladly did so; and just as the train was starting he said to me that perhaps I might need money for travelling expenses, and put a sovereign in my hand. This so took me by surprise that I nearly dropped it. How I inwardly praised the Lord for a direct answer to prayer just when I was not expecting it! My letter was already written, and soon was in the post. The battle was fought, the victory won, and my faith strengthened for work in China. The next day I was introduced to a gentleman who, on shaking hands and wishing me God-speed, left a half-sovereign in it. Two days later another gave me two pounds, and so time after time the Lord supplied all my wants until we left for China. Only the Lord knew my need, and it was years before I told anyone of it but my godly mother."

HALF-A-CROWN FOUND IN THE SAND.

An evangelist tells that when he was a boy he often read the Bible to his aged great-grandmother. She was a godly woman, and taught him to love and trust the Lord. His parents were very poor, and one morning there was not anything for breakfast. His mother with a sad heart dressed the children, and sent them down to play by the seashore till help came. He watched the seabirds as they wheeled around him, and he remembered Christ's words, "Your Heavenly Father feedeth them. Are ye not much better than they?" He thought if God provided for the birds He could as easily feed him. He knelt down and prayed that the Lord would send food. After wandering along the shore he began to build sand-houses with the other children. On lifting a handful of sand he saw something bright, and found it was half-a-crown. With a happy heart he hastened home with it to his mother, and soon they had a good breakfast. This answer to prayer in boyhood has had its effect on him throughout a long and active life. He has been engaged in evangelistic work for many years, and has been used in bringing numbers to Christ and in establishing believers in their faith.

MONEY AMONG THE COALS.

Many years ago a poor woman living in the country found one night that she had not any supper in the house for her children. The food was all done, and she had not any money with which to buy more. She comforted her little ones as best she could, and put them to bed, saying she would awaken them when help came. She knelt down and prayed to God to send deliverance. As the fire was getting low in the hearth, she went to an outhouse for coals. When she brought them in she was surprised and overjoyed to see a bright shilling lying on the top of them. To her it was as direct an answer to her prayer as if the shilling had dropped from heaven. She had prayed to a God whom she knew not, and the Lord had so manifestly and so graciously answered her that from that moment her life was changed, and she became and still continues a firm believer in the living God. She says she never found a shilling among the coals before or since. She purchased some food and soon had a supper prepared. There were glad and thankful hearts in the humble house that night. Her children are now all grown up, and are doing well in the world. She still lives, and goes about a country village as an angel of mercy, and is often found by the bedside of the sick and dying, ministering to them, and trying to instil into their hearts the same faith in God which has so transformed and gladdened her own life.

THE LORD PREVENTED HIM.

Two lady missionaries were located at a town in the North of China, where it was difficult to get money sent with regularity, and their funds ran low. At last matters came to a crisis, but they could only pray and wait. Their servant asked for money to buy their food, but they had to tell him they did not have any. He went to the merchant and told him the ladies' cash was all done, and the man, touched by their extremity, offered to lend them some. They, however, would not accept his kind offer, and they told him it was against their principles to owe any man anything. They had come to China trusting in the Lord for supplies, and they would wait on Him, for they could neither borrow money nor go into debt. A brother missionary was at this time passing near their station, and had supplies with him for them. As there was to be a conference at a town not very far distant, he thought he would meet them there and give them the money, and thus save himself a journey of several miles. On the morning of the day when their supplies failed he was fifteen miles away, and was preparing to go to the conference, but he felt as if the Lord were preventing him. He had it laid strongly upon him that he must visit the ladies, and he told his travelling companion, a military man, that he must go and see them. He went, and arrived just in time to relieve their wants. They had been faithful to their God, and He had remained faithful to them. They said nothing of their need to the missionary at the time, but afterwards they told him the whole story.

TEN DAYS' PRAYER.

Several years ago I was much interested in one of my fellow-workmen. His wife and her mother became unwell, and I was afraid they might be in want. It was a delicate matter to ask them if they were in need, and I could only pray that if it were so the Lord would raise up friends for them. I was reading at the time in Jeremiah, and found from the xlii. chapter that the prophet had to wait ten days before he got an answer to his prayer. I thought if Jeremiah, who spoke face to face with God, was kept waiting so long, I should take courage and plead on. I did so, and trusted that by the tenth day my prayer would also be heard. One day I was called into the master's office on business, and while there the master's son and one of the clerks began to talk of my fellow-workman. They asked me how he was getting on, and one of them wondered if his religion would be keeping him right now, for he added, "Christianity does not give him his wages." They wished to know if he was in need of money, for he had been obliged to stop work and stay at home to nurse the sick ones, and money was going out but none coming in. The son was evidently much interested in the case, and talked it over with his father. I was called in again, but could not give them any definite information, as he had never mentioned his needs to me. I told them I feared he must be in want. The master asked my friend's address and called on him. He was much touched by what he saw and heard during his visit, and before leaving handed him £5. I was soon told the good news, and, to my great delight, found it was the tenth day since I began to cry to the Lord to raise up friends for them. I had prayed in faith that on this day the Lord would answer, and He graciously did so.

T. S.

HER LAST BISCUIT.

A devoted missionary lady had penetrated into Tibet, and there she remained for the sake of the souls of its inhabitants, in spite of endeavours to drive her out, and to kill her by starvation or by poison. Once when she was reduced to her last biscuit, a messenger came asking her to go and see a man twenty miles off. He was ill, and had heard of her medical skill. In all the simplicity of her strong faith, she told her Heavenly Father that she could not walk twenty miles on one biscuit, but that she would set out in dependence on His providence. She did so, and though she nibbled as slowly as possible at that biscuit it was soon gone. But as she walked on she perceived on the rough road a piece of popcorn.

With a grateful heart she picked it up and ate it. Other small pieces were found as she proceeded, and presently she saw a man some distance ahead with a bag on his back, from which doubtless her supplies had dropped through a hole. But he was too far distant to hear her call, so she could not make him aware of his trifling loss, which had been her great gain. That food enabled her to reach the sick man, and God blessed to his recovery the remedies she applied. The grateful people fed her well while she was with them, and sent her home again with abundant provisions.

A PAROCHIAL BOARD INFLUENCED.

A missionary was much interested in a widow who had been left with several children without the means of supporting them. He applied to the inspector of poor for relief for her, but was refused. After one or two calls on members of the Parochial Board trying to interest them, the case seemed to be hopeless, and he went home thoroughly discouraged. He was in great distress about the matter, but he knew the Lord could turn men's hearts like water, and he betook himself to prayer. He spent hour after hour pleading that on the morrow, when the meeting for the decision was to be held, the Lord would undertake for the poor widow and her children. His faith was not very strong, however, and he let two days pass before making enquiries. When he did call, he found that the feeling of the Board towards the widow had completely changed, and they had agreed to support her and her family. The missionary's faith was greatly strengthened by this answer to his prayer. May it also encourage the reader to lay all his difficulties before the Lord, and confidently expect help from Him. God waits to be gracious, and will not suffer any who put their trust in Him to be confounded.

HER LAST SHILLING.

Those who live near the Lord, and are willing to follow His leading, are often used to bless and help others. A young man went to his work one day with a shilling in his pocket. He

SCRIPTURE TESTIMONY
The sheep know and hear His voice
JOHN 10:3-4 · JOHN 10:16

was not in the habit of carrying money with him, but the Lord had need of this shilling for one of His children.

In the afternoon, while engaged as usual, a voice seemed to say, "Give the shilling to Mrs H."—a woman who had been converted from a life of drunkenness. He had occasionally seen her on the street, but it was always during the day, and he wondered how he would find an opportunity of giving her the money at night. Besides, he had never spoken to her: yet he was fully persuaded that the Lord meant him to give it. An unseen Hand was at work, and as he went along the street the woman passed him going in the same direction. The temptation was strong to let her go on, but he resisted it, and tapping her on the shoulder, he said, "Here is a shilling for you." She looked up, and said, "But who are you?" "Never mind," was the reply, "I am one of the Lord's bairns." She then told him she had spent her last shilling in buying some Gospel literature to give away; and she said, "I was just asking the Lord for some money, and He has answered me already, and has given me my shilling back again. It is just like Him." With a grateful heart she left, rejoicing in one more token of her Heavenly Father's willingness to give to those who ask. He who commended the widow as she put her two mites into the treasury looked with favour on that poor woman's loving heart, which prompted her to give her last shilling to help His cause. And as the young man went his way might he not hear the gracious words of the Master, "Inasmuch as ye did it unto one of the least of these my brethren, ye did it unto Me"?

AN ACCEPTABLE GIFT.

A friend writes:—"Knowing that you are specially interested in 'Answers to Prayer,' I feel constrained to lay before you the following facts from my own experience one day. I had had several experiences of the same kind before, but I feel that I must relate this one to the honour of our faithful Lord and Master.

"My dear wife came to me asking if I could give her some money to pay an account that was due. I gave her the sum, all that was left of my quarter's salary. When giving it, I said, 'That's it all; what are you going to do till next month?' With one of her happy smiles, she said, 'I don't know.' I, however, felt a little anxious about the matter, and so took it to the Lord in prayer. I felt, while telling Him about it, what a small thing it was for Him—who made the heavens and the earth, and redeemed me by His blood—to give, and that He could not deny it, as His promise was sure. I had to address a women's meeting that afternoon. After the address, I was asked to tea by a kind lady who was present. When coming away to catch the train she put £2 in my hand. It may seem a small matter to some, but you can understand what thankfulness and comfort it brought to me.

"Praise Him! Praise Him!"

A MINISTER IN NEED.

A Christian minister, living in Northern Indiana, being in want, knelt in prayer again and again before his Father in heaven. His quarterly allowance had been with-

SCRIPTURE TESTIMONY
God answers prayer
LUKE 18:7 · JOHN 15:7 · ACTS 12:5 · JAMES 5:15

held, and want stared him in the face. Constrained by urgent need, and shut up to God for help, he pleaded repeatedly for a supply of his temporal wants. Now see how extraordinary was the plan of the Lord to send relief:—

"In one of the lovely homes of Massachusetts, while the snow was falling and the winds were howling without, a lady sat by the side of the cheerful fire knitting a stocking for her grandson, and her husband opposite to her was reading aloud a missionary paper, when the following passage arrested the attention of the lady, and fastened itself in her memory. The words ran thus:—'In consequence of failure to obtain my salary when due, I have been so oppressed with care and want as to make it painfully difficult to perform my duties as a minister. There is very little prospect, seemingly, of improvement in this respect for some time to come. What I say of my own painfully inadequate support is substantially true of nearly all your missionaries in this State. You, of course, cannot be blamed for this. You are but the almoners of the churches, and can only appropriate what they furnish. *This, however, the Master will charge to somebody as a grievous fault*: it is not His will that His ministers should labour unrequited.' This extract was without name or date. It was simply headed, 'From a Missionary in Northern Indiana.' Scores of readers probably gave it only a passing glance. Not so the lady who sat knitting by the fire and heard her husband read it. The words sank into her mind and dwelt there. The clause—'This, however, the Master will charge to somebody as a grievous fault', especially seemed to follow her wherever she went. The case, she said, haunted her. She seemed to be herself that very 'somebody' who was to answer at the bar of God for the curtailed supplies and straitened means of this humble minister.

"Impelled by an unseen, but, as she believes, a divine presence and power, after asking counsel and guidance of the Lord, she took 25 dollars, which were at her own disposal, and requested her husband to give it to Rev. Dr H--- for the writer of the above communication, if he could devise any way to obtain the writer's address.

"Dr H--- is a prompt man, who does not let gold destined to such an end rest in his pocket. Familiar with the various organisations of the benevolent societies, and only too happy to have an agency in supplying the wants of a labourer in Christ's vineyard, he soon started the money on its errand. Early in April the lady in her rural home had the happiness of receiving the following note, of which we omit nothing save the names of persons and places:—

"Dear Madam,—I have just received a draft of 25 dollars as a donation from you. This I do with profound gratitude to you for this unselfish and Christ-like deed, and to Him who put it into your heart to do it. How you, a lady a thousand miles away, could know that I was and had been for some time urged by unusual need to pray for succour and worldly support with unwonted fervency is a matter of more than curious enquiry. It is an answer to my prayer, for the Lord employs the instrumentality of His children to answer prayer, and when it is necessary He moves them to it. This is not the first or second time that I have been laid under special obligations by Christian sympathy and timely aid."

"Does not this little incident illustrate the power of prayer? The man of God, weary and heavy laden, in his closet in Indiana, spread his case before the Lord. A disciple in Eastern Massachusetts, a thousand miles away from the spot where the prayer was offered, who did not know anything about him or his work, is touched with his wants, and moved to send him immediate aid."

A NATIVE MISSIONARY'S TESTIMONY.

The Rev. T. B. Pandian, a native missionary from Madras, writes:—"Every man who has been in the inner chamber of God, and realised his privileges, will always be ready to bear testimony to the marvellous dealings of God with him. My experience as a Christian and a worker in the cause of Christ, though not a long one, recalls many happy instances of answers to my prayers.

"On looking back I find in the difficulties, trials, discouragements, and temptations through which I passed, I had but one means of getting my temporal and spiritual needs supplied—that is by prayer.

"I first commenced to pray during my visit to the heathen village where I was born, and I especially prayed for light and knowledge to be given me, as I was utterly ignorant of anything bright and hopeful in life, and surrounded by heathen influences. How thankful I am to say that my prayer was answered, for the Lord opened the eyes of my understanding, and has guided my every step hitherto. When I was working in the city of Madras, I was in great need of financial help, which I made known to the Father of Mercies. One morning, having lifted up my eyes towards heaven, I left my home to conduct a meeting, and on my return I found a letter waiting me from a missionary friend, who in a few words expressed his regret for not having written me for a long time. He thought a line would encourage me, and he enclosed a cheque, which brought indeed most timely help.

"On another occasion I was in need of funds to publish my book, which cost a considerable amount. I, however, went to the Lord with the hope of getting what I wanted; but I was utterly ignorant of the party who was directed to help me out of my trouble. A gentleman residing in one of the South Indian cities kindly undertook to pay my expenses to a neighbouring town to attend a meeting there. Although it appeared difficult to comply with his request, I yielded to his suggestion, and to my joy and surprise on arriving at the town I had more than the sum I required put into my hand.

"There was a time when thick clouds of doubt surrounded me as to the divinity of Christ. This was the darkest period I have ever experienced. Still the Lord upheld me by His hand, and removed the clouds, making me again to behold the King in His beauty, whose glorious mission on earth I am endeavouring to proclaim.

"I could give many instances of direct answers to prayer, even in my sojourn in Britain. When men try to shut the door, I look to God, who has opened so many favourable doors, and I still pray and trust for His direction and help, and for strength and knowledge.

"What a blessing it is for us to know that we have a Father in Heaven, who is ever willing to listen to the cries of His children, whatever may be their circumstances in life."

OLD MARGARET.

From "*Old Margaret, a Saint at Last*" by Dr Elder Cumming, we take the following:— "Many were the answers to prayer for herself and others which brightened her path. Some have felt a blessing following them, they knew not why, until they traced the source of it to dear old Margaret's prayers. Among the things she much wished for at one time was a clock which would tell the passing hours, and by whose striking her husband (who was blind) could know what time it was when left alone. 'The old couple,' says a friend, 'had no idea of time, and often they used to start too early, and wander about in the park tired and hungry, before people who could buy their oranges were astir.' So the two agreed to pray to God in this difficulty also, and very soon Margaret saw a bonnie clock (called a 'wag-at-the wa') in a shop window. She was delighted with it, went home and told James, and then sallied forth with all her money to get it. But to her disappointment she found the price far beyond her little store, and she had to give it up. Looking round the shop, however, she discovered a dusty, rusty-looking old clock, which the man said she might have for a trifle. She carried it home in triumph, dusted it, oiled it, and set it agoing, and its works being good it went for more than twenty years, and only stopped after her own spirit had gone where a thousand years are as one day and one day as a thousand years.

"From that day she recognised an answer to prayer in almost everything. Sometimes it was finding a sixpence on the high-road when there was not a crust of bread in the house; sometimes it was a friend calling and leaving the exact sum to pay the rent (which was due that evening, and must be paid), though the friend had no knowledge of the need. One left her room refreshed and strengthened by communion with her who communed so much with God. She spoke to God on all subjects audibly, and sometimes before she opened her door one expected to find a visitor with her. It was Margaret speaking to God.

"A well-known minister gives a striking account of the power of prayer in this humble dwelling in words which I cannot reproduce here. He tells how her prayers followed him step by step; how she asked things for him which there seemed no earthly prospect of obtaining, but many of which have already come. He describes these prayers as if they had been moulding his life all unknown to him; and mentions that one or two yet remain to be answered—as to which only time can tell. Margaret traced these answers to her prayers with much thankfulness, and so happy did she feel with reference to one of them that she said 'she was ready to go to heaven from the church door.'"

LET US ASK GOD.

The *American Messenger* relates an instance of a poor man in a village, who, with a family of young children and a wife in very feeble health, found it extremely difficult to obtain

SCRIPTURE TESTIMONY
God answers prayer
LUKE 18:7 · JOHN 15:7 · ACTS 12:5 · JAMES 5:15

a livelihood. He was at length compelled to work by the week for a shoemaker in the city, returning to his family every Saturday evening, and leaving home early on Monday morning. He usually brought home his wages in provisions for his family during the following week, but one cold and stormy night in the depth of winter he went towards his humble dwelling with empty hands though a full heart. His employer had declared himself unable to pay him a penny that night, and the shoemaker, too honest to incur a debt without knowing how he could pay it, bent his weary steps homewards, trusting that He who hears the ravens when they cry would fill the mouths of his little ones. When he entered his cottage, cold and wet with the rain, he saw a bright fire, the tea-kettle was sending forth its cloud of steam, and a pitcher of milk sent by a kind neighbour was waiting for the bread so anxiously expected by the children. The sad father confessed his poverty, and his wife in tears begged him to make some effort to get food for them before the Sabbath. He replied, "Let us ask God to give us our daily bread. Prayer avails with God when we ask for temporal good as when we implore spiritual blessings." The sorrowing group knelt around the family altar, and while the father was entreating for the mercies they so much needed, a gentle knocking at the door was heard. When the prayer was ended the door was opened, and there stood a woman in "the peltings of the storm " who had never been at that door before, though she lived only a short distance from it. She had a napkin in her hand which contained a large loaf of bread, and half apologising for offering it, said she had unintentionally made a larger batch of bread than usual that day, and, though she hardly knew why, she thought it might be acceptable there. After expressing their sincere gratitude to the woman, the devout shoemaker and his wife gave thanks to God with overflowing hearts. While the little flock were appeasing their hunger with the nice bread and milk, the father went to an adjoining house to tell his artless story, and he again returned to his home with a basket heavily laden, and a heart full of gratitude to a prayeranswering God.

THE LEPERS' PRAYER MEETING.

SCRIPTURE TESTIMONY
Don't be anxious, instead make requests known to God
PHILIPPIANS 4:6

We take the following from a letter to the *Missionary Pence Association*:—Some time ago there was great scarcity in one of the hill districts in India where there is an asylum for lepers. So great did this privation become that the missionary in charge was obliged to refuse to admit any more patients. He wrote asking if it were possible for us to give him an additional grant to enable him to tide over this difficulty. But at the time we had not a penny in hand for extra work, barely enough for current expenses. With sad hearts we carried this burden to the Lord at our monthly meeting for praise and prayer, asking Him soon to give us the joy of being able to "wire" to our friend that help was coming, so that he might again admit the sufferers who came to him for help.

That was on the 1st of the month. On the 12th of the same month, of their *own wish*, the lepers in that asylum observed an "all-day" of prayer and fasting, the latter, they said, to show God that they meant what they said when they prayed. That day was strictly observed by Christians and *non*-Christians alike.

The Father heard the cry of need, and on the 20th, just eight days after, He gave us the unspeakable joy of sending, and them of receiving, a telegram which ran, "Admit lepers, help coming," we having in the meantime received £100 for their special need.

Shortly afterwards one of the Christian lepers said to the missionary, "We had a day of prayer."

"Oh, yes," replied our friend, "a very blessed day." "And God heard us, did He not?"

"Yes," again answered the missionary, "He did indeed, and we have been thanking Him ever since."

"Oh, yes," replied the leper brother; "but we haven't had a day *all* thanksgiving as we had a day *all* prayer."

Our friend told us he felt quite rebuked, and set at once about repairing this oversight by arranging for a Thanksgiving Day, which in its turn proved to be also a memorable one.

Readers will not wonder that shortly after this quite a number of these dear souls publicly confessed Jesus as their Saviour, and were baptised into His name; and, better still, it could be said that scarcely one heathen had been left in that large asylum.

A. B.

MONEY FOR THE COTTAGES.

A missionary in North Africa needed premises in which to open a new branch of work, and having seen some empty cottages which

SCRIPTURE TESTIMONY
God provides exactly what is needed
2 CORINTHIANS 8:15 · PHILIPPIANS 4:19

appeared suitable, he called at the house of the landlord with a view to making an offer of purchase. He found that the landlord was absent in Gibraltar, and his wife, a bigoted Romanist, refused to negotiate on any terms with a Protestant missionary. After consultation and prayer with his fellow-workers it was arranged that Mr P. should go to Gibraltar by next morning's steamer and see the landlord personally about the matter before his wife had time to prejudice him by letter. Accordingly, early next morning Mr P. dressed suitably for the journey, packed his travelling bag, and having breakfasted, retired for a brief season of prayer for God's guidance and blessing on his undertaking. After a while, to his wife's surprise, he came to her, saying that, in answer to prayer, the Lord had strongly impressed him that he was not to go to Gibraltar, though He had not yet shown him the reason. She gently remonstrated, reminding him of the advice of the other missionaries, but he replied, "he could not dare to go with his present conviction of the Lord's will." He therefore at once resumed his usual dress and commenced the daily routine of mission work. About two hours afterwards he received a telegram from a friend in Gibraltar asking him to meet the three o'clock steamer from there by which his sister would arrive, and he would be much obliged if Mr P. would kindly show her over the town, and especially all the branches of work in his mission. The missionary was duly at the landing-place when the steamer arrived, and the first person to step from it on shore was the landlord of the cottages, so that if Mr P. had started that morning they would have passed each other on the way. Of course Mr P. accosted him immediately, and it was arranged they should meet at the cottages next morning at six o'clock. The meeting took place, and the landlord asking a price for his property which Mr P. felt to be quite reasonable, he agreed to it, but explained that as all large sums of money were banked in Gibraltar he could only give part of the amount now, and would pay the remainder in a fortnight. The landlord replied that that arrangement would not suit him, as he wished to purchase a business for himself in Gibraltar, and had only returned in the hope of getting some ready money for the purpose, and should go back by steamer that morning at eleven o'clock. As the Lord's leadings had been so clear hitherto, Mr P. felt assured that it must

be His will for him to have the cottages, and therefore, though he did not
know where the money was to come from, he promised the landlord that
he should have the full amount by eleven o'clock. They parted, and Mr P.
went along the road towards his home praying that the Lord would show
him what step to take next, when he was unexpectedly met by the native
Arab teacher of the mission, who inquired—"Well, Mr P., what about
the cottages?" He explained how matters stood, and the teacher replied
that he had some savings by him which he did not need at present, and
which, though far from being the full amount, would help towards it. Mr
P. accepted the offer of the loan, and accompanied him to his house. Next
door resided one of the lady medical missionaries, to whom Mr P. said
he would tell the present state of affairs while the teacher was getting his
money. On hearing Mr P.'s account, Miss J. said she had likewise a small
sum of money by her for which she had no immediate need, and would
gladly lend it. The teacher and the lady accordingly produced their respec-
tive contributions, and on the money being counted out it was found that
the two sums together exactly made up the required amount, so that after
united thanksgiving to God for His gracious and striking answers to prayer,
Mr P., according to promise, at a quarter to eleven o'clock placed in the
hands of the landlord the full purchase money of the cottages.

                                                            E.R.V.

EMPLOYMENT FOUND.

A Christian man, who had been out of work for a considerable time,
found himself seriously straitened, there being only food enough in the
house for each of the family to take a little. He left the house with a
somewhat anxious mind, and went round several places asking for work,
but got the usual reply that there was "nothing to-day."

Standing for a little while at the end of a street he saw a man corning
along who sometimes had given him a job, and he thought—I hope he
will speak to me to-day; but the man passed on without speaking.

"I felt," said he, "quite prostrate; there was nothing at home, and I
could not get anything to do. I had put my case into God's hands, but no
way had opened, and it seemed very dark. Just then a gentleman came

along, and stood at the end of the street opposite to me. He looked up and down the street for a minute, and then came over to me and asked if I knew a certain place of business. I said I did. 'Will you take me there? ' he then asked. 'O yes,' I answered. When we got there he told me to wait for him, and on coming out asked me to show him to another firm which he mentioned.

"He kept me going with him till about four o'clock, when, putting his hand in his pocket, he handed me 4s. 6d., saying 'This will clear you and me.' I need hardly say how I wondered when going home. I had only gone through a few streets, done nothing at all, as I thought, yet here I was with 4s. 6d., which was more than ever I had got for a hard day's work. We had a better supper that night than I had expected, and we praised God, who can supply all our needs."

THE WONDERFUL DELIVERANCE OF DANIEL LOEST.

SCRIPTURE TESTIMONY
God provides exactly what is needed
2 CORINTHIANS 8:15 · PHILIPPIANS 4:19

John Daniel Loest, a celebrated German tradesman of Berlin, Germany, was, by the aid of the Lord, so prospered in his worldly circumstances that by steady industry he raised himself to a position among the most respectable tradesmen of Berlin, where he kept a well-frequented fringe and trimming shop.

He was always benevolent, willing to help others, and both fervent in spirit and constant in prayer, asking the help of the Lord in the minutest details of his business. Yet there once occurred in his experience a season of severest trial, which demanded his utmost trust and unfailing confidence in God. He seemed almost forsaken and hedged in by circumstances impossible to overcome. But his deliverance so astonished him that he was lost in wonder at the mysterious way in which the Lord helped his business and sent him all that he needed.

By means of acquaintances of high social character, whom he fully trusted as good Christians, never suspecting there could be any degree of hypocrisy, he became security for a Christian lady of good property to the amount of 600 thalers. The attorney assured him that there was not the shadow of a risk in going security for her, as her property would be more than ample to cover any claim.

Months elapsed and the circumstances were forgotten, when Mr Loest was most unpleasantly reminded of them by receiving an order from the court to pay in on the following Tuesday the 600 thalers for which he had become security, under penalty of execution.

He now discovered that he had been designedly mystified, and there was no escape. The 600 thalers must be paid before next Tuesday. He had just accepted a bill for 300 thalers to be paid on the ensuing Saturday. And on the first impulse, in his perplexity, he hoped to get out of his dilemma by hurrying to a rich friend to obtain a loan. On his way to his friend's home he stumbled on another acquaintance who had lent him 400 thalers on a mere note of hand, and he saluted him with the news that he must call for repayment of that sum on the following Friday, as he required it to pay for a parcel of goods which would arrive that day. "You shall have it," said Loest, as he hurried on to his friend. The friend was at home, but before Loest could utter his errand, he is addressed thus, "It is lucky you came, my friend, for I was just going to send for you, to request you to make provision to pay me back the 500 thalers you owe me, for I must needs have it on Wednesday to pay off a mortgage on my house which has just been called up." "You shall have it," replied Loest calmly, yet his heart became heavier every moment.

Suddenly it occurred to him that the widow of a friend just dead was possessed of large means, and she might be inclined to help him. But, alas, disappointments thickened fast upon him. Loest owed the deceased friend 500 thalers for note, and 300 thalers for goods just delivered. As he entered the room of the widow she handed him an order from the Court of Trustees, under which he was bound to pay up the 500 thalers on Thursday, and, continued the lady, before the poor man had time to speak a word, "I would earnestly entreat you to pay the other 300 thalers early on Saturday to me, for there are accounts constantly pouring in on me, and the funeral expenses;" here her voice faltered. "It shall be cared for," said Loest, and he withdrew, not having had an opportunity to utter one word as to the business that took him thither. He had failed at every turn; not one thing was for him, all seemed against him. But though the waves surged, and rose, and oppressed, yet they did not overwhelm his hope; the more the discouragements, the greater became his faith that all things were appointed for his good, and though he could not guess how, yet even the trial would result by God's own working to the honour and glory of His great name.

Yet here was his situation. Six hundred thalers to be paid on Tuesday, 500 on Wednesday, 500 on Thursday, 400 on Friday, 300 on Saturday morning, 300 on Saturday afternoon; in all 2600 thalers. It was already the Saturday previous, and his purse contained only 4 thalers. There was only one prospect left; he went to a rich money-lender, and in response, his request for relief in his many difficulties was met with a reply of irony and sarcasm from one who loved to indulge his enmity to the Christian faith. "You in monetary difficulties, or any difficulties, Mr Loest? I cannot believe it; it is altogether impossible! You are at all times and in all places boasting that you have such a rich and loving Master! Why don't you apply to Him now?" And the hardhearted man could not conceal his pleasure at this opportunity of testing a Christian.

Loest turned away; hard as the random taunt and remark of his opponent was, it recalled him to a sense of his duty and his forgetfulness of the fact that he had not hitherto asked God for help in his special circumstances. With cheerful steps he hurried home, and in long and imploring prayer asked for help and forgiveness in this, his neglect of trust in One so rich and generous. He was refreshed and comforted, and the Sunday was one of peace and sweetness. He knew and felt assured "The Lord would provide."

The eventful week opened, and on Monday he arose with a cheerful thought in his heart. Ere he had had full time to dress he noticed with great surprise that both his sister and the assistant in the store seemed, notwithstanding the earliness of the hour, to have fully as much as they could do in serving customers and making up parcels, and he at once hastened into the shop to give them assistance. And thus it continued all day. Never, in his experience, could Loest remember such a ceaseless stream of customers as poured on that memorable Monday into his rather out-of-the-way shop. Cooking dinner was out of the question; neither master nor maid had time for that; coffee and bread taken by each in turn served instead of the accustomed meal, and still the customers came and went; still three pairs of hands were in requisition to satisfy their wants.

Nor was it for new purchases alone that money came in. More than one long-standing account, accompanied by excuses for delayed payment, and assurances that it had not been possible to settle it sooner, increased the contents of the till, and the honest-hearted debtor on whom this unwonted stream of money flowed in felt induced every minute to call out, "It is the Lord."

At length night came, when Loest and his literally worn-out assistants, after having poured out their hearts in thankful adoration in family prayer, sat down to the first meal they had that day enjoyed in common. When it was over the brother and sister set themselves to count over the money which had been taken. Each hundred thalers was set by itself, and the result showed six hundred and three thalers, fourteen silver groschen. This was sufficient to pay the first debt next day and leave but 10s. 8d. over—a trifle less than they commenced the day with.

Loest was lost in wonder and grateful emotion evoked by this gracious testimony of how faithfully his Lord could minister to him in his earthly necessities.

How countless must be His host of ministering servants, seen or unseen, since he can employ some hundreds of them and send them to buy of Daniel Loest to-day or pay him those bills which they owed. What a wondrous God is ours, who in the government of this great universe does not overlook Loest's mean affairs, nor forget His gracious promise—"Call upon Me in the day of trouble and I will deliver thee." Tuesday was a repetition of Monday's splendid business, and brought in the 500 thalers which he needed the next morning to pay off the mortgage of his friend's house due that day. Wednesday's sales gave him 500 more thalers, which he was obliged to have ready to pay on Thursday morning into the Court of Trustees. Thursday's sales brought him 400 thalers —just the amount he had given promise to pay the next day for goods delivered. And Friday's sales gave him just 300 thalers with which to honour the widow's demand on Saturday to pay funeral and contingent expenses.

During these days of wonderful business and deliverances, after each indebtedness was discharged, there still was left in hand a sum not exceeding 12s. or 15s. On Saturday morning, after he had sent the 300 thalers to the widow, he had left precisely 2 thalers, or 26 silver groschen (six shillings and eightpence sterling), the smallest balance he had yet had; and what seemed most alarming, the rush to the shop seemed to be entirely over, for, while during the five days past he had had scarcely time to draw his breath from hurry and bustle, he was then left in undisturbed possession of his place. Not a single customer appeared. The wants of the vicinity seemed to have come to an end, for not a child even entered to fetch a pennyworth of thread or a few ells of tape. This utter cessation of trade was as unusual and out of the accustomed shop business as the extra rush had been.

At five o'clock that afternoon was due the debt of 300 thalers to his scoffing creditor. Three o'clock came, and still there was but 6s. 8d. in the till. Where was the money to come from? But Loest sat still and "possessed his soul in patience," for he knew the Lord would choose the best time, and he desired to be found waiting and watching for His coming. That last hour ran slowly on. At a quarter to four, almost the last few moments of painful suspense, a little old woman came in, and asking for Mr Loest, said to him, half in a whisper, "I live here close by quite alone in a cellar, and I have had a few thalers paid me, and now I want you to be so good as to keep them for me. I have not slept over night since I had them; it is a great charge for a woman like me."

Loest was only too glad to accept the money, and offered interest, which she declined. She hurried back, brought the money, counted it on his table, and there were just 300 thalers—6 rouleaux of 50 thalers each.

She had scarcely left the house with the receipt in her pocket ere the clerk of his creditor, with his demand in his hand, entered Loest's presence. He received his 300 thalers, and both parted speechless with amazement. Loest was lost in wonder at the marvellous way and the exactness of time in which the Lord had delivered him, while the creditor was astonished thus to find that Loest's mighty Friend had not failed in his hour of need.

Thus in one short week, from a beginning of 5 thalers, God had so exactly supplied his business needs that he had paid all his obligations of

2,600 thalers, saved him from failure, saved his honour and good name, and now all was peace.

The history of Loest and other providences which helped him in his business are given more at length in a little book, "The Believing Trades-man," published by the Religious Tract Society of Berlin.

The sketch illustrates the necessity of looking to God daily for help and strength, success and deliverance, in our business occupations as well as those of our souls, and most effectively proves that those who use their business and business proceeds to honour the Lord will be blessed with His favour. It teaches, in short, the sublime lesson that money and prosperity are gifts from the Lord, and must be considered as such, acknowledged with thankfulness, and used to glorify the Giver.

Whenever the Christian learns to love the gift more than the Giver, the Lord often takes it away to remind him of his need of dependence upon Him, but whenever the Christian loves the Giver because of His gifts, and spends his means to please his heavenly Father, he becomes the Father's steward, and his lap is filled with bountiful blessings, as we know by experience. "The Lord is my Shepherd, I shall not want."

BIBLE WOMEN'S WORK AND PRAYERS.

There being no appropriation for the Bible women one year, my co-labourer felt it her duty to dismiss them from the service, and called them together for that

SCRIPTURE TESTIMONY
God provides exactly what is needed
2 CORINTHIANS 8:15 · PHILIPPIANS 4:19

purpose in September. They replied that they had been called of God to teach the heathen about them the way of salvation, and that they felt they must continue the work. And so, though humanly speaking they knew not where their daily bread was to come from, they continued the Bible work.

At the close of the month of October the kind-hearted missionary in charge of the work in this part of the field, hearing of their need, advanced the money for their rice from his own pocket.

It was soon after this that I returned to Himeji, and I was met at once by this need of the Bible women, but could not see any way out of the dilemma except to write to the Board in America and await their reply.

Meantime not one word of complaint did the Bible women utter, but went cheerfully about their daily duties; and thus the days sped by, the end of another month was at hand, and still there was not any money to buy their food. Two or three days before the end of the month a travelling companion of mine on the Pacific, who still lingered in Japan, came down to Himeji to see the mission work here, and upon leaving handed me a little roll of bank notes to be used in the work "where most needed." When I opened the roll after the guest's departure I was astonished to find just exactly the sum needed to supply the Bible women to the end of November.

I gave them the money at the first opportunity and told them how I came by it. Then with tears of joy and prayers of thankfulness to God they opened their hearts to me, and told of their trials of faith and of their needs. One woman said she had been living on boiled wheat with no rice for some time, but even with this economy she had finally spent her last sen, and that very morning had cooked and eaten the last bit of food in the house. Then she knelt down and asked God to provide her with a dinner if He wished her to continue the work for Him, for she had nothing more of her own.

"But," she said, "my faith was very faint, and I am ashamed to confess that as I walked through the street this morning I was planning how I should work to earn money for myself instead of doing the work God has given." This was said with downcast face. Then she looked up and added, while her face lighted up with a smile of perfect trust, "How wonderfully God has provided!" "Let us sing 'God will provide,'" some one suggested. Then followed a season of thanksgiving prayer. Miss Barlow gave them the reference, "The labourer is worthy of his hire"—precious words that had a new and added meaning to them just then.

We can all learn a lesson of simple faith from these trusting Bible women. (Luke x. 21.)

ELLA R. CHURCH.

THE LORD'S "FRIENDS IN NEED."

The following tells of missionary trials in India. The Lord had tried the faith of certain of these men very severely, but they had found Him to be the faithful God—the fulfiller of the promise "Call upon Me in the day of trouble; I will deliver thee, and thou shalt glorify Me." At one time nine of the missionaries lived for a week on four rupees, when they had chupatties (substitute for bread), water, and praise. On the ninth day they had not enough food for dinner, but they set the tables by faith. Fifteen minutes before dinner time a boy came in with four rupees and a basket of flour. Needless to say, the place rang with "Hallelujahs." During the afternoon a letter arrived from Mr M'Gavin with a ten rupee note enclosed. They also received the joyful news that 640 rupees had been received in answer to prayer. That evening Mr M'Gavin arrived from Poona. He told them that the money received (640 rupees) had not been enough to meet all the needs; that they had prayed for 200 more, and shortly afterwards had received 205 rupees from South Australia. Miss Parsons writes—"I leave you to imagine the atmosphere of joy and praise we were in when he told us that not only had all this come in answer to prayer, but that Mr Reeve had written saying that the Lord had given him £500 for the purchase of land at Mahablashwar for a hill station for our holidays."

HOW THE ACCOUNT WAS PAID.

A Christian man, who was engaged in a small business, was once very hardly pressed for money. On balancing his accounts he found he was owing £7, but he did not know where he could get the money. He had laboured hard in the Lord's cause, and had striven to deal honestly and uprightly, but some losses he had sustained had thrown him behind. He gave himself to prayer, and pleaded for help. He had been asked to hold evangelistic services in a neighbouring town, and when he arrived a letter awaited him. He opened it, and found it contained £5. He got £1 for his services, and a friend in the train handed him five shillings. The parties to whom the money was due, when they heard of his position, offered to reduce the account. It was the turning-point in his life. Since that time he has been wholly engaged in evangelistic work, and has been much blessed in it. At times when his faith is tried he can look back at the way in which the Lord delivered him and take courage.

THE DROUGHT IN KHAMA'S COUNTRY.

Perhaps the most remarkable chapter in the book published by Messrs Hodder & Stoughton, entitled "Twenty Years in Khama's Country," is the sixth, wherein is described "the last rain-making and other heathen rites in Shoshong, and the drink devil turned out." We extract the following answers to prayer:— "Praying and trusting, working and growing," wrote Mr Hepburn, "is just as efficacious among these degraded tribes as among ourselves for producing robust Christians. . . . Famine, people dying, the veldt as hard as flint, not a cloud in the sky, no water in the river bed, scarcely enough to drink, even when you take turns to sit all night for it, the hearts of the people dead within them, the Boers writing threatening letters to Khama. It was a hard time for Khama.

"'What shall I do, Monare?'

"'Do what a Christian only can do, Khama—lay it all before God.'

"I pointed him to the examples of Hezekiah and Nehemiah in their times of distress.

"The Boers' letter, in which they charged Khama with being the cause of their leaving home, and upon whose head they threw the blame of all the bloodshedding that was about to take place, was laid before God publicly. In like manner we pleaded before God publicly for rain. A neighbouring chief sent Khama a taunting message—

"'You are the wise man. Go on praying—that's the proper thing to do. You are the man with wisdom.'

"It was hard for Khama to hold his ground. We held a week of prayer, and the blessing of rain came in torrents. Again the spiritual windows of heaven had been opened, and again the water was flowing— this time the water of life. I can see and have seen that God hears and answers prayer to-day as much as in the times of patriarchs, prophets, and apostles. Water wont flow in the desert, and especially it wont flow up a sandy hill in the desert, if you pray ever so earnestly for it, you say? I'm not so sure about that! Perhaps it will if your necessities absolutely require it, and you have not become too learned to be able to pray for it in the simplicity of your heart. The Trek- Boers got into the desert, and were dying for want of water, and their cattle died in thousands. There was necessity at any rate. Some poor, uneducated, simple-minded Boers are climbing up, one side of a long, heavy sand-hill; the hot African sun is blazing overhead; the sky is clear of every speck of cloud. Here is a single tree by the wayside.

"'Let us kneel down and pray for rain under this tree.'

"'But the rain season is over.'

"'Let us pray for it; God is good.'

"They knelt down and prayed together. There were doubters to grumble even there.

"'We might have been far on if we had not stayed here to pray for rain which wont come,' they said.

"But there was a missionary two days off with the waggon, who accidentally heard on the very morning he was to trek from a certain pan of water that the Boers were dying from want of water in the thirst desert. He off-loaded his waggon at once, and sent back a waggon-load of water; and while the poor, ignorant Boers are praying on the one side of the hill the waggon is climbing the other."This time it is manna in the wilderness. The Boers are starving in the wilderness, and the Capetown people hear of it, and send a ship round with provisions and other necessaries. Was there no prayer in the wilderness?

"Again the water supply was failing at Shoshong. The women were sitting in crowds round the wells waiting their turn. . . . The feeling of oppression silenced me. I had not heard the least mention of the state we were in. We had had our public service at the time of digging, and had prayed for the regular yearly rains. , . . My evangelist, Khukwe, and I commenced a week of prayer together early on the Sunday morning. At this meeting it was announced that this week was to be spent in prayer to God for rain. There was no compulsion. Those would come who felt that God only could give the rain. The clouds had come up on Sunday morning, but they all went away, and the sun blazed in all its South African glory.

"'Why, they have driven the clouds away,' said the Makaluka rain-maker.

"All that week the sun blazed in brightness, and on the following Sunday afternoon I heard from Khukwe's address to the people what the Makaluka rain-maker had been saying, and that the Makaluka god was angry, and was going to give us no more rain because all these years he had given it and Khama would not acknowledge him.

"As I sat and listened the wind was blowing down the kloof—a strong, steady wind from the north—the direction of the Makaluka god's mountains, and I had noticed across the valley to the south that the clouds had begun to show themselves almost as soon as I had sat down from interpreting for Mr Cochin, the young missionary previously mentioned. All the time Khukwe was speaking I watched the clouds."

Then follows Mr Hepburn's own address, and the incident concludes thus:—

"That night it rained a beautiful, heavy, groundsoaking rain. All that week and the next we had very heavy rains. For a long time the people talked about it, and about the Makaluka rain-maker and his threat. It was an unfortunate threat for the Makaluka god. The clouds came up and covered us over, and poured out rain for twenty-seven days.

"If *that* was not *answering prayer*, then I don't know *how* God is to answer prayer."

IN JESUS' NAME.

SCRIPTURE TESTIMONY
Ask Me anything in My name
MATTHEW 18:19 · JOHN 14:13-14 · JOHN 16:23-24

In The *Hebrew-Christian* we have a touching account of how a Jew learned to pray in the name of the Lord Jesus. It was at a time when his wife was very ill. He had no money in the house with which to buy bread for his hungry children. They cried all night long for the food he could not give them; and at last he chastised his little ones to keep them quiet that their mother might not be disturbed. Many, many times he prayed to the God of Abraham, Isaac, and Jacob for help in his time of need, but no answer came to his oft-repeated cry. At last, he somehow became convinced that he must pray in the name of Jesus, or God would not hear him. He went into his bedroom to pray again, this time in earnest, and with a heart burning with love for his Saviour as never before. Down on the floor he knelt and prayed, he knew not how long, crying, "Lord, in the name of Jesus Christ, for Christ's sake, have mercy upon me." Shortly afterwards a boy came from his employer of a year and half before, saying that his master wanted Mr Kearn back to his work, and wanted him at once. "I cannot leave my wife alone so ill, and my children crying for food," answered Mr Kearn, "but if I had money to get a woman to stay here I would go at once." Then though he knew his former employer never paid wages in advance, he said to the boy, "Go and ask him to send me a few dollars in advance, and I will come to work to-morrow morning." The boy came back in a few hours, and, to the man's astonishment, handed him fifteen dollars. When telling his story, J. Kearn added, "I was glad, and believed with my whole heart that Jesus helped me. I saw I must pray in His name alone, and the wish rose in my heart to come nearer to Him." Mr Kearn has now been publicly baptised, and has become a consistent member of the church of Christ.

DON'T WORRY; THE LORD WILL PROVIDE.

The following instance is recorded by *The Christian*, New York, as true, and to a remarkable degree indicates how thoroughly God knows our minutest needs, and how effectively

> **SCRIPTURE TESTIMONY**
>
> *Don't be anxious, make requests known to God, and He will give peace*
>
> PHILIPPIANS 4:6-7

He makes those who reproach His name ashamed of their unbelief:—

"An elderly Christian woman, who was a 'widow indeed,' who trusted in God, and continued in prayers and supplications day and night, was once brought into circumstances of peculiar straitness and anxiety. She had two daughters, who exerted themselves with their needles to earn a livelihood; and at that time they were so busily engaged trying to finish some work that they had neglected to make provision for their ordinary wants, till they found themselves one winter's day in the midst of a New England snowstorm, with food and fuel almost exhausted, at a distance from neighbours, and without any means of procuring needful sustenance. The daughters began to be alarmed at the dismal prospect, but the good old mother said, 'Don't worry, girls; the Lord will provide. We have enough for to-day, and to-morrow may be pleasant.' And in this hope the girls settled down again to their work.

"Another morning came, and with it no sunshine, but wind and snow in abundance. The storm still came, no one came near the house, and there were no tokens of any relief for their necessities. The girls became much distressed, and talked anxiously of their condition, but the good mother said, 'Don't worry; the Lord will provide.' But they had heard that story the day before, and they knew not the strong foundation upon which that mother's faith was built, and could not share the confidence she felt. 'If we get anything to-day the Lord will have to bring it Himself, for nobody else can get here if they try,' said one of the daughters impatiently; but the mother said, 'Don't worry.' So they sat down again to their sewing—the daughters to muse upon their necessitous condition, and the mother to roll her burden on the Everlasting Arms.

"Now, mark the way in which the Lord came to their rescue just at this moment of extremity and put it into the heart of one of His children to go and carry relief. Human courage would never have ventured to face such a storm, but waited for a pleasant day. But divine wisdom and power made the Lord's servant carry just what was needed, in the face of adverse circumstances, and at the time it was needed. Mr M. sat at his fireside, about a mile away, surrounded by every bounty and comfort needed to cheer his heart, with his only daughter sitting by his side. For a long time not a word had been spoken, and he seemed lost in silent meditation, till at length he said, 'Mary, I want you to go and order the cart yoked, and then get me a bag; I must go and carry some wood and flour to Sister C.'

"'Why, father, it is impossible for you to go. There is no track, and it is more than a mile up there. You will almost perish.'

"The old man sat in silence a few moments, then said, 'Mary, I must go.' She knew her father too well to suppose that words would detain him, and so complied with his wishes. While she held the bag for him she felt perhaps a little uneasiness to see the flour so liberally disposed of, and said, 'I wish you would remember that I want to give a poor woman some flour when the storm clears off.' The old man understood her, and said, ' Mary, when the Lord says stop I will do so.'

"Soon all things were ready, and the patient oxen took their way to the widow's home, plunging through the drifted snow, and dragging the sled with its load of wood and flour. About four o'clock in the afternoon the mother had risen from her work to fix the fire, and looking out of the window, she saw the oxen at the door, and knew that the Lord had heard her cry. She said not a word—why should she? She was not surprised! But presently a heavy step at the threshold made the daughters look up in astonishment as Mr M. strode unceremoniously into the room, saying, 'The Lord told me, Sister C., that you wanted some wood and flour.' 'He told you the truth,' said the widow, 'and I will praise Him for ever.'

"'What think you now, girls,' she continued, as she turned in solemn joy to her unbelieving daughters. They were speechless—not a word escaped their lips. But they pondered that new revelation of the providential mercy of the Lord, and from that hour they learned to trust in Him who cares for His needy in the hour of distress, and who from His boundless stores supplies the wants of those who trust in Him."

A HOUSE FOUND.

Mrs Mary R., an aged widow, who has to earn her living, was told she would have to leave her little house in a few months, as it was to be pulled down. She took the matter to the Lord, and reminded Him every night and morning of His care for His children, and asked Him to open up the way for her and give her a home. She was not very able to look for a house after her day's work, but two or three that she did go to see were either uninhabitable or unsuitable. So she left herself in the Lord's hands, trusting that He would provide for her. Two or three months passed, still no house had been found, but she knew God was her Father, and that He would answer her prayers in His own time. One night while looking at "Answers to Prayer" in *Trust magazine*, the widow read about a farmer who carried a quantity of flour and wood to an old woman and her two daughters who were isolated without food or fuel in the depth of a winter snow-storm. It occurred to Mary's mind that God could give her a house just as easily as He had provided for the starving women, and kneeling down she asked Him again to open up the way for her, and send her as plain an answer. While sitting thinking about it in her chair she fell asleep, and after a time was awakened - by a knock at the door. On opening it she saw Miss C., a kind friend, who exclaimed, "Oh, Mrs R., I think I have heard of a house for you now," and after describing it, said she knew the lady who owned it, and if Mary thought it would suit her, she would write to the lady that night. So next day, instead of going to her work, Mary went to see the lady, and took the house. The same night when Mary was visiting an invalid sister, a friend came in with a present for the invalid; and, turning to Mary, said, "And, Mary, mother sent you this for your Christmas," and put in her hand the exact money to pay the first month's rent. She now praises God for not only answering her prayer in such a direct way, but far above all she thought or asked for.

A CHILD'S LIFE SAVED.

SCRIPTURE TESTIMONY
God answers prayer
LUKE 18:7 · JOHN 15:7 · ACTS 12:5 · JAMES 5:15

Mrs John G. Paton, in her "Letters and Sketches from the New Hebrides," tells of an answer to prayer when all the missionaries were together on their way to the Synod. She writes—"As we were sitting at tea a native came overland with a mail from the other side. The letter was from Mrs Goodwill to Mrs Inglis, telling her that little Tommy was dying, and bewailing her husband's absence, little dreaming that by stress of weather he was still on the same island, and would himself read her sorrowful epistle. We had a silent perusal of it round the table, as it entered so much into the detail of the darling child's sufferings that it could not be read aloud. How clearly then we saw the guiding Hand in the storm! Mr Inglis proposed that instead of the sermon usually read on Wednesday evenings there should be a meeting for prayer on behalf of the dear child. He conducted it, and each of the missionaries, except Mr Goodwill and Dr Steele, made earnest supplication that the child might be spared. I don't believe there was a dry eye in the room, and poor Goodwill seemed prostrate, his tears dropping the whole evening. After the closing prayer, he said in as steady a voice as he could command, "I thank all you dear brethren for your kind sympathy and prayers,' and bidding us good night, he walked off to his room. In answer to prayer, the child was restored to health and strength."

THE "DAYSPRING" SAVED.

"As we approached Aneityum, all at once a great grating was heard, and a quivering of the vessel from stem to stem. The 'Dayspring' was on the reef. There we stuck for nearly four hours, with consternation on every face. I felt most of all for the captain, who had been on duty the whole night, and is always so very cautious; but the narrow entrance between those hidden reefs is both deceptive and dangerous. The sailors worked as one man, and the missionaries, having given all the help they possibly could, assembled in the cabin and kept praying in turn to the Lord for our relief. Blessed was the sound to us all when the captain shouted, in a voice falsetto with excitement, 'Hallelujah! she's off! she's off!' He admitted, however, that John was the very first to feel the delightful 'lifting,' and to praise the Lord for answer to his servants' prayers. It was but another illustration of how, in all God's dealings with His children, prayers and pains go hand-in-hand to bring us the blessing."

SAVED FROM THE FLAMES.

A remarkable instance occurred at Saiong, China, of the way God honours faith. There was a terrible fire in the town, and a large number of houses were burned to the ground, leaving the poor families homeless. The people were greatly terrified, seeing the flames advancing and no means apparently of arresting their progress. In one house, right in their path, was an old Christian woman. She climbed on to the roof, and, stretching her arms out to the sky, she cried aloud to Jesus to save her. Next day it was discovered that, though the houses all round were burned, hers was untouched. This event has much impressed even the heathen, and has led the Christians to have more simple faith in God.—*From the Life of Robert and Louisa Stewart.*

A GODLY MINER.

SCRIPTURE TESTIMONY
The sheep know and hear His voice
JOHN 10:3-4 · JOHN 10:16

George B. is a godly miner, and in his lifetime has often proved the truth of God's promises. Some years after his marriage, he was brought into very straitened circumstances through illness in his family. His wife was prostrate with fever and a bad abscess, and required close attention and nursing. It was during a long strike. Nothing could be earned, while the cost of medicine and necessaries exceeded one pound every week. Very soon the little store of savings was exhausted; and one day the husband was face to face with the fact that all the money in the house was fourpence, while the needs of the family were as great as ever. The neighbours were almost as poor, and there was not any one to whom he could apply. He was in despair, and knew not where to turn. All at once there flashed into his mind the promise of God, that no righteous man would ever need to beg his bread. He had prayed before, but now a new light dawned upon him, and, kneeling down at his sick wife's bedside, he laid his need before God, and claimed the fulfilment of His promise. That very night help came. His aged father called, and said that all through the afternoon he could not get rid of a presentiment that George might be needing something, and left a half-sovereign. Hardly had he left, when in stepped a friend from a village two miles away. He explained how, during the day, he had felt an overpowering sense of George B.'s need; and how, acting on the impulse, he had gone round a few of his personal friends and fellow-teachers in a Mission Sunday School, of which George B. was superintendent, and had collected a sum of money which he herewith handed over to his friend, who received it with tears in his eyes, and gratitude in his heart to the great God who had sent an almost instant answer to his cry. Now, dear reader, the incident here narrated is true, for the writer knows all the parties mentioned. Indeed, George B. is the writer's father.

A. B.

THE LOST RECEIPT FOUND.

A poor woman lived in a small cottage who had paid a large sum of money to a tradesman—a dishonest tradesman—and this man pressed her a second time for the money. The poor woman was certain she had paid the money, but she could not find the receipt anywhere, and the tradesman said, "Unless you find that receipt you will have to pay it; I shall send the bailiff, and will sell you up." What did the poor woman do? She went straight to God and said, "Oh, my heavenly Father, Thou knowest the distress I am in, and Thou knowest that it will ruin me if my little cottage and place are sold up; oh, my heavenly Father, undertake for me, for I know I paid that man; and my Father, have mercy on me, and find this bill for me."

As she rose from her knees, the sun shone out gloriously, and in flew a butterfly through the cottage door, and after it came quite a little child—a little bit of a child. The child caught at the butterfly, but it flew behind a cupboard, and then the child screamed and yelled, trying in vain to get at it. The poor woman sought to quiet the child, but the child would not be quieted; and a neighbour coming in said, "Oh, Mrs---, what is the matter with the child?"

"Well," she replied, "a butterfly flew in, and the child wants to get it; it is behind that heavy cupboard there, which I cannot move." "Oh," said the woman, "let us move the cupboard and between them they shifted the heavy press, when something fluttered down to the ground. It was a bit of paper that had been between the press and the wall, and when the old lady took it up, she beheld the receipted bill.

I do not think the tradesman gained much by that transaction.

DESTITUTE, BUT NOT FORSAKEN.

Mrs Lundie, in her *Children of the Manse*, tells the following story of a poor woman, who lived on the banks of the Tweed, whom she had often tried to approach on the subject of religion, but without much success. One day, however, she begged Mrs Lundie to come in, and having shut her door and turned the key that they might not be interrupted, she began: "O, Mrs Lundie, what a lofty heart this is of mine! I thought I would rather perish than make my complaint to any one. I thought that God above knew if we were to live we must be fed, and so I waited as if it belonged to Him to send down manna on me and my five fatherless children, though I neither humbled myself nor prayed for bread.

SCRIPTURE TESTIMONY
God answers prayer
LUKE 18:7 · JOHN 15:7 · ACTS 12:5 · JAMES 5:15

"At last, one Saturday, when it was very cold, and snow on the ground, I had only fourpence in the world, and there were six of us. I almost thought of sending one of the girls up to you to ask a loan of a shilling, though I had no prospect of repaying it; but I was too proud for that even; so I sent her to bring three-quarters of a barley scone, a candle, and some onions; we had some coals and salt, and this was our provision for the Lord's-Day.

"I mourned on that Sabbath more than ever before, and began to think that I had come short in not asking help in prayer. ... I tried at times that day to pray, but my heart was so hard it would neither melt nor feel. I divided the little piece of bread into two, and then shared the half to us all in the morning, and the other half in the evening, and I made the children read chapters, say their prayers, and go to bed early. After that I burned out my candle looking through the Bible for examples of the destitute being provided for, and concluded with a heavy heart that no prophet would ever come to me; if he did, he could not multiply meal for me, as I had not even a little in the barrel. At last I lay down and slept, I think, from hunger. On the Monday morning I sent four of the children away to school with nothing but a drink of warm water. Their complaints of hunger and cold, and the tears of the two younger, fairly broke my heart, and though I said I hoped to have something for them when they came home at noon, I had really no hope. I shut little Mary outside the door and bid her go and play, and then I locked myself in and took my Bible, but I could not read. At last my eye lighted on the words, 'Call on Me in the day of trouble; I will deliver thee, and thou shalt glorify Me.'- I thought this was my day of trouble, and I had not called on God, which might be the reason I was not delivered; so I laid the open book on that chair and kneeled down, but my heart was so full I only rained tears on the chair and cried, 'O Lord, thou knowest that we are starving! help, Lord, for Thy mercy's sake.'

"And while I knelt, and wept, and said a few words now and then, little Mary came running and banging the door, with a cry of great joy, 'Mother, mother, I have found a big fish!' I opened the door, trembling, for I did not know what she meant, when she took hold of my apron and led me to a pool of water left in a hollow by the river, and there, sure enough, lay a stranded salmon, so heavy that I could scarcely lift it.'

Mrs Lundie goes on:—"I remember the time very well. Thaw came in the night; the snow melted fast; the ice in the river broke up hastily; the water spread over the banks, and nearly up to the doors of that row of cottages. The fish had been swept out of the channel and left in a hollow place; the water flowed away quickly and left the salmon for the poor widow. She carried it up to the largest inn and sold it. When it was weighed it was 19.5 lbs., and she got many shillings for it—enough to feed her family many days. I said, 'That was a wonderful provision; I am sure you felt that it came straight from God.'

"'Yes,' she said. 'Had any one given me double the price into my hand I fear I should not have seen the hand of God in it.'

"She then told me that as soon as she had purchased some provisions and prepared them for the children, she shut the door again and kneeled down to give thanks, and vowed never again to forget that prayer is the way, and that God on whom we depend has all things in His hand."

We do not call this a miracle, yet how did it come? It was an answer to prayer, and we may learn from this true story that the Lord knows the wants of His people, and can supply them now as well as on the day when Peter took the tribute-money out of the mouth of the fish, and His power over water and the creatures that dwell therein is still turned to the help of those who call on Him.

> "The birds without barn
> Or storehouse are fed;
> From them let us learn
> To trust for our bread.

His saints what is fitting
Shall ne'er be denied
So long as 'tis written
The Lord will provide."

THE CHRISTMAS BOX.
By a Minister's Wife.

SCRIPTURE TESTIMONY
Our Father in heaven gives good things
MATTHEW 7:9-11

I remember a day during one winter which stands out like a boulder in my life.

The weather was unusually cold. Our salary had not been regularly paid, and it did not meet our needs when it was. My husband was away travelling from one district to another most of the time.

Our boys were well, but my little Ruth was ailing; and at best none of us were decently clothed. I patched and repatched, with spirits sinking to the lowest ebb. The water gave out in the well, and the wind blew through the cracks of the floor.

The people in the parish were kind and generous, but the settlement was new, and each family was struggling for itself. Little by little, at the time when I needed it most, my faith began to waver. Early in life I was taught to take God at His Word, and I thought my lesson was well learned. I had lived upon the promises in dark times, until I knew, as David did, Who was "my fortress and my deliverer." Now a daily prayer for forgiveness was all that I could offer.

My husband's overcoat was hardly thick enough for October, and he was obliged to ride miles to attend meetings or funerals. Many a time our breakfast was Indian cake and a cup of tea without any sugar. Christmas was coming; the children always expected their presents. I remember the ice was thick and smooth, and the boys were each craving a pair of skates. Ruth, in some unaccountable way, had taken a fancy that the dolls that I made were no longer suitable; she wanted a large, nice one, and insisted upon praying for it. I knew it was impossible; but, oh, how I wanted to give each child its present! It seemed as if God had deserted us. But I did not tell my husband all this. He worked so earnestly and heartily, I supposed him to be as hopeful as ever. I kept the sitting-room cheery with an open fire, and tried to serve our scanty meals as invitingly as I could. The morning before Christmas James was called to see a sick man. I put up a piece of bread for his lunch—it was the best I could do—wrapped a plaid shawl round his neck, and then tried to whisper a promise, as I often had: but the words died away on my lips. I let him go without it. This was a dark, hopeless day.

I coaxed the children to bed early, for I could not bear their talk. When Ruth went I listened to her prayer; she asked for the last time most explicitly for her doll, and for skates for her brothers. Her bright face looked so lovely when she whispered to me, "You know, I think they will be here early to-morrow morning—early, mamma," that I thought I could move heaven and earth to save her from the disappointment.

I sat down alone and gave way to the bitterest tears.

Before long James returned, chilled and exhausted. He drew off his boots; the thin stockings slipped off with them, and his feet were red with cold. Then, as I glanced up and noticed the hard lines in his face, and the look of despair, it flashed across me—James had let go, too! I brought him a cup of tea, feeling sick and dizzy at that thought. He took my hand, and we sat for an hour without a word. I wanted to die and meet God, and tell Him His promise was not true—my soul was so full of rebellious despair.

There came a sound of bells, a quick step, and a loud knock at the door. James sprang up to open it. There stood Deacon Pike.

"A box came for you by express just before dark. I brought it round as soon as I could get away; reckoned it might be for Christmas. At any rate, I thought, they shall have it to-night. Here is a turkey my wife asked me to fetch along, and these other things, I believe, belong to you."

There was a basket of potatoes and a bag of flour. Talking all the time, he hurried in the box, and then with a hearty "good-night" rode away. Still without speaking, James found a chisel and opened the box. I drew out at first a thick red blanket, and we saw that beneath was full of clothing. It seemed at that moment as if Christ fastened upon me a look of reproach. James sat down and covered his face with his hands.

"I can't touch them," he exclaimed, "I haven't been true just when God was trying me to see if I could hold out. Do you think I could not see how you were suffering, and I had no word of comfort to offer? I know not how to preach the awfulness of turning away from God."

"James," I said, clinging to him, "don't take to heart like this. I've been to blame. I ought to have helped you. We will ask Him together to forgive us."

"Wait a moment, dear, I cannot talk now" then he went into another room.

I knelt down and my heart broke; in an instant all the darkness, all the stubbornness rolled away. Jesus came and stood before me, but now with the loving word "Daughter!" Sweet promises of tenderness and joy flooded my soul. I was so lost in praise and gratitude that I forgot everything else. I do not know how long it was before James came back; but I knew that he, too, had found peace.

"Now, dear wife," said he, "let us thank God together." And then he poured out words of praise —Bible words, for nothing else could express our thanksgiving. It was eleven o'clock. The fire was low, and there was the great box, and nothing touched but the warm blanket we needed so much. We piled on some fresh logs, lighted two candles, and began to examine our treasures. We drew out an overcoat. I made James try it on; just the right size, and I danced awhile round him, for all my lightheartedness had returned. Then there was a cloak, and he insisted on seeing me in it. My spirits always affected him, and we both laughed like foolish children. There was a warm suit of clothes also, and three pairs of warm woollen hose. There was a dress for me, and yards of flannel; a pair of Arctic overshoes for each of us, and in mine was a slip of paper—I have it now, and I mean to hand it down to my children. It was Jacob's blessing to Asher— "Thy shoes shall be iron and brass, and as thy days, so shall thy strength be." In the gloves, evidently for James, the same dear hand had written—"I, the Lord thy God, will hold thy right hand, saying unto thee, Fear not, I will help thee."

It was a wonderful box, and packed with thoughtful care. There was a suit of clothes for each of the boys, and a little red gown for Ruth. There were mittens, scarfs, and hoods. Down in the centre, a box —we opened it, and there was a great wax doll. I burst into tears again, and James wept with me for joy. It was too much. Then we both exclaimed again, for close behind it came two pairs of skates. There were books for us to read—some of them I had wished to see—stories for the children to read; aprons and underclothing, knots of ribbon, a gay little tidy, a lovely photograph, needles, buttons and thread, actually a muff, and an envelope containing a ten-dollar gold piece. We cried over everything we took up. It was past midnight, and we were faint and exhausted even with happiness.

I made a cup of tea, cut a fresh loaf of bread, and James boiled some eggs. We drew up the table before the fire—how we enjoyed our supper!—and then we sat talking over all our life, and how sure a help God had always proved.

You should have seen the children the next morning. The boys raised a shout at the sight of their skates. Ruth caught up her doll and hugged it tightly without a word; then she went into her room and knelt by her bed. When she came back she whispered to me—"I knew it would be here, mamma, but I wanted to thank God just the same, you know."

"Look here, wife; see the difference!"

We went to the window, and there were the boys out of the house already, and skating with all their might.

My husband and I both tried to return thanks to the church in the East which sent us the box, and have tried to return thanks unto God every day since.

Hard times have come again and again, but we have trusted in Him, dreading nothing so much as a doubt of His protecting care. Over and over again we have proved that they who seek- the Lord shall not want any good thing.

THE WIDOW'S SON.

A clergyman's widow in England was anxious as to the future of her second son, a youth sixteen years of age. His health failed through over-study, and the doctor recommended entire rest for a time. At the end of a year he felt so well that he was desirous of turning his attention to some particular line in life, and chose the sea. Mrs A. thought of the navy, but had no influence, and despaired of getting admission for her son. Nothing daunted, however, she went to London, and laid her case before one of the Lords of the Admiralty, who said that merit alone decided, and that no amount of influence would have the least effect. A large number of young men applied for nominations to the coveted office, that of assistant paymaster, and when the examination was over Arthur A. was greatly surprised to find that he had passed second, having only six marks less than the one who was first. Five candidates were elected.

No sooner did Arthur pass than his mother was informed that his outfit would cost £60 at least—a sum which she could not afford, as she had six children to provide for. She consulted an uncle, who seemed to think Arthur must now give up all idea of appointment. On the street, when returning home, there flashed into Mrs A.'s mind the promise, "Before they call I will answer." An hour after the postman brought a letter, which was from a rich cousin, and before opening it she said, "The money has come! Arthur, let us kneel down and thank God," which they did. The letter contained a cheque for £50, and a few days later a second cheque for £50 came from a kind brother-in-law. Both friends had seen the notice of Arthur's success in the newspaper, and sent the money as an encouragement. "Whoso is wise and will observe these things, even they shall understand the loving-kindness of the Lord."

WAITING ALL DAY.

A lady, who lived on the north side of London, set out one day to visit a poor sick friend living in Drury Lane, and took with her a basket provided with tea, butter, &c. The day was fine and clear when she started, but as she drew near Islington a thick fog came on and somewhat frightened her, as she was deaf, and feared it might be dangerous in the streets if she could not see.

Thicker and darker the fog became; the lamps were lighted, and the omnibus went at a walking pace. She might have got into another omnibus and returned, but a strong feeling which she could not explain made her go on. When the omnibus reached the Strand she could see nothing. At last it stopped, and the conductor guided her to the footpath. As she was groping her way the fog cleared up just at the entrance of Drury Lane, and even the blue sky was visible. She now easily found the narrow court, rang No. 5 bell, and climbed to the fifth storey. She knocked at the door, and a little girl opened it.

"How is grandmother?"

"Come in, Mrs Allen," answered the grandmother.

"How did you get here! We have been in thick darkness all day."

The room was exceedingly tidy, and the kettle was boiling on a small clear fire. Everything was in perfect order; on the table stood a little tea-tray ready for use. The sick woman was in bed, and her daughter sat working in a corner of the room.

"I see you are ready for tea," said the lady; "I have brought something more to place upon the table."

With clasped hands the woman breathed a few words of thanksgiving first, and then said, "Oh! Mrs Allen, you are indeed God's raven, sent by Him to bring us food to-day, for we have not tasted any yet.

I felt sure He would care for us."

"But I see that you have the kettle on the fire ready for tea?"

"Yes, ma'am," said the daughter; "mother would have me set it on the fire, and when I said, 'What is the use of doing so? you know we have nothing in the house,' she still would have it, and said, 'My child, God will provide. Thirty years He has already provided for me through all my pain and helplessness, and He will not leave me to starve at last; He will send us help, though we do not see how.' So mother has been waiting all day, quite sure that some one would come to supply our need. But we did not think of the possibility of your coming from such a distance on such a day. Indeed, it must be God who sent you to us."

"LORD, HELP ME!"

A gentleman once asked a poor boy, "Do you pray to God?" "No, I don't know how."

"If I teach you a prayer will you use it every day?" "Yes, but my head is thick."

The prayer was very short—-only three words: "Lord, help me."

"Please, sir, will that do for everything?—if I am cold and hungry?"

"Then tell God, and say, 'Lord, help me.'"

"When they met again Mr Milton asked, "Did you pray?" "Yes."

"What did you say?" "Lord, help me, because Mr Milton says You will."

"Why did you mention my name?"

"I thought the Lord knew you, and would be more likely to mind me if you were my friend."

Shortly after the boy told his kind friend how bitterly he felt the cold, and asked if he might pray for a great-coat.

"Yes, we may tell God everything."

But in a few days the boy came, looking very sad. "I have asked, but God has not given me a greatcoat."

Mr Milton pitied the boy, and longed to give him one, but he only said, "Go on praying."

The day following the poor boy marched up, clad in a warm coat, his face shining with joy, and exclaimed, "Look, sir! Did not God hear me quickly?"

"Where did you get that?"

"When I left you I prayed again, and said, 'Lord, don't you remember how I asked for a great-coat, because I was so cold and the weather keeps bad, and I have none; please send me one. Lord, help me!' When I went out all shivering, a gentleman said to me, "How cold you look, lad and he took me to the shop and bought me this. Isn't it a beauty?" he added, his eyes glistening with joy.

Mr Milton was hardly less pleased than the boy, and they knelt and thanked God together.—*Friendly Greetings.*

MORE PRECIOUS THAN FOWLS OR LILIES.

About the year 1870, I left my home in Ireland to make my way in the world. I decided to go to Scotland, and on leaving my father gave me a Bible and a few shillings, and said that as long as he had a roof over his head I would get a welcome back again. I went to Glasgow, and stayed for a time with a student whom I knew. I was a compositor to trade, and he accompanied me for about a week in my search for work, which, however was a vain one, for no opening could I find. A minister who knew my father wrote me from Edinburgh telling me of a vacant situation there. I went over, only to find that the work was altogether different from that to which I was accustomed, so that I had to decline it. When I went to see the minister, he was from home, but I took lodgings, and pursued my search. One day I found that after paying my landlady I had only sixpence left. What was I to do? Return home I felt I could not, so I took my Bible and turned to the 12th chapter of Luke, where our Lord tells how the fowls are fed and the lilies are clothed by Him, and reminds us that we are much more precious to Him than they are. A sweet sense of the Lord's presence was with me as I read, and I knelt down and prayed earnestly that He would undertake for me and provide work. He seemed to take me by the hand and lead me out to a street where I had never been before. I stopped before a stationer's shop, went in, and on asking for work I was at once taken into the employment of the firm. I stayed there a year and a half, and it was one of the happiest times of my life. I was full of thankfulness to God for so manifestly answering my prayer.

A SAILORS' REST OBTAINED.

The town of Dunkirk, in the north of France, is much frequented by sailors of all nations. The town is a very wicked and drunken one, and the sailors are exposed to every form of temptation. There was not a Protestant place of worship or Sailors' Rest to which the men could go. One day four sailors knelt down and pleaded with God that some place might be opened where they could meet each other and be safe from the sin and temptation which beset them when landing from their vessels. An account of the need of a Sailors' Rest in Dunkirk was inserted in a religious magazine in this country. A lady read it, and was so touched by the appeal that she offered to pay the rent of a suitable place for three years. Another friend came forward and offered to furnish it, and in less than a month from the time the four sailors knelt in prayer a full answer was given. The place became a centre of blessing, but as the three years—the time for which the rent was promised— drew to a close earnest prayer was again offered that help might be given. For a time there seemed not to be any answer, but one day a gentleman who knew their circumstances offered to build a suitable house and lease it to the mission on the same terms as they were then holding their suite of rooms. His offer was gladly accepted, and excellent accommodation was provided. The mission, which was begun in prayer, is still carried on in the same spirit, and is much blessed.

FIVE GUINEAS FOUND.

SCRIPTURE TESTIMONY
The prayer of a person in right relationship with God is effective
JAMES 5:16-18

A fisherman in the isle of Portland, having had a very bad fishing season, was in great distress. His son-in-law, T. C., who was the Parish Clerk, was a man of decided piety, and of great prayerfulness. At family worship one morning he prayed most earnestly that God would send help to his father-in-law. His wife said to him—"Tom, thou hast prayed very fervently to-day; I believe God will hear thy prayers." The next day his father-in-law was digging for bait in the mere opposite the parsonage, and almost the first spadeful of sand and mud he took up had in it five guineas of the early part of George III.'s reign! Tom's wife heard of the providential discovery before her husband, and on his return to dinner said to him —"Sure enough God has heard thy prayers, for father has found five guineas almost the first spadeful he dug up." Tom's father-in-law was thus enabled to discharge his debts and to supply himself with needed food. Never before nor since had money been found in that mere. One of these guineas has been preserved by the present incumbent of St John's, Portland, as a memento of the Divine faithfulness in answering prayer, and as a proof that "the effectual fervent prayer of a righteous man availeth much."

A LADY'S WILL.

On one occasion the London City Mission had a deficiency in its general receipts of about £4,000; and, as it is a plan of that Society to spend all that the Christian public confide to its care, *but no more*, its Committee began seriously to think about the necessity of reducing the number of its missionaries. It was, however, felt that this would be a circumstance deeply to be deplored, and many a prayer was offered that the Lord would be pleased to avert such a calamity. These prayers were heard and answered in the following remarkable manner:—In the district of Belgravia some papers had been circulated announcing a meeting to be held on behalf of the "Belgrave Association of the London City Mission." One of these papers was seen by Mrs W., a lady not previously acquainted with the Society. She saw the name of Dr--- as one of the speakers, and out of curiosity went to hear him, for she had long had a desire to do so. His address so interested her that she gave a subscription of £5. Shortly afterwards she was taken ill, and was advised to make her will. The London City Mission having just before occupied so much of her thoughts, she resolved to divide the £20,000 three per cents, which she had in the funds between it and three other Societies. The will was accordingly made, and she died shortly afterwards. The £5,000 three per cents, was paid over without delay to the Mission, and after selling out and paying the £500 legacy duty, it brought into the Society £4,173 15s., at the very time needed to prevent the large reduction of missionaries, which so many had been praying to the Lord to avert.

IN DESTITUTION.

The following is taken from "A Woman's Work:" "One Sabbath, at forenoon service, Miss Fletcher's eyes and heart were irresistibly drawn towards an old woman who was evidently pinched with care and bowed under some load of pressing anxiety. She felt that she ought to give that old dame some money, and mentally resolved to do so, if the opportunity presented itself, at the evening service. Arriving at home she found that her pocket-money consisted of exactly one napoleon, and though loath to part with the whole of it, she felt she could neither break it nor leave it behind, but must take it with her to church. This she did, half hoping that the old woman would not be among the worshippers again. But there she was, with the mute and unconscious but irresistible appeal as plainly written on her face as ever. On coming out of the church Miss Fletcher somehow found herself side by side with her; and it was the work of a moment to slip the gold piece into the astonished old lady's hand and run off without waiting for thanks. It afterwards emerged that the woman at that very time was in the utmost destitution. She had been presenting her case to God in prayer, and was leaving the church in the confidence that He had pitied and had heard her—when the answer was given in this unlooked-for way."

II. PRAYER FOR SPIRITUAL BLESSINGS.

A HUSBAND'S CONVERSION.

A GODLY WOMAN had a very ungodly husband, and was much distressed by his conduct. Instead of getting better he grew worse, and latterly he forbade

SCRIPTURE TESTIMONY
Holy Spirit convicts people of their sin
JOHN 16:8

her to speak to him on religious subjects. She prayed much for him and reasoned with him, but her prayers and entreaties were of no avail. In great distress of mind she went to her minister and told him how her husband had prohibited her from trying to win him to Christ. The minister replied that he might forbid her to speak, but he could not prevent them praying for him. The doors of heaven were still open, and the prayer of faith could gain admittance. They prayed earnestly for him, and his wife went home to continue her pleadings. One Sunday morning some time afterwards he rose and went out to spend the day in his usual way. As he passed along he saw a tract lying on the street, and, stooping down to look at the title, he saw the words, "One shall be taken and the other left." The phrase seemed very personal, and evidently applied to himself and his wife. She would be taken and he would be left; would it actually come some day to this? If he continued his present wicked life he knew it would. The thought pierced him like an arrow. His peace was gone, and there was no pleasure for him that Sunday. He turned homeward and went at once to bed. He lay troubled and uneasy, for when conviction of sin comes home to a man's heart all the bravado leaves him. In the evening as the bells were ringing for worship he rose and told his wife he was going to church with her. She was greatly astonished, but also greatly delighted. Perhaps her prayers were to be answered after all. A higher power was dealing with him now. They went together to church, and the minister who had encouraged her and prayed with her was the preacher. But what was her husband's amazement as he heard the text given out, "One shall be taken and the other left." Surely the hand of God was in this. The words had stared him in the face in the morning, they had arrested him and prevented his habitual sin of Sabbath-breaking, they had sent him all day to bed in distress of soul, and now the minister read them from the Word of God, as if meant specially for him. It was too much for him; humbled and penitent, he there and then accepted God's offered salvation. There was joy in heaven, and joy in the heart of his praying wife, because her husband was converted and her prayers of years were answered. The change in his life was great. He wished now to do something to show his gratitude to the Lord who had mercifully saved him. He began work among the young, and for many years laboured zealously for their salvation.

ALL SAVED.

"Surely goodness and mercy shall follow me all the days of my life." These words are truly the experience of the friend of whom I write. In her earlier days, in a comfortable position, she received many tokens of the Lord's favour, and with her husband, and family of five sons and two daughters, knew little of trouble. But the sudden removal of her husband changed her circumstances, and the burden of her family's wants weighed heavily on her. Her concern was intensified by the death of her eldest son when he was beginning to be a help to her. These were dark days, for on her own labour the family almost entirely depended. Still her face did not lose its sunshine, and through the darkness she traced the outline of a Father's hand. Years passed away, and anxiously she watched and longed to see her children brought to the Saviour. For nearly twenty years she pleaded earnestly, and at last her two daughters and eldest and youngest sons gave themselves to the Lord, though not all at the same time. Subsequently another blow fell upon her. A deadly and terrible disease seized her, accompanied with great pain. But to her a heavier burden than that of physical suffering was her two unsaved sons, and it is of them I wish to tell more particularly. One was in London, and the other, who was the object of her special pleading, was in Australia. A year and a half passed away, and her entreaties to her distant son to come home seemed lost upon him, and she wondered if the absence of ten years had cooled his affection. But still she prayed for them, and her prayers were so far answered that her son in London removed to a neighbouring town, and marrying, settled down to a quieter life than he had led in the Metropolis. And her joy can be imagined when one day most unexpectedly her son from abroad came home to her safe and sound. He had a strange tale to tell of his home-coming. Through stormy weather the ship was driven out of her course, and was so long in arriving that she was posted as overdue. On board all was confusion. The captain lost knowledge as to his whereabouts, and they were in imminent peril of being stranded on the Goodwin Sands; but through timely help they were saved from a watery grave, and reached Gravesend in safety. But not yet were all dangers passed: a heavy fog fell on them in the Thames. They were run into by another steamer, and once more death threatened them; but the mother's prayers were to be *all* answered, and her boy reached home in safety—safe in body, but not safe in soul. Still she prayed that God would fulfil all her desires, and that ere the end of her pilgrimage both of her lads might be the Lord's. God has granted her request. At one of Mr Moody's meetings her married son and his wife gave themselves to Christ, and a few weeks later the other son also accepted the Saviour. Could other words than those I began with better describe my dear friend's feelings towards God. . . . *All the days of her life*, and not least at the very end. What a happy family: not one amissing on that day when she shall say, "Here am I and the children whom Thou hast given me."

J. N.

SEVEN SAVED.

A prominent Christian worker died, leaving a widow with a family of eight young children. She was well-nigh crushed under the blow, but she knew her God and could cling to the promise that He would be a father to the fatherless and a husband to the widow. She daily carried her troubles to the throne of grace, and her many hours of care and burdenbearing were known only to herself and the Lord, who, in a very remarkable manner, directed and sustained her. Her family attained to good positions in life. From their childhood she had prayed earnestly for their conversion, and also asked the prayers of friends on their behalf. A letter from one of her sons abroad gave an account of his conversion, which filled her with gratitude. He said, "One Sunday afternoon I was reading a small book which M. gave me. I began looking back on the past four or five months, and they appeared to have been hedged in on every side with tokens of God's mercy. There was a work of grace going on all that time, but my stubborn heart would not yield. M. used to say that I was a puzzle, having it all in my head and shutting my heart against it; and so it was. I could see that I had been very near the point of decision at that time; I could also see that I must now decide the question once for all, because I knew that if I gave in the least bit to the world all desire for a higher life would leave me. I decided for Christ; so praise God for another wandering sheep brought into the fold. I know you will all rejoice exceedingly at my having come to this decision. I pray that I may be out and out for Christ."

The mother prayed six years before she saw any of her children converted, and there are now seven of them brought to the Lord. There is only one who has not openly confessed Christ, and she is unceasing in her prayers for him. Herself a woman of faith and communion with the Lord, she has called down much of the blessing of heaven on her family.

A MOTHER'S PRAYERS.

A Christian worker says:—"Through many years I have had requests to pray for the conversion of some loved one, and I have adoringly to bear testimony to the faithfulness of our Heavenly Father in answering prayer. Since my conversion I have been favoured to see no fewer than eight of my own relatives and my dear adopted daughter brought *to* the Lord Jesus, and all gone to be *with* Him, joined eventually there by my much-loved wife. Have I not cause to sound an encouraging note and say, 'PRAISE YE THE Lord?'

"Oh, remember His own word, 'Ask and ye shall receive.' The answer to prayer may seem to us to be delayed, but it will come. Many, many instances I could give of apparently delayed answers—nevertheless they did come. I give one illustration of this:

"I was called upon to visit a man who had met with a very serious accident. On going I found he had lived a sad life, and was utterly careless about eternal things. Seeing his life was in danger, I sought to press the truth of his lost condition and his need of salvation upon him. He appeared quite callous; he certainly listened, and that was all. I saw him repeatedly, yet all seemed in vain. His Christian mother was in much distress about his spiritual state. She assured me that for years she had prayed for him. Weeks passed, and to all appearance he remained in the same unconcerned frame of mind—becoming weaker and weaker in body. One of his sisters told me that his mother had always prayed for him, and that when a lad, she had known his mother get out of bed at night to pray on his behalf. A few days before he departed the Holy Spirit convicted him of sin, and that very deeply, so that he continually cried to the Lord to have mercy and to save him. At last the answer came. Peace with God, through the Lord Jesus Christ, flowed into his poor troubled soul, and his joy became boundless—he was filled with praise, glorifying God, and so passed away."

"If six or sixty prayers are passed,
Pray on and never faint;
A blessing surely comes at last
To cheer a drooping saint."

AT THE ELEVENTH HOUR.

A godly man, who had spent a lifetime in evangelistic work, had a wife who gave him much concern. She had little or no sympathy with Gospel

SCRIPTURE TESTIMONY
The blood of Jesus cleanses us from all sin
I JOHN 1:7

work, and her conduct was very unbecoming. Her husband felt the trial keenly, but took refuge in his Bible and his God. For many years he prayed for her, but, although the Lord used him much in the salvation of others, his own wife remained quite careless, and his prayers for her seemed to go unanswered.

But a change was about to take place. Bodily weakness and a sickbed are often used to bring wanderers to the fold, and it was so in her case. She became very unwell, and her life was despaired of. Her husband was away from home, but was summoned, and only arrived in time to be recognised by his dying wife. He spoke to her, and heard her faintly whisper, "The blood cleanseth from all sin." He fell on his knees, and as she passed away he committed her spirit to the Lord. He said that as he prayed the heavens seemed to open over him. The vision was so clear and distinct that it left not even the shadow of a doubt that she had been received up into glory, and that his years of prayer had been answered. He was so overjoyed that he would gladly have gone home himself. It was years after his wife's death when he related this, but he said that the effect of the manifestation still remained with him.

A BROTHER'S PRAYERS.

An earnest Christian was anxious for the salvation of his sister. She lived in a public-house, and all its influences were against her. The brother gave himself to prayer for her, believing that, hard though the case seemed to be, nothing was impossible with the Lord. He met her on the street one day, and exhorted her to seek first the Kingdom of God and His righteousness. The words laid hold of her, and she could not shake off the impression they had made. She got no rest, and although she was in a state of anxiety and had fallen into ill-health, her brother was not allowed to visit her. He heard that she had become much worse, and resolved that, if possible, he would get into the house and see her. He made the attempt and got to her bedside. He pointed her to Christ, and his joy was great when she told him that even if he had not come she would have met him in glory. His prayers and his earnest words on the street had resulted in her conversion. She died trusting in Christ for salvation. Unbelief makes us think at times that some cases are beyond the reach of grace, but faith pleads on and expects God to glorify Himself in rescuing the worst.

THE JUST SHALL LIVE BY FAITH.

A minister lost his wife by death. He felt the stroke very keenly, and was much depressed in spirit. He had carried his trouble to the Lord, but had not found relief. With a heavy heart he followed her body to the grave, and felt as if he were burying all life's joys with her. While he stood surrounded by the mourners the words, "The just shall live by faith," came to him with great power. In a moment he realised that the Lord doeth all things well; that for some wise purpose He had taken away his wife, and would make His grace sufficient for him in the future. For the first time since her death his heart was at rest, and his prayers and tears were answered.

"IF ANY TWO OF YOU."

A young woman living in a country district was converted a few years ago. She found another likeminded with herself; they both met once a week for prayer, and for two years

SCRIPTURE TESTIMONY
All great movements of God are birthed in prayer
ACTS 1:14 · ACTS 4:31

pleaded with the Lord for blessing. Meetings were very rarely held in the district, but an evangelist ultimately visited it. The services were very successful, and numbers were converted. The two young women were foremost in the work, and did much to make it a success. They were greatly blessed themselves, and had the joy of seeing an abundant answer to their two years of prayer. The revival of the Lord's work greatly depends on the praying bands scattered over our country. If His people would meet oftener together in twos and threes and give themselves to wrestling, believing prayer, we would soon see the tide of worldliness and unbelief which is rapidly setting in upon us turned back. The only power that can save men is the power of God, and that is given in answer to the prayers of faith. When believers take to their knees victory is near.

A MOTHER AND HER TWO DAUGHTERS.

A mother who was anxious regarding the salvation of her two daughters often prayed for them. They attended a church where the Gospel was faithfully preached, but the minister's words failed to awaken them. Mr D.

L. Moody visited the town, and many professed conversion. The mother was much troubled lest the time of blessing should pass and her children remain unsaved. She wrote a letter to Mr Moody requesting his special interest in them. She also asked the lady with whom he was staying to use her influence with him to plead for them. The Lord loves importunity, and He blessed the mother's efforts. In the evening meeting as the requests for prayer were read out Mr Moody specially referred to the widow's request for her daughters, and prayed earnestly for them. That night they were in the meeting, and were awakened. Friends spoke to them. They were both converted, and the mother's prayers of many years were answered.

ORIGIN OF A REVIVAL.

SCRIPTURE TESTIMONY
The believer is to be persistent in prayer
LUKE 11:5-10

A man living in a country village became distressed about its spiritual condition. He did not know much about evangelists or Evangelistic Associations, but he knew of one Society which sent out men to labour in villages. All he could do was to go to his God and plead with Him that an evangelist might be sent from that Mission. The prayer of faith is always heard, though the suppliant may never see the answer. It was so in this instance. The man died, and was taken to his rest, but several months afterwards an evangelist from the Society he had named arrived in the village, and began a series of meetings. During the first fortnight he lodged in a certain house, but at the end of that time he was told he would require to look out for other lodgings, as the landlady had friends coming who would want the room. After inquiry he found he could stay with the sister of the man who had died, and for three weeks he lived in the room that had been occupied by the man who had so earnestly prayed that he should be sent to the village. To the evangelist that room must have been as the very ante-chamber of heaven, fragrant with the prayers of the man of God, and sanctified by the presence of the Lord Himself. The meetings were successful, and conversions followed. The man of prayer was gone, but the Lord gave the answer in His own time.

CONVERSION OF A SERVANT GIRL.

A young woman in domestic service having been brought to the Lord some years ago was filled with joy, and was anxious that others should share it with her. She began to witness for Christ, and to tell of the great change He had wrought in her heart. She was specially interested in a young girl who was serving with her in the same house, and often spoke to her about her salvation, urging her to give her heart to Christ. But she was only mocked and laughed at, and all her efforts seemed in vain. Time passed, and she removed to a place in another part of the country. When bidding farewell, her fellow-servant became greatly distressed, and said, "I will have no one now to speak to me about my soul." This was the first time that the faithful words had made any apparent impression. Greatly encouraged, the Christian pleaded on for four years, and then received a letter from her young companion telling that she had become a follower of the Lord Jesus Christ. Her earnest entreaties and her four years of prayer were rewarded. If we diligently seek the Lord He will be found of us, and will give us the desires of our hearts.

FRUIT AFTER THREE YEARS.

There are many forms of Christian work in which any one anxious to serve his Lord may engage, and it is a cause of great strength to us if we know we are in the very place where the Lord would have us. Mr D., an earnest worker, was in the habit of setting apart some time each Sabbath for personal dealing on the streets with young men who did not go to church. He would enter into conversation with them about their salvation, and would try to win them for the Lord. He found many of them quite willing to listen, and some were evidently impressed. Some time after a friend advised him to get work in connection with his church or mission, and to give up the more unusual one of accosting people on the street. He was troubled at this suggestion, as he thought he was engaged in the very service to which God had called him. He was in the habit of laying all his concerns before the Lord in prayer, asking His guidance. He pleaded earnestly for Divine direction in this matter, seeking for some special token of the Lord's will. One day shortly afterwards, while coming out of a shop, a young lad accosted him and asked if he were Mr D. Being answered in the affirmative, he asked if he remembered speaking to a young man on the street about his salvation three years before, "Because," said he "I am that young man. I decided for Christ at that time, and have been trusting Him ever since." Mr D.'s heart was filled with thankfulness that his prayer had been so speedily answered, and that the Lord had so manifestly set His seal to his work. It decided him to continue a service which he loved so much, and to which no one but himself seemed to be specially devoted. Truly, if we acknowledge the Lord in all our ways He will direct our paths.

WHAT A LETTER DID.

A worker says:—"There was a young lad under my charge for a time in whom I took a special interest. He became deeply impressed, and I was hopeful he had undergone a change of heart. He left for a foreign country and prospered. In 1891 I saw a letter he had written to a mutual friend, but I was much pained to find it was all about worldly matters, and did not contain any reference to spiritual things. His case lay heavily on my heart, and for several months I pleaded with God for his salvation. I wrote him an earnest letter telling him my fears, and urging him to seek the Lord. For a considerable time I did not get any answer, but it came at last, and was as follows':—'I was very glad to receive your kind and welcome letter. It was the best one I have ever got, for it went to my heart. I could not put it aside, but had carefully to think it over. I have never written a letter with more pleasure than I write this one, for I can now say "The Lord is my refuge and strength, in Him will I trust." Before I got your letter I was going deeper and deeper into sin, but I thank God He has put a new life in me. I have joined the Y.M.C.A., and the young men are a great help to me. When they heard I had found the Lord they made me a present of a Bible.' The above letter cheered me greatly. It came as the answer to many prayers, and I now give it to encourage others to plead on in faith, and the Lord will in His own good time and way grant them their petitions."

INTERCEPTED AND SAVED.

A lady who was very much used by the Lord in the salvation of souls, met, when visiting in her district, a young militiaman who had led a wicked life, and was just out of prison. He was to leave for his regiment on the following day, and the lady, thinking that probably she might never have another opportunity, spoke very solemnly to him about his sins, and urged him to turn to God. Kneeling down, she prayed earnestly that he might be kept from evil companions and be brought to repentance. He left next day and became so intoxicated that he fell and injured his leg severely. He was taken to an hospital, where he lay several weeks. He felt that God had brought him low in order to convince him of his sinfulness. He was angry with the lady, and he afterwards said that her prayer caused him to lie six weeks with an injured knee. He, however, returned home with an awakened conscience, from which he did not get any rest till he found pardon and peace through the blood of Christ.

A REMARKABLE BLESSING.

James Brainerd Taylor was converted at the age of fifteen, and six years afterwards he experienced a remarkable blessing from the Spirit. This is his own account of what

SCRIPTURE TESTIMONY
No longer I who live, but Christ who lives in me
GALATIANS 2:20

then occurred:—"It was on the 23rd of April 1822, when I was on a visit to Haddam, in Connecticut. Memorable day! The time and place will never—no, never—be forgotten! I recur to it at this moment with thankful remembrance. For a long time my desire had been that the Lord would visit me, and fill me with the Holy Ghost—my cry to Him was, 'Seal my soul, for ever Thine.' I lifted up my heart in prayer that the blessing might descend. I felt that I needed something I did not possess. There was a void within which must be filled, or I could not be happy. My earnest desire was then, as it has been ever since I professed religion six years before, that all love of the world might be destroyed—all selfishness extirpated—pride humbled—unbelief removed— all idols dethroned—everything hostile to holiness and opposed to the Divine will crucified; that holiness to the Lord might be engraved on my heart, and evermore characterise my conversation. My mind was led to reflect on what would probably be my future situation. It occurred to me 'I am hereafter to be a minister of the

Gospel. But how shall I be able to preach in my present state of mind? I cannot—never, no, never, shall be able to do it with pleasure, without great overturnings in my mind and soul.' I felt that I needed that for which I was then, and for a long time had been, hungering and thirsting. I desired it, not for my benefit only, but for that of the Church and the world. At this very juncture I was most delightfully conscious of giving up all to God. I was enabled in my heart to say, Here, Lord, take me, take my whole heart and seal me Thine—Thine now, and Thine for ever. 'If Thou wilt Thou canst make me clean.' Then there ensued such emotions as I never before experienced. All was calm and tranquil, and a heaven of love pervaded my whole soul. I had a witness of God's love to me, and of mine to Him. Shortly afterwards I was dissolved in tears of love and gratitude to our blessed Lord. The name of Jesus was precious to me—'twas music in my ear. He came as King, and took full possession of my heart; and I was enabled to say, "I am crucified with Christ; nevertheless I live; yet not I, but Christ liveth in me.' Let Him as King of kings and Lord of lords reign in me, reign without a rival for ever."

REND THE HEAVENS.

In a letter in the *Christian*, Dr Newman Hall says—In the course of a delightful walk among the hills on Easter Monday, a Welsh pastor related the following example of the influence of prayer in promoting a revival of spiritual life without recourse to any external agency. It is a custom occasionally to gather the small Sunday schools of a country district to the central school or chapel for examination in the Scriptures, prayer, and singing. Such an assembly was to take place on a hill pointed out. A man of much prayer, on arriving, was greeted by the presiding minister, who hoped for a very happy and profitable season. He replied he was sure of it, as he felt that prayer for much of the Divine presence would be answered.

After the usual exercises of worship, the question was asked, "What is the chapter for the day?" "Sixty-fourth of Isaiah." "What is the first verse?" "Oh, that Thou wouldst rend the heavens; that Thou wouldst come down!" seven hundred voices repeated together. "Say it again," said the minister. They said it again with renewed emphasis. "Say it again." And the third time they repeated the prayer. There were immediately signs of very deep emotion. The expected lesson could not be proceeded with. That one verse was enough. The whole of the allotted time and much more was occupied with prayer, praise, and exhortation, and of confession of sin and faith in Christ by young and old. It was the beginning of a revival in the neighbourhood lasting several months, and resulting in the admission of hundreds to the churches. Many in the churches at Tredegar are known as "children of the revival."

SOME ONE WITH HIM.

Another case was as follows:— Some years ago a famous preacher, a God-sent evangelist, was announced to preach. Great numbers assembled, and, the hour having struck, were getting impatient. The preacher was

SCRIPTURE TESTIMONY
Holy Spirit directs believers in ministry
MATTHEW 10:19-20 · ACTS 8:29 · ACTS 13:2 · ACTS 15:28 · ACTS 16:6-10 · ACTS 20:22 · ROMANS 8:14

in his bedroom at the house of the farmer on whose grounds the service was to be held. The latter sent to summon him, but the servant returned saying that he had got some one with him in his room, and was begging him to come with him, and was saying, "If you do not go with me I will not go up hence," or something to that effect. The godly farmer said, "Oh, it is all right; we shall have God's presence to-day." And it was so. A remarkable power attended that day's ministry. Many were pricked to the heart, and cried for mercy. It was the beginning of a long-continued period of spiritual revival, during which not only a multitude of sinners were converted, but the whole tone of the spiritual life of the believers was raised in personal devotion, attendances, active zeal, and righteousness of life. It cannot be wrong to avail ourselves of methods to promote revivals which are Scriptural and have been proved efficacious, but we must be on guard against thinking more of methods than of objects—of creating a revival ourselves rather than of seeking it from heaven—of looking to some human agency more than to the Divine Plead of the Church—to freshness, eloquence, music, excitement, rather than to the Holy Spirit, to kindle and fan the sacred flame. Very often real and lasting revivals have begun within a church rather than from foreign aid and fire kindled from without.

SECRET PRAYER AND FASTING.

Jonathan Edwards says of the "Life of David Brainerd":— "The reader of that life will see how much Brainerd recommends the duty of secret fasting, and how frequently he exercised himself in it: nor can it well escape observation how much he was owned and blessed in it, and of what benefit it evidently was to his soul. Among the many days he spent in secret prayer and fasting, of which he gives an account in his diary, there is scarcely an instance of one which was not either attended or followed soon with apparent success and a remarkable blessing in special influences and consolations of God's Spirit, and very often before the day was ended."

HOW THE PRODIGAL RETURNED.

Mr D. L. Moody, the evangelist, tells the following story of a mother who came to him greatly burdened, and being asked the nature of her trouble, said—"I have an only boy who is a wanderer on the face of the earth. I don't know where he is. If I only knew I would go round the world to find him. You don't know how I love that boy. This sorrow is killing me." Mr Moody advised her to tell God all her trouble, for she could reach her boy by way of the throne, even though he were at the uttermost parts of the earth. He then told her of a mother who lived down in the southern part of Indiana. Some years previously her son came up to Chicago. He was a moralist; but it needs more than morality to keep one right in a great city. He had not been long there before he was led astray. A neighbour of his father came up to town, and found him one night in the streets drunk. When that neighbour went home at first he thought he would not say anything about it to the boy's father, but afterward thought it was his duty to tell him. It was a terrible blow to the father. When the children had been put to bed that night he said to his wife, "Wife, I have heard bad news from Chicago to-day." The mother dropped her work in an instant, and said, "Tell me what it is." "Our son has been seen on the streets of Chicago drunk." Neither of them slept that night, but they took their burden to Christ, and about daylight the mother said, "God has given me faith to believe that our son will never come to a drunkard's grave." One week afterwards that boy left Chicago—*he could not tell why*. An unseen power seemed to lead him home, and his first words were, "Mother, I've come back to ask you to pray for me. Soon afterwards he went back to Chicago to live and work for Christ.

A FATHER FOUND.

One day a young coloured girl came in great distress to the Sailors' Institution in London, asking if they could tell her anything about her father, who was a sailor. He had been away from home some days, and her mother was very anxious about him. He was out of work, and had for some time tried to get a ship, but without success. After wearily pacing the docks, and going home to report his usual want of success, his wife irritated him by her reproaches. He had borne it for a time; but at last he had determined to leave her altogether, and had been away from home for some days when the girl called at the Sailors' Institution. The person in charge became much interested in the girl and her story, and brought her into the prayer meeting which was then going on. As she sat in front of him with her woe-begone face his heart was touched, and he was led to pray most fervently that the father might be found. While thus engaged in prayer the door opened, and some one entered and sat down quietly beside him. And how great was his joy when on opening his eyes he saw father and daughter sitting side by side. Truly this was a fulfillment of the promise, "Before they call I will answer, and while they are yet speaking I will hear."

D. C.

HEAVENLY JOYS.

John Flavel was alone on a journey, his mind greatly occupied with self-examination and prayer, and thus describes what befell him:—"In all that day's journey he neither met, overtook, nor was overtaken by any. Thus going on his way, his thoughts began to swell and rise higher and higher, like the waters in Ezekiel's vision, till at last they became an overwhelming flood. Such was the intention of his mind, such the ravishing tastes of heavenly joys, and such the full assurance of his interest therein, that he utterly lost all sight and sense of this world, and all the concerns thereof; and for some hours he knew no more where he was than if he had been in a deep sleep upon his bed. Arriving in great exhaustion at a certain spring, he sat down and washed, earnestly desiring if it was God's pleasure that this might be his parting place from this world. Death had the most amiable face in his eye that ever he beheld, except the face of Jesus Christ, which made it so; and he does not remember, though he believed himself dying, that he ever thought of his dear wife or children, or any earthly concernment. On reaching his inn the influence still continued, banishing sleep. Still, still, the joy of the Lord overflowed him, and he seemed to be an inhabitant of the other world. But within a few hours he was sensible of the ebbing of the tide, and before night, though there was a heavenly serenity and sweet peace upon his spirit, which continued long with him, yet the transports of joy were over, and the fine edge of his delight blunted. He many years after called that day one of the days of heaven, and professed he understood more of the life of heaven by it than by all the books he ever read, or discourses he ever entertained, about it."

A SON CONVERTED.

In the "Devotional Remains of Mrs Cryer" there is the following remarkable answer to prayer "At Sheffield there resided a Christian gentleman who, with his wife, one son, and two daughters, were converted to God. The conversion of the son occurred as follows: One day the father was out driving a friend, Mr A., to some place not far distant, and almost as soon as they got out of the town he burst into tears, exclaiming, 'O, Mr A., what must I do? What will become of my lad? I have plenty of earthly goods—God has prospered me beyond all my expectations; but most gladly would I forego it all and begin the world without a penny if the soul of my son could be saved, or its salvation promoted thereby.' This son was an attorney, very dissipated, and withal an infidel. Mr A. was deeply affected. The father added—'Only this morning I spoke to him seriously in my own room, but could make no impression.' It was agreed there was nothing now but fervent prayer that could prevail, and they resolved to try its efficacy there and then. Immediately they began, just as they were, in the gig, by the wayside, to pour out their souls to God on his behalf, and they were favoured with special access to the throne of grace. When they reached the place appointed the gentleman left Mr A., and returned home the same night. Next morning Mr A. received a letter from the father, blotted by tears of joy and gratitude, informing him that when he returned to Sheffield to his astonishment he found that that morning, at the time they were praying, as his son was on his way to his office he was suddenly so arrested by the power of God that he could not take another step; there he stood in the public street, under the deep awakening of the Spirit, inwardly crying for mercy, and there and then he was truly converted to God. Since that time he has walked at liberty and adorned his Christian profession."

TWO CHINAMEN IN TROUBLE.

Two Christians, Mr Uang and Mr U., were sent by the native Church at Ta-ning to a small town in the district of Jong-ho. They were both simple farmers, and very poor scholars, but

SCRIPTURE TESTIMONY
God answers prayer
LUKE 18:7 · JOHN 15:7 · ACTS 12:5 · JAMES 5:15

Mr Uang especially is a man filled with love to the Lord and souls. At first they had a very trying time. No one would come into the Opium Refuge to break off opium, and all treated them with suspicion, so that they had little opportunity for preaching the Gospel. At the end of about a month and a half their money was all done, and only one had come into the Refuge. Mr U. returned to Ta-ning to seek Pastor Chang's advice, and ask if he could give them a little more money. Mr Chang advised them to give up the place and come home. When Mr U. returned with his message Mr Uang was much cast down, and said he would not go home until someone believed the Gospel. He decided to send to his own home asking them to send some coarse flour and a few hundred cash. They then spent the whole of the Sunday in fasting and prayer. From Saturday to Monday no food was touched, and they pled with the Lord to give them some souls before they returned home, and also to influence the people to come into the Refuge to break off the opium.

The day following, a man came from a village ten li distant, saying that his child was very ill, and asking if they could do anything for him. They replied by telling him about the true God, who could heal the child if he would trust Him. They offered to pray for his child, and after further conversation they all knelt down together, and these two men poured out their hearts in earnest prayer, asking that God would glorify His name. They believed the promise that "If two of you shall agree on earth as touching anything that they shall ask, it shall be done for them."

The man left them and went home, and to his delight his child was almost immediately well. He returned to tell Mr Uang and Mr U., and from that time the whole family became interested in the Gospel. Not long afterwards the two brothers destroyed their idols and with their families began to worship the true God. They have since passed through a time of severe trial. One of their children died, and the neighbours all said it was because they had offended the gods by destroying their idols. Thank God, they have come through the fire. The faith of Mr Uang and Mr U. was much strengthened by this answer to their prayers, but still no one came to the Refuge. So they decided to spend the next Sunday in fasting and prayer, and the Lord again heard them, for that very day a man came to say that he and several others wanted to break off opium. It was the depth of winter, and the sky could be seen through the roof of the room in which the two had, for the Lord's sake, been living. "We cannot come here," the man said, and offered a place of his own. The two brethren recognised the Lord's hand and an answer to prayer in all this, and their hearts were filled with joy and thanksgiving. During the following month, two or three families gave up idolatry, and most of the men who broke off opium in the Refuge gave promise of being truly converted.

AS A LITTLE CHILD.

An agent of the London City Mission says:—"I entered a wheel-wright's shop where two men were engaged at work. One of them I

SCRIPTURE TESTIMONY
The believer is to be persistent in prayer
LUKE 11:5-10

knew to be a Christian; the other, a broad-shouldered fellow, six feet high, was not. To the latter I specially addressed myself, and while the weather and other topics were being discussed he was most civil; but when I inquired about his spiritual welfare, he suddenly changed colour, grew perfectly white with passion, and, swearing, seized a large hammer to strike me. The Christian young man, fearing for my safety, asked me to retire. I said, "No, I will stand it out." At length the man cooled down a little, and I said, "Well, friend, if I may not speak with you about your soul, I can pray for you." This I did for three weeks, when one morning, on answering a knock at my door, there stood my tall friend. I asked him inside, and seeing he looked downcast, I inquired as to his state of mind, when he burst into a flood of tears. We had earnest prayer together, and he left the house a changed man, as humble and docile as a little child. He has since been a regular attender at public worship, and gives every evidence of being a sincere Christian."

A YOUNG WOMAN'S CONVERSION.

A colporteur relates the following:—"Calling at a house on my usual rounds some time back, the occupant said, 'I want a Bible to give to a young woman leaving home for the first time, and I am going to pray that God may bless it to the salvation of her soul. Will you pray for her too?' I said I would, and that I always prayed when I got home that the Lord would bless the Bibles, books, and tracts to the readers. When I called next month, the person to whom I had sold the Bible told me that the Lord had graciously answered our prayers, and the young woman to whom the Bible had been given had, through reading it, been converted, and had written her such a nice letter."

THE SPIRITUAL BANKRUPT.

One of our busy bankers, ever ready to turn a listening ear to the cry of a soul for light, however pressing his secular work, was interrupted by a mechanic, who entered

SCRIPTURE TESTIMONY
Holy Spirit renewal for the repentant
JAMES 4:8-10 · JAMES 5:16 · 1 JOHN 1:9

his office, evidently borne down by a heavy burden. His first remark was, "Mr---, I am bad off, I'm broke, I must have help." Of course the banker expected to be asked for pecuniary aid. "Tell me what you need. Are you in financial straits?" "Worse than that," was the reply; "I'm a spiritual bankrupt," and tears and sobs shook the strong man as he sat in the presence of his friend, the personification of grief.

The story he told has its thousands of counterparts. Said he, "Myself and my wife are members of church. We have not been inside its walls for more than two years. I have drifted out and away into darkness, and am not at rest. Will you, can you, help me?"

"But tell me the cause of this backsliding. Where did the departure begin, and what has brought you to me in such a condition?"

"Well," he said, "my little girls were at Sunday School last Sunday. On their return I asked them the lesson for the evening. Their reply was 'prayer,' and turning to me one of them said, with such an appealing look, 'Papa, you used to pray with us; why don't you now?' This question for three days has sounded in my ears, day and night; I cannot sleep, I am restless. What shall I do?"

"Where did you leave off?"

"With the omission of family prayer. At first morning devotion was omitted. I was in haste to get to my work. I excused myself for lack of time. Then at the evening I gradually left off the habit on the plea of weariness, or some other excuse. The neglect of Sabbath service followed, till at last I am here with no rest, no comfort, no peace. Neither my wife nor myself have been to church for two years."

The practical answer of the banker was, "Begin where you left off. Commence to-night. Call your family together and pray with them."

"But I cannot; it is far harder than at the first."

"Very well, if you will not do this you will have no rest, and I hope you will continue in this condition till you again resume the duty which you never should have laid aside."

With a few kindly words they parted, but not till the tired soul had made the promise desired. The burden was taken up, duty became a pleasure, new life and joy came into the household, and with loving harmony the family are now walking onward toward their Father's home.

THE FIRST TO LEAVE.

The mother of a missionary in the foreign field told the following instance of Answered Prayer:—

"He was the first of a large family to leave the home nest. Well do I remember the heartbreak it caused to have him leave for another situation in a distant town.

"He was not converted at that time, and was what people call 'a wild young fellow.'

"Coming back from the station, to which I had gone to see him away, my heart felt *sure* that now he was beyond my influence and care.

"Then the thought came, '*This is unbelief.* Surely God can save him *there* as well as here.'

"Standing still in a quiet part of the road, I just looked up to God, and cried, 'Oh, Spirit of the Living God, convert my son; save him *just* where he is, for Jesus' sake. Amen.'

"Then I went home, lightened. You know the rest," she added, "how at an open-air meeting he was brought in, then God led him step by step, till now, praise His Name, he is proclaiming the message to the heathen in S."

Mothers, keep praying for your absent sons.

A PRAYING PEOPLE.

A minister told me that in one of his former charges he was surrounded by a band of godly praying people, who helped him greatly in the work. He remembered one occasion, when some of them gave themselves to special prayer for a blessing on the services of the Sunday. They cried most earnestly for conversions, and told him before the service began that they were convinced the Lord was to bless. And they were not disappointed. At the Sunday forenoon service there were seven anxious souls; in the evening, eleven; a considerable number of young people in the Sunday School were under deep impression, and several professed to accept Christ. The memory of that day is still an inspiration to the minister, and he traces the blessing given to the importunate prayers of the people.

J. H. S.

PRAYER FOR AN AUNT PREVAILS.

When I was converted nearly sixty years ago and found Jesus to be the Pearl of great price, I felt an anxious desire for my unconverted relatives. I had an aunt who did not know the Saviour. I mentioned her case to a friend who was converted about the same time as myself, and we agreed to pray for her regularly every day at the same time, using every means in our power to bring her under the influence of the truth. We continued to do so for three months, but we had great difficulties to contend with, as she was one of those who do not believe that any one can know that their sins are forgiven. She could not understand why we were so earnest about her salvation, but the Holy Spirit was gradually withdrawing the veil from her mind, and she became more and more anxious. About that time a series of evangelistic meetings were to be held in the town, and before they began a few of God's people met daily at noon to plead for an outpouring of the Holy Spirit. She attended these meetings, and when she heard us praying so earnestly for our unconverted friends a deep impression was made, and she asked the all-important question, "What must I do to be saved?" Of course we directed her to the Lamb of God that taketh away the sin of the world, and she was enabled to appropriate Jesus as her Saviour. She lived for many years a consistent Christian life, and died rejoicing in the hope that she was going to be with Christ. I firmly believe that our importunate pleadings for this soul led to her conversion. We looked upon it as an answer to our prayers. It encouraged me to pray and labour for the conversion of others, and I have received many tokens for good from my gracious Father.

A. S.

PRAYER AND CORRESPONDENCE.

Several years ago I was led to pray for the conversion of a young man, Archie R., who had gone out to California. A month or two afterwards I felt constrained to write to him. Shortly thereafter I received a reply stating that a few weeks previous, while passing along a street, he had been arrested by the singing and speaking at an open-air meeting. He listened to the Word, the arrow of conviction went home to his heart, and he there and then surrendered himself to the Lord.

Subsequently, when in London, I met a visitor from that country, and in the course of conversation learned he came from the place where my friend lived. On enquiry about Archie I received a most cheering report.

A. B.

THE WRONG TRADE.

A barber in the town of L--- occasionally had among his customers men under the influence of strong drink, and he rarely missed an opportunity of pointing out to them the evils of intemperance. Being then a young teetotaler, I rejoiced at this, but ere long my joy was turned to disappointment on learning that the barber had become a publican.

Having heard of the great things God had done in answer to prayer, I decided to pray over this man, and also wrote him a letter.

A year passed, and still my prayer remained unanswered; but God answered in His own good time. By and by the late barber's sign-name was painted out, and on enquiry I learned that, conscience- smitten, he had come out of the whisky trade, and was now seeking to earn a livelihood in a more honourable way. The public-house he vacated was one of the most lucrative in the town, so that it was not a question of "not paying," but a clear case of God speaking to the man in answer to prayer.

A. B.

A SWEARER'S CONVERSION.

On board a vessel bound for Madras, many years ago, were two ladies, both earnest Christians, but strangers to each other until they met as passengers on this East Indiaman. They agreed to spend together a portion of every day in searching the Scriptures and prayer. They remembered their friends at home, their own needs, the cause of the Redeemer throughout the world, and their fellow-passengers and the crew of the ship. They also sought opportunities of doing good while on the voyage.

Among the passengers was a young man who had received a good training, but who had broken away from early restraints, and was leading a reckless life.

It was laid upon the hearts of these good women earnestly to pray for and seek his salvation. One day this young man uttered an imprecation in the hearing of one of them. She enclosed a copy of "The Swearer's Prayer" in an envelope, and sent it to him with her compliments. He read it, and acknowledged his sin. They together sought further conversation with him. At first he was impatient, but afterwards he listened to their appeals. But his heart was untouched. "You talk to me like my mother," said he. "She is a very religious woman, and I dare say I have often grieved her because I did not follow her example, but preferred the pleasures of the world." He ended the interview by saying, "I am determined to take my fill of worldly pleasures, so it will be of no use to try to alter my resolution." And he acted in the spirit of it. Even when the vessel struck upon a rock, and the passengers apprehended instant death, and some were praying, and others almost frantic with fear, he remained hard and impenitent.

The ship floated off, and reached her destination in safety. For three months the ladies neither saw nor heard anything of the young man. At the end of that period, a missionary called on them with the message, "A young man to whom one of you gave a tract on the voyage out, wishes to see you." They made further inquiries, and found that a great change had taken place in him, and that he was desirous to tell them of it. "They have heard me blaspheme the name of Christ," he said, "and I now wish them to hear me confess His name, and own Him as my Saviour."

Accompanied by the missionary they visited him. Great was their joy and gratitude as he told them of what God had done for his soul. With deep emotion he related the chief points of his history, in substance as follows:—"From my earliest infancy I was the object of my mother's earnest prayers. Two brothers and a sister also have of late been most anxious for my conversion. But I shut my heart against the affectionate counsels of my mother, as also against her godly example. I resisted all their appeals, and told my mother and brothers and sister not to annoy me with their admonitions, for I was determined to hold by the world.

"The evening before I left England my mother took me into her room, and prayed earnestly for me, asking the Lord to grant me His pardoning and converting grace. She gave me a letter to a missionary, asking him to speak to me as often as he could about my soul's salvation. Knowing the purport of the letter, I refused to take it, to my mother's no small grief.

"On arriving here, I gave myself up to sinful pleasures, uniting with a number of dissipated young men. I was laid upon a sick bed as the result of my dissolute conduct. Then it was that my conscience awoke from its slumbers. I thought of opportunities slighted, mercy despised and rejected, and my life as being one daring defiance of God my Maker. My mind was filled with remorse. I thought of my mother's instructions and prayers, and wept. But tears brought me no relief. I tried to pray, but could not. Again and again I tried, but failed. The remembrance of my sins was indeed grievous. I feared there could not be mercy for me, as I had sinned so daringly, against the beseechings of Christian friends and the entreaties of the God of love. The agony and darkness of my soul continued for several days. At length I resolved to seek out the very missionary to whom my mother wished me to take a letter. I did so, and I laid my case before him, and he it is who has brought you here.

"He prayed with me, he pointed me to Jesus the Lamb of God; he set before me the freeness of the grace of Christ, and the efficacy of His blood to wash away even my crimson sins. He had several interviews with me; God graciously blessed his message; my mind was enlightened, and my heart opened to receive Christ as my Almighty and loving Saviour. I was filled with peace and holy joy, and I can now rejoice in that love which has followed me all through my sinful career, and has plucked me as a brand from the burning."

The young man thus rescued from the ways of evil, and brought to God, lived many years to adorn his profession, and now, with all those used by the Lord in his conversion, including his dear mother, adores in brighter worlds the grace which saved him.

The young man refused to take the letter of his mother to the missionary, but that very missionary was afterwards sought out by him, and was the means of leading him to Christ and salvation.

Notwithstanding the hardened opposition of her wayward son to everything good, the godly mother and another of her sons retired every day during the voyage to pray that God would put it into the heart of some on board to care for his soul, and speak to him of Jesus and His great salvation.

While they were yet speaking the Lord put it into the heart of the two ladies to do so; and in the salvation of the young prodigal prayers also were answered.

MR MOODY AND THE EDINBURGH INFIDEL.

SCRIPTURE TESTIMONY
The believer is to be persistent in prayer
LUKE 11:5-10

Mr D. L. Moody, while conducting a prayer meeting in Northfield, gave the following illustration of the power of prayer to subdue the most unlikely cases of sin and unbelief:—

While in Edinburgh, a man was pointed out to me by a friend, who said, "Moody, that man is Chairman of the Edinburgh Infidel Club." So I went and sat down beside him, and said—"Well, my friend, I am glad to see you at this meeting. Are you not concerned about your welfare?" He said he did not believe in a hereafter. I said, "Well, you just get down on your knees and let me pray for you." "But I don't believe in prayer." I tried unsuccessfully to get the man down on his knees, and finally knelt down beside him and prayed for him. Well, he made a good deal of sport over it, and I met him many times in Edinburgh after that. Some considerable time afterwards, while in the North of Scotland, I met the man again. Placing my hand on his shoulder, I asked, "Hasn't God answered the prayer?" He replied, "There is no God. I am just the same that I have always been. If you believe in a God and in answer to prayer, do as I told you. Try your hand on me." "Well," I said, "God's time will come; there are a great many praying for you; and I have faith to believe you are going to be blessed."

Six months after being in the Highlands I was in Liverpool, and there I got a letter from a leading barrister in Edinburgh, telling me that my friend, the infidel, had come to Christ, and that of his club of thirty men, seventeen had followed his example. How it happened he could not say, but whereas he was once blind, now he could see. God had answered the prayer. I didn't know how it was to be answered, but I believed it would be, and it was done. What we want to do is to come boldly to Christ.

After Ten Years.

SCRIPTURE TESTIMONY
Pray for all people, that they may come to Christ
I TIMOTHY 2:1-4

At one time I had to take a long sea voyage to Australia for the benefit of my health. On my arrival there I was met by a young man, a relative of my own, at a house where I was to stay. He was a tall and muscular fellow, full of life and energy, and possessed of all the frankness and generosity which is so characteristic of colonials. I very much enjoyed his company, and we had talks on many subjects. He was not a Christian, but spoke freely on religious matters. I thought what a splendid Christian he would make if converted, and I began to pray daily for him. I returned home, and some correspondence passed between us, but it soon ceased. Ten years afterwards I received a letter from him telling me of his conversion. I was delighted to receive it, and to learn that my prayers had been answered. I wrote back telling him how glad I was to get the good news, and also saying that for ten years, ever since I had been with him in Australia, I had prayed for his conversion. In due course I received a letter from him full of gratitude. It was a surprise to him to learn that all those years, thousands of miles away, a friend had been praying daily for him. As he had formerly been foremost in the world's pleasures, he now threw himself as heartily into the Lord's work. Although a professional man, and at the head of a growing business, he gave freely of his time and strength in trying to spread the Gospel which had done so much for him.

J. H. S.

ALMOST TOO SACRED.

Mr D. L. Moody, at one of his meetings, said:—"I can myself go back almost twelve years, and remember two holy women who used to come to my meetings. It was delightful to see them there, for when I began to preach I could tell by the expressions of their faces they were praying for me. At the close of the Sabbath services they would say to me—"We have been praying for you." I said, "Why don't you pray for the people?" They answered, "You need power." "I need power," I said to myself, "why, I thought I had power." I had a large Sabbath School, and the largest congregation in Chicago. There were some conversions at the time, and I was in a sense satisfied. But right along the two godly women kept praying for me, and their earnest talk about "the anointing for special service" set me thinking. I asked them to come and talk with me, and we got down on our knees. They poured out their hearts that I might receive the anointing of the Holy Ghost. And there came a great hunger into my soul. I knew not what it was. I began to cry as never before. The hunger increased. I really felt that I did not want to live any longer, if I could not have this power for service. I kept on crying all the time that God would fill me with His Spirit. Well, one day in the city of New York—oh, what a day!—I cannot describe it; I seldom refer to it; it is almost too sacred an experience to name. Paul had an experience of which he never spoke for fourteen years. I can only say, 'God revealed Himself to me, and I had such an experience of His love that I had to ask Him to stay His hand.'

"I went to preaching again. The sermons were not different; and I did not present any new truths, and yet hundreds were converted. I would not be placed back where I was before that blessed experience if you would give me all Glasgow."

MRS BEECHER STOWE'S PERSEVERANCE.

Mrs Phelps says:—"The most beautiful story which I ever heard about Mrs Stowe was told me, as such things go, from lip to lip of personal friends who take pride in cherishing the sweetest thoughts and facts about those whom they love and revere. During the latter part of her life Mrs Stowe has been one of those devout Christian believers whose consecration takes high forms. She has placed faith in prayer, and given herself to the kind of dedication which exercises and cultivates it. There came a time in her history when one who was very dear to her seemed about to sink away from the faith in which she trusted, and to which life and sorrow had taught her to cling as only those who have suffered and doubted and accepted can. This prospect was a crushing grief to her, and she set herself resolutely to avert the calamity if and while she could. Letter after letter—some of them thirty pages long—found its way from her pen to the foreign town in which German rationalism was doing its worst for the soul she loved. She set the full force of her intellect intelligently to work upon this conflict. She read, she reasoned, she wrote, she argued, she pleaded. Months passed in a struggle whose usefulness seemed a pitiable hope, to be frustrated in the effort. Then she laid aside her strong pen and turned to her great faith. As the season of the sacred Christmas holiday approached she shut herself into her room, secluding herself from all but God, and prayed as only such a believer, as only such a woman may. As she had set the full force of her intellect, so she set the full power of her faith, to work upon her soul's desire. One may not dwell in words upon that sacred battle. But the beautiful part of the story, as I have been told it, is that a few weeks after this a letter reached her, saying, 'At Christmas time a light came to me. I see things differently now. I see my way to accept the faith of my fathers; and the belief in Christianity, which is everything to you, has become reasonable and possible to me at last.'"

A DAY TO BE REMEMBERED.

Christmas Evans, the fervent Welsh preacher, has left us the record of a most gracious visitation of the Holy Spirit which he experienced. "I was weary of a cold heart toward Christ and His sacrifice and the work of His Spirit; of a cold heart in the pulpit, in secret prayer, and in the study. For fifteen years previously I had felt my heart burning within me, as if going to Emmaus with Jesus. On a day ever to be remembered by me, as I was going from Dolgelley to Machynlleth and climbing up towards Cadair Idris, I considered it incumbent on me to pray, however hard I felt my heart, and however worldly the frame of my spirit was. Having begun in the name of Jesus, I soon felt, as it were, my fetters loosening, and the old hardness softening, and, as I thought, the mountains of frost and snow dissolving and melting within me. This engendered confidence in my soul in the promise of the Holy Ghost. I felt my whole mind relieved from some great bondage; tears flowed copiously, and I was constrained to cry out for the gracious visits of God, by restoring to my soul the joy of His salvation, and that He would visit the churches in Anglesea that were under my care. I embraced in my supplications all the churches of the saints, and nearly all the ministers of the principality, by their names. This struggle lasted for three hours; it rose again and again, like one wave after another, or a high-flowing tide driven by a strong wind, until my nature became faint by weeping and crying. Thus I resigned myself to Christ, body and soul, gifts and labours, all my life —every day and every hour that remained for me; and all my cares I committed to Christ. The road was mountainous and lonely, and I was wholly alone and suffered no interruption in my wrestling with God. From this time I was led to expect the goodness of God to the churches and to myself. The result was that when I returned home the first thing that arrested my attention was that the Spirit was working also in the brethren in Anglesea, inducing in them a spirit of prayer, especially in two of the deacons, who were particularly importunate that God would visit us in mercy, and render the Word of His grace effectual among us for the conversion of sinners."

DESIRE FOR SOULS.

SCRIPTURE TESTIMONY
Spiritual burden for a lost people group to be saved
ROMANS 9:1-3

The following is taken from the diary of David Brainerd, the Apostolic missionary: — "April 19, 1742. I set apart this day for fasting and prayer to God for His grace; especially to prepare me for the work of the ministry, to give me divine aid and direction in my preparations for that great work, and in His own time to send me into His harvest. Accordingly, in the morning I endeavoured to plead for the Divine presence for the day, and not without some life. In the forenoon I felt the power of intercession for precious immortal souls, for the advancement of the kingdom of my dear Lord and Saviour in the world, and withal a most sweet resignation and even consolation and joy in the thoughts of suffering hardships, distresses, and even death itself, in the promotion of it; and had special enlargement in pleading for the enlightening and conversion of the poor heathen. In the afternoon God was with me of a truth. Oh, it was blessed company indeed! God enabled me so to agonize in prayer that I was quite wet with sweat, though in the shade and the cool wind. My soul was drawn out very much for the world; I pleaded for multitudes of souls. I think I had more enlargement for sinners than for the children of God, though I felt I could spend my life in cries for both. I had great enjoyment in communion with my dear Saviour. I think I never in my life felt such an entire weanedness from this world, and so much resigned to God in everything. Oh, that I may always live to and upon my blessed God! Amen, amen."

A MANIFESTATION OF GOD.

G. V. Wigram, for many years lived morally but without a conscious sense of the presence of Christ, till one evening there fell upon him a powerful manifestation

SCRIPTURE TESTIMONY
Jesus reveals Himself
ACTS 9:4-7

of the Spirit. He was kneeling at his bedside, absent-mindedly saying his prayers, when he says—"Suddenly there came on my soul a something I had never known before. It was as if One, Infinite and Almighty, knowing everything, full of the deepest, tenderest interest in myself, though utterly and entirely abhorring everything in and connected with me, made known to me that He loved myself. My eye saw no one, but I knew assuredly that the One whom I knew not had met me for the first time and made known to me that we were together. There was a light which no sense or faculty of my own nature ever knew; there was a presence of what seemed infinite in greatness—something of a class that was apart and supreme, and yet at the same time making itself known to me in a way that I as man could thoroughly feel, taste, and enjoy. The light made everything light, Himself withal; but it did not destroy, for it was love itself, and I was loved individually by Him. The exquisite tenderness and fulness of that love discovered to me the contrast I had been to all that was light and love. I wept for a while on my knees, said nothing, then got into bed. The next morning's thought was 'Get a Bible.' I got one, and it was henceforward my hand-book."

"I WILL DO IT FOR GOD."

With regard to the custom of binding the feet in China, the following answer to prayer is given by Mr Stanley Smith:—"It seems fitting that the first city woman to leave this foot-crushing custom should be the wife of Mr Liu, who was the first man in the city to confess Christ. Seven years elapsed between his coming out from the world and his wife taking a like step. In the providence of God I was led to give a series of about forty addresses to the native Christians on prayer, by which the spirit of prayer was considerably stimulated in our midst. Among other objects of prayer some of us seemed very specially to have Mrs Liu laid on our hearts. Her natural disposition was such as to lead people to suppose that she would rather die than open her feet, for she was exceedingly timid, and very tenacious of all native customs, and stubborn in the matter of yielding to God. Her husband had for years longed for her conversion, and of late the point of resistance to God was mainly on the feet. "Anything but that" was her constant cry. Her case has more than ever convinced me that it is most unsatisfactory to baptise women with bound feet. If it is possible to unbind them and they refuse, they have certainly not overcome the world. Much prayer for her became the order of the day. One night Mr Glover and I waited on God till midnight, while her husband was pleading with her; but it seemed as if God heard not, and she seemed more determined than ever. In the hour of prayer which Gracie, Glover, and myself held daily for the work, prayer for her filled up much of the time. What made us so urgent in this case under the Spirit of God was that God's glory was so greatly involved in the case. The Lius' were to leave the district very soon, but at the last moment something transpired about the house they were going to occupy, and kept them two months longer with us, and we said, 'The Lord means to bring Mrs Liu to Himself in these months.' So we foreigners had special prayers for Mrs Liu, and felt that our prayers were answered in heaven though not on earth. Coming out I met Mr Liu near my door, and he told me he had had an experience in prayer quite new to him, and he felt his prayer for his wife was answered. He told me this before I mentioned our similar experience. But some days passed, and the answer was not yet made manifest. One night I spent at an adjoining village, and on returning home next day we met the cart coming for us, and a note was put into my hands from Gracie, saying that that very morning Mrs Liu had put on shoes and stockings. Chin and I got down on our knees in the fields, and gave thanks to God. In reply to my question she said, 'I never would have done it for man, but I'll do it for God.' The outcome of this step was remarkable. Her old step-mother had been invited here to talk about this step, and we thought she would be against it, so we made special prayer about her coming. The old woman strongly advised her to take the step, and said she herself would follow suit, though she is of the age of 65 years. She has known the Gospel for some time."

A YOUNG MAN CONVERTED.

I was asked to visit a young man who had been in my Bible Class ten years before, and was now unwell. On my first visit he did not appear to be very anxious about his salva-

SCRIPTURE TESTIMONY
For God so loved the world that He gave His only Son
JOHN 3:16

tion. I read the Scriptures, pointed him to Christ, and prayed with him. A week later I paid him a second visit, but still without any apparent result. Earnest prayer was offered up for him at the Daily Prayer Meeting, and by friends in private. About a fortnight after my last visit I received a message one Saturday morning, asking me to call as he was worse, and wished to see me. I went in the forenoon and found him much weaker. The pale, emaciated face and sunken eyes showed that the fell disease was doing its work. He was much depressed, and was suffering a good deal. I quoted the text, "Him that cometh unto Me I will in no wise cast out," and assured him of a welcome from the Lord. He said he wanted to be saved, but he did not know how to come. I quoted the passage in Isaiah, "He was wounded for our transgressions, He was bruised for our iniquities, the chastisement of our peace was upon Him, and with His stripes we are healed," and explained how Christ took the place of sinners and died for them, and that faith in His sacrifice brought salvation. He was still unable to see the way. I had a prolonged interview with him, and several times engaged in prayer and asked the Lord to reveal Himself to him. I quoted the text, "For God so loved the world, that He gave His only begotten Son, that whosoever believeth in Him should not perish, but have everlasting life." And I repeated it, substituting his name for "world." I told him that Christ, out of love to him, shed His blood on the cross, and that coming to Christ simply meant believing, or trusting, or giving himself to Him. How could he doubt such a Saviour? Could he not say, "Jesus, I will trust Thee—trust Thee with my soul," and do it? He lay looking up, his face became rigid and fixed, and, with a voice full of resolution, he said, "I will, I will." The Lord responded to his act of faith and revealed Himself to him, and in a moment a change was apparent. His face relaxed, tears began to trickle down his wasted cheeks, and he said, "I see it, I see it! oh, how simple! I'm saved." His countenance lit up with joy, and he broke out, "I'm happy, happy now." His mother, who was in the next room, attracted doubtless by the unwonted sounds, came in at this moment, and he turned to her with a beaming, tear-stained face, and stretching out his thin, wasted hands, cried, "Oh, mother, I'm saved, I'm saved!" The poor mother hastened to the bed, threw her arms around him, and kissed him. I silently withdrew, and left them weeping and rejoicing. During the rest of his life he lay in a state of triumph; doubt and fear had entirely left him. He was much in prayer, and commended Christ to those who came to see him. He was heard singing,"Ring the bells of heaven," and he explained that that hymn was sung in the olden days in the Bible Class when any of the young men were converted. He suffered much before he died, especially during the last few days. As his weakness increased his speech became almost inaudible, but his lips were seen to move, and when asked if he were speaking he said, "No, I was just speaking to Jesus," and to the very end he whispered His name.

J. H. S.

SAVED FROM DRINK.

SCRIPTURE TESTIMONY
Salvation transforms
2 CORINTHIANS 5:16-17 · GALATIANS 6:15

Dr S. I. Prime says in *The Power of Prayer*—"A young man held a good position in a large publishing house in a certain city. He was about thirty years old, a married man, and happy in all the relations of life. Years passed away, and there came a dark place in his life. Intemperance of the most depraved kind made his career most dreadful. He disappeared, and was not heard from for some time. He separated himself from his family, and from all good.

"He was met in Boston one day by an old friend, after long years, who noticed a marked difference for the better in his appearance. On being

spoken to, he said 'I am a changed man. I one day got up in the morning, after a night of wakefulness; and, thinking over what a wretch I had
become, and how miserable I had made my poor wife and children, I
resolved to go to the barn, and there, all alone, to pray that God would
take away utterly for ever my accursed thirst for rum, and to pray till I felt
assured that my prayer was heard. I went down on my knees, and on them
I stayed until I had asked God many times to take away all my appetite for
rum and tobacco, and everything that was displeasing to Him, and make
me a new creature in Christ Jesus—a holy, devoted Christian man, for
the sake of Him who died for sinners. I told God I could not be denied; I
could not get up from my knees till I was forgiven, and the curse was for
ever removed. I was in earnest in my prayer.

"'I was on my knees two hours—short hours as they seemed to me; two
blessed hours, for I arose from my knees assured that all the dreadful past
was forgiven, and my sins blotted out for ever. Oh, I tell you, God hears
prayer. God has made me a happy man. I left all my old appetite in the
barn. In that old barn I was born again. Not one twinge of the old appetite
has been felt since then.'

III. PRAYERS OF CHRISTIAN WORKERS.

MISS LAURA GRUNDBERG, THE RUSSIAN CHILDREN'S FRIEND.

Miss Laura Grundberg gives an account in the *Christian* of her faith work among destitute children in Russia, and relates the following answers to prayer:—

"Children were sent us almost every day till we had twenty-one, and no permission from Government. The authorities heard about it, and of course paid us a visit. We asked for permission, which was not granted, and we were ordered to close the Home within a week. This we did not do, because we did not believe it was the Lord's will. In answer to our prayers He gave us the xci. Psalm. We knew we were safe, and instead of shutting the Home we admitted more children. God's ways are not our ways, and little I knew where He would lead me, till I found myself face to face with one of the Grand Duchesses, who was so exceedingly kind that I altogether forgot before whom I stood: She took up my case most kindly, promising to do what she could. On the Emperor's birthday the permission to keep a 'private home' was brought me.

"Our home was too small, so we began to ask God for another house. The children asked for a house with a garden around. Four years we continued in prayer. At the end of two years I was led to ask God whether it was His will to give us a larger house, or if I should stop praying for it. When

95

I opened my Bible these words were given, 'Furthermore, I tell thee that the Lord will build thee an house.' Now we knew what the Lord was going to do, and prayed two years longer. Through time we moved into our new God-given home. He gave us two houses, instead of one, and a park instead of a garden.

"We had also been asking for a cow, the children asking for a 'big cow.' One morning a note was handed to me with these words—'To-morrow a cow will be brought; the Lord has provided the money; to Him be all the praise.' When the animal came she turned out to be as the children had asked, 'a big cow.' The day I left Russia a goat was sent us; for this we had not prayed.

"I must tell you how I came to England. That is as wonderful as anything the Lord has done for us. One day the children asked me if I was going away soon, and if I was going for good. I told them I was not going away at all. Some time after, Dr Selheim asked me the same question, and while he yet spoke a lady came to ask me the same. Then I said—'As soon as the Lord sends me the money I will go.' The following Saturday money was sent me to go to England. So I am here, knowing that the Lord will do far more than I can ask or think, and I ask you, dear friends, to praise Him for the past, and to pray for the Baby Home in St Petersburg."

JOHN WESLEY'S PRAYER OF FAITH.

SCRIPTURE TESTIMONY
Ask Me anything in My name
MATTHEW 18:19 · JOHN 14:13-14 · JOHN 16:23-24

John Welsey's leadership, like Christ's, like Paul's, was pre-eminently the leadership of prayer. It is seen in all the minor incidents of his life, as well as in the great epochs.

As a matter of habit and rule, his ordinary private praying consumed two hours a day; but all the intervals and interstices were filled by prayer. We submit a few facts from his journal as illustrative of the prominence and potency of prayer in his leadership.

I.—*It perfected strength.*

He states—"In the evening we cried mightily to God that brotherly love might continue and increase, and it was according to our faith." Being much weaker than usual, the service of the day being equal to preaching eight times, he prayed God to send him help. A clergyman came and offered his service. "So when I ask for strength," says Wesley, "God gave me strength; when for help, he gave me this also." Seized with a pain in the midst of his preaching, so that he could not speak, "I knew my remedy," he says, "and immediately kneeled down.

In a moment the pain was gone, and the voice of the Lord cried aloud to sinners."

II.—*It swayed the elements.*

The elements as well as sickness were often in his way; prayer removed the hindrances. "Just as I began to preach the sun broke out, and shone exceedingly hot on my head. I found if it continued I should not be able to speak long, and I lifted up my heart to God. In a minute or two it was covered with clouds, which continued till the service was over." And he says—"Let any who please call this chance, I call it an answer to prayer." It was raining, and Wesley and his congregation were crowded out of the church, and the rain ceased the moment they came out. He says in regard to this incident, "How many proofs must we have that there is no petition too little, any more than too great, for God to grant!"

III.—*It healed the sick.*

How many records like the following we find! One of his Kingswood teachers lay near death, and found no help from medicine. "We poured out our souls in prayer to God; from that hour she began to amend." The physician told him a friend could not live over night. "I went and found all crying, his legs being cold, as it seemed, dead already. We all kneeled down, and called upon God with strong cries and tears. He opened his eyes, and called for me, and from that hour he continued to recover his strength."

IV.—*It gave songs in the night.*

Many times he gathered his company and prayed all night, or till the mighty power of God came on them. "About three in the morning, as we were continuing instant in prayer, the power of God came mightily upon us, so that many cried out for exceeding joy, and many fell to the ground. As soon as we were recovered a little from that awe and amazement at the presence of His majesty, we broke out with one voice, 'We praise Thee, O God; we acknowledge Thee to be the Lord.'" On another occasion he says, "After midnight about a hundred of us walked home singing, rejoicing, and praising God." How often does he record, "We continued ministering the Word of God and in prayer and praise till the morning!" One of his all-night wrestlings alone with God is said to have greatly affected a Catholic priest, who was awakened by it, or overheard it.

John Wesley was a man of culture, and a theologian; but the secret of his success does not lie in any of these. His power lay in his praying. His organising force, his quenchless zeal, his spiritual wisdom, his power, were all secured by his prayers. God honoured and endowed Him, because he honoured God by his praying. God made him great, because he made himself little by prayer.—*St Louis Christian Advocate.*

INCIDENTS IN THE LIFE OF JAMES GILMOUR.

I.— *The Russian Escorts.*

SCRIPTURE TESTIMONY
God is able to bring good from any circumstances
ROMANS 8:28

The following experiences of answered prayer are from the Diary of the late James Gilmour, of Mongolia. He says:—

"I desire to look back on the way by which the Lord has led me for the last year. In September 1870 I was looking out eagerly, anxiously for some one who was going to Russia that I might go with him. I could find no one. I made it a subject of prayer, and at last when I was on my knees in came M'Coy to tell me of a Russian who was going up without delay. I saw the Russian, and arranged to go and started. 'While they are yet speaking I will hear.'

"On the journey between Pekin and Kalgan I was alone, and could only speak a little Chinese, yet I got on very well; and though my money was in a box on the back of a donkey, yet it came in all safe, none lost. In Kalgan

I had difficulty at first about finding camels, but at length the Russian postmaster turned out to be going home. The time when was uncertain, quite; his departure depended on the coming of his successor. I prayed about this, and one day was informed that the successor had arrived much earlier than was expected, and that we were to start in a day or two. We did start, and after a prosperous journey, arrived safely at Kiachta."

II.— *"Thy way, not mine, O Lord"*

"There we found Grant and Hegemann, two Englishmen. I went to live in Grant's country house at Kudara. A difficulty arose about a teacher. I prayed about this, and strolling along came upon a tent in which was a man out of employment, and he being educated I engaged him to be my teacher. In Kiachta, after some delay, I got a teacher, but not to my satisfaction. After I had been with him a time Grant remarked one day that I did not seem to be making much progress in the language. This stung me to the quick, and made me go down into Mongolia. Here I was directed to the tent of Grant's contractor, and with him I made arrangements to live. I thank God for not permitting me to get a good teacher in Kiachta. Had I got a good one there I would simply have remained there, and I am sure would not have learned half as much as I did in the house at Mongolia, would have got none of the insight I gained into the style of Mongolian life, and would not have got the introductions I had there to numerous Mongols. At the time I was immensely chagrined that I could not get a proper teacher, but now, after the lapse of only a few months, I can see good reason for thanking God for leading me by that way. This should teach me to trust God more than I do when things seem to thwart my purpose.

"Again I was under a great disappointment about the delay that occurred in the sending of my passport from Pekin. In consequence of its not coming I was unable to go to Urga with Lobsung and Sherrub in February. I felt it much at the time, but some months after I learned that they had suffered excessively on the road, so much so that had I gone with them I might have got my feet frozen and died with the cold. Here again I have to praise God for not giving me my own way."

III.—*Bullet Wounds—A Startling Answer.*

SCRIPTURE TESTIMONY
God using circumstances and timing to communicate
ACTS II:II

"One day a messenger came from the cavalry camp outside the town. He had come to take me to treat two soldiers who had received bullet wounds in an encounter with Mongolian brigands. I had never seen a bullet wound in my life, but I knew I could do more for the wounded men than any Chinese doctor, so I went. The wounds were then forty-eight hours old, and I dressed them as best I could, paying a daily visit for about a fortnight. Two wounds, though deep, were merely in the flesh; with these I had no difficulty. The third was a bone complication. I knew nothing of anatomy, had no books, absolutely nothing to consult—what could I do but pray? And the answer was startling! The third morning, when in the market-place attending to the ordinary patients, but a good deal preoccupied over the bone case, there tottered up to me through the crowd a *live skeleton*, the outline of nearly every bone quite distinct, covered only with yellow skin, which hung about in loose folds. I think I see him yet—the chin as distinctly as if it had bleached months on the plain. The man was about seventy, wore a pair of trousers, and had a loose garment thrown over his shoulders. He came for cough medicine, I think; if so, he got it; but I was soon engaged fingering and studying the bone I had to see to that afternoon. I was deeply thankful, but amidst all my gratitude the thing seemed so comical that I could not help smiling, and a keen young Chinaman in the crowd remarked in an undertone, 'That smile means something.' So it did. It meant, among other things, that I knew what to do with the wounded soldier's damaged bone; and in a short time his wound was in a fair way of healing."

PRAYER IN CHURCH WORK.

SCRIPTURE TESTIMONY
Believers praying together for many days
ACTS I:I4

The Editor of the *Missionary Review*, writing from the Metropolitan Tabernacle, says:—"Here in this great Tabernacle we have had an exhibition and illustration of the power of importunate and believing prayer. In May 1892 Pastor Charles H. Spurgeon was attacked with a violent and virulent influenza. After partial recovery, in June, he was the victim of a relapse that brought him to the very jaws of death. His recovery was pronounced impossible by human means, and this great congregation of six thousand souls united in daily prayer to God for him. For *twenty-one weeks* daily meetings for prayer assembled in the Tabernacle early in the morning at seven o'clock, and again at the same hour in the evening. They were thronged, and not only by Mr Spurgeon's own people, but by Christians of every name. No sublimer spectacle has appeared to human eyes since Apostolic days than this union of disciples in believing prayer.

"This Tabernacle is most emphatically a *house of prayer*. Here are numerous rooms under and around the great audience-room, where for almost forty years this one servant of God has held forth the Word of Life; and in these rooms prayer is almost ceaselessly going up. When one meeting is not in progress another is. There are prayer meetings before preaching, and others after preaching; Evangelistic Associations; Zenana Societies—all sorts of work for God find here a centre, and all are consecrated by prayer. Before I go upon the platform to address these thousands, the officers of this great church meet me and each other for prayer as to the service; and one feels upborne on the strong arms of prayer while preaching. No marvel that Mr Spurgeon's ministry has been so blessed. He himself attributes it mainly to the prevailing prayers of His people. Why may not the whole Church of God learn something from the Metropolitan Tabernacle of London as to the power of simple Gospel preaching, backed by believing supplication?"

DR CULLIS' FAITH WORK.

The following answers to prayer are taken from among a large number recorded by Dr Cullis in his journal, and they show in what

SCRIPTURE TESTIMONY
God's work will not lack God's supply
PHILIPPIANS 4:19

a variety of ways and by what different agents the Lord provided what was required for the purchase and maintenance of the Consumptives' Home.

"A day or two ago I received a note from a stranger asking me to call on her to-day. I did so, and found a young lady sick with consumption. She said she was going to die soon, and as she had a little money she thought she would like to give it where it would do most good. At her request, her mother had visited various charitable institutions, and the Lord had shown her that the Consumptives' Home was the place to give her money. She made some inquiries regarding the work, and then, taking her purse, she presented me with five hundred dollars. I was not surprised at the gift, though it was so large an amount, for I expect great things of the Lord. I had asked for large donations this month, and though they had been small until to-day, I felt they would come.

***

"A day long to be remembered. How shall I render sufficient thanks to my Heavenly Father for the great blessings He has this day bestowed upon me? This forenoon two ladies called, and informed me that a friend had authorised them to furnish the new house with everything needed at his expense. They declined to give his name. But the name of God is always known. His be the praise, and may His blessing rest upon the kind friend. This is a great help, and another proof that God hears and answers prayer. For several weeks I have been asking for means to furnish the house, and the Lord in His goodness, instead of sending the money to purchase all these things, puts it into the heart of this friend to do it all, thus saving me much trouble and care. What a faithful Promiser!

***

"After paying for the necessary articles this morning my funds were entirely exhausted. At the Home the Matron asked me for money to pay the domestics. I had to tell her I had not a dollar in the world. On reaching my residence I found a lady waiting to pay a bill for professional services. That enables me to send the amount needed to the Home.

***

"A friend called and gave me five dollars, and in less than an hour a cheque was sent me for two hundred dollars. An unknown donor sent twenty tons of coal, so settling the question about fuel for the winter. On returning to my house in the forenoon I found a clergyman waiting, he having brought a gift of one hundred dollars from an invalid lady for the Children's Home. At noon I received a cheque for one hundred dollars from a firm in the city. Oh that we could always ask in faith, nothing wavering, for He is faithful that promised.

***

On reaching my house I found a lady waiting, who, handing me a package, said, 'My son has lately returned home, bringing this valuable fur collar. Having become interested in your work, he wishes to give it to be sold for its benefit.' I had been praying that morning for fifty dollars, due to a carpenter at work on the building, and after the lady had gone I said to myself, this is not the fifty dollars I prayed for, but I thanked God for the gift, and asked him to send speedily a purchaser. During the afternoon a friend called, and, showing him the fur, I told him it was for sale for the benefit of the work. He immediately said he would buy it, but went away without further comment. Later in the afternoon he returned, took the fur, and, without asking the price, sat down and filled out his cheque for one hundred dollars.

***

"Saturday always brought Sunday's supply along with its own. One Saturday, Dr Cullis found that flour was needed at the Children's Home. He told the Matron he had not a cent, but expected some money from the Lord before the day was done. Just as he finished speaking the door bell rang, and a lady entered and handed him fifty cents, saying, 'I came much out of my way to bring this to you. I was impressed that I must do it.'

"A sewing machine was very much needed, and Dr Cullis asked the Lord to send one. Afterwards, reflecting that he had money enough in hand for the purpose, he concluded to buy one. Just then a new and very complete machine came in, sent by the Company that made it. Whereupon the Dr says, 'How like a tender, loving Father as He is, does the Lord supply every need; no want is too small to reach His ear.'

***

"On one occasion the Dr found himself unable to pay the annual instalment of one thousand dollars on Willard Street Chapel. When the money fell due it was not forthcoming, though asked of the Lord. The party to whom it was owing granted a certain time. But daily prayer still failed to bring in the money, and Dr Cullis felt constrained to offer the Chapel for sale. This he cheerfully did, though in his heart he did not think the Lord would allow it to be sold; and it was not. The work of conversion went on within its walls, and though it stood advertised for a whole month no offer was made for it, and when the trial of faith had wrought its fruits, the Lord sent the money.

***

"The removal of the consumptives from Willard Street to the new Home on Boston Highlands was a serious thought to Dr Cullis. The weather was severely cold, and he earnestly prayed for a change. We tell the result in his own words:—'I asked the Lord that the weather might be moderated, and see how wonderfully the Lord answered. For many days it had not only been intensely cold, but on account of fierce winds the dust had blown in clouds, stinging and piercing every pore. During the night there was a slight fall of snow, which served to lay the dust, and the morning of our departure opened mild and pleasant, such as we had not known for weeks, so that scarcely an overcoat was needed. On going to the Home I found two of the patients so feeble that it hardly seemed safe to move them; I feared they might die in the carriages. I again called upon the Lord that His strength might be given them. And the Lord hearkened and heard. The patients were moved in comfort and safety, and none the worse for the ride of four miles. They were ushered into a perfect summer atmosphere at the new Home, the heat from the steam apparatus permeating every room with a softness that was grateful to all."

SAVED FROM CANNIBALS.

SCRIPTURE TESTIMONY
Deliverance from enemies and circumstances
LUKE 1:71

Rev. J. Hudson Taylor relates the following:— "The voyage to China was a very tedious one. We lost a good deal of time on the Equator from calms, and when finally we reached the Eastern Archipelago (the monsoon being against us, it was needful to take the eastern passage), we were again detained from the same cause. Usually a breeze would spring up after sunset, and last till about dawn. The utmost use was made of it, but during the day we lay still, with the sails flapping, often drifting back, and losing a great deal of what we had gained in the night.

"This happened notably one day when we were in a dangerous position to the north of New Guinea. Saturday night had brought us to a position some thirty miles off the land, but during the Sunday morning service, which was held on deck, I could not fail to notice the captain look troubled, and frequently go to the side of the ship. When the service was over I learned from him the cause—a four-knot current was carrying us rapidly towards some sunken reefs, and we were so near that it seemed improbable that we should get through the afternoon. After dinner the long-boat was put out, and all hands endeavoured, without success, to turn the ship's head round from the shore. As we drifted nearer we could plainly see the natives rushing about the sands, lighting fires here and there. The captain's horn-book informed us they were cannibals, so our position was not a little alarming.

"After standing for some time silent on the deck, the captain said to me, 'Well, we have done everything that can be done; we can only await the result.' The thought occurred to me, and I replied, 'No, there is one thing we have not done yet.' 'What is it?' he said. 'Four of us on board are Christians (the carpenter and our coloured steward, as well as the captain and myself). Let us each retire to his own cabin and in agreed prayer ask the Lord to send us a breeze. He can as easily send it now as at sunset.' The captain agreed to the proposal. I went and spoke to the other two men, had some united prayer with the carpenter, and we all four retired to wait on God. I had a good, but very short, time in prayer, and felt so satisfied that the prayer was heard that I could not continue asking; so very soon I went on deck. The first officer, a godless man, was in charge of the deck. I went up to him and asked him to let down the corners of the mainsail. He asked me, 'What would be the good of that?' I told him we had been asking a wind from God, that it was coming immediately; and we were so near the reefs by this time that there was not a minute to lose. With a look of incredulity and contempt, he said, with an oath, that he would rather see a wind than hear of it! But while he was speaking I watched his eye, and followed it up to the royal topmast sail, and there, sure enough, the corner of the sail was beginning to tremble in the coming breeze. I said to him, 'Don't you see the wind is coming? Look at the royal!' 'No, it's only a cat's- paw,' he replied (that is a mere puff of wind). 'Cat's-paw or not,' I rejoined, 'pray let down the mainsail, and let us have the benefit of it.' This he was not slow to do; in another minute the heavy tread of the men on the deck brought up the captain from his cabin to see what was the matter; and sure enough the breeze had come. In a few minutes we were ploughing our way at six or seven knots an hour through the water, and the multitude of naked savages whom we had seen on the beach had no wreckage that night. We did not altogether lose that wind until we passed the Belew Islands."

MR D. L. MOODY AND AN INVALID'S PRAYER.

SCRIPTURE TESTIMONY
All great movements of God are birthed in prayer
ACTS 1:14 · ACTS 4:31

At a meeting of the Glasgow Y.M.C.A., Mr Moody said—"In 1871 I came to London to spend three or four months with Christian people in study. I just wanted to get acquainted with my Bible, as I thought some people in England had a better knowledge of Scripture than we had on my side of the Atlantic. I was in the Sabbath School Union of the Old Bailey one Sunday afternoon when a minister came in. He was a Congregationalist, or an Independent, as you would call him. He asked if I would preach for him that day. I agreed to do so. His church was in the northern part of London. I preached to an ordinary congregation. There did not seem to be any unusual interest. I thought it was very odd. I did not think the congregation responded much to what I had said. In the evening I preached again. I could not understand it, but it seemed, after all, as if the power of the unseen world fell upon that congregation, and when I got through I asked all those who would like to be Christians to rise. I had no thought till that minute that they would rise in hundreds as they did. I said to myself, 'They don't understand this invitation.' I repeated the invitation, and said, 'Would you just step right into this room at the back of this pulpit?' They went in hundreds into the room, and could not all find seats, so many were they. I said to the minister, I did not understand it. And the minister said, 'Neither do I.' We talked and prayed with them. I thought I would apply another test. I said, 'All who want to become Christians meet your pastor to-morrow night.' I started for Dublin next day, and on Tuesday I got a despatch from the minister. He said there were more on the Monday night than on the Sabbath. They all wanted to be Christians. I afterwards laboured among them for ten days, and hundreds united themselves to that church. That turned my steps with Mr Sankey to this country in 1873. Let me tell the sequel. There was just one solitary member of that church who was bedridden.

She took it into her heart to pray to God to revive that church. She could not labour: she could pray. Thank God, the weakest members of God's Church can pray. They may not be able to stand upon a platform or go into the homes of the poor, nor enter any counting-house; but, thank God, they can reach God by prayer. That lady had been praying. She had seen an American paper that referred to something I had done in America. She said to herself, 'I might go and pray that the Lord would send Mr Moody to our church.' She began to pray, and on Sunday her niece asked her to guess—that is an American word—who had preached for their pastor. She guessed a number of ministers as having exchanged with their pastor Finally, as she could not guess the right name, she was told it was Mr Moody from America. The lady replied, 'I know what that means; that is an answer to prayer.' When they brought her dinner she refused to eat. 'No, I must spend this afternoon in fasting and prayer;' and all that afternoon she was holding me before God, and that evening whilst I was preaching she was praying. It was that bed-ridden saint that called the power of God upon that congregation. Let us call that power down. Why should not the God of Elijah give answer to prayer? I want all who have not got the power of prayer to remember that you can have it if you ask it. Pray God to forgive your sins and to give you power. If you walk up one of the streets of New York, or the streets of any American city, you will see a notice, 'This shop to rent, with or without power.' That means there is a boiler at the back, and if a man wants to manufacture he can hire the shop with or without power. You who are Christians can have this power of God or not. You can take your choice; God will give you the power if you ask it, and have it not."

DR PIERSON'S EXPERIENCE.

At a memorial service held at the Metropolitan Tabernacle, Dr Pierson said:—"When I first heard Mr Spurgeon, I received a wonderful inspiration from his manner and his matter in preaching and in praying. I undertook to live a new life in Christ, but in my congregation I was continually beset by opposition from some who claimed to be children of God, led on by worldly-minded men outside the church membership entirely. I tell you solemnly that, however you account for it, Divine chastisements were visited upon that band of opposers, and it showed me the sacredness of the Christian ministry, and how we need not defend ourselves, but commit our cause unto the Lord God Almighty. And since we are here like a band of brethren, I want to say to you, further, that I had another remarkable illustration of how, when we cultivate spiritual insight and spiritual instinct, we can depend upon God to interpose for us. I was once in a church where there was a deadly feud between certain members and officers, and it was so bitter that the opposing parties would not even sit on the same side at the prayer meeting. After eighteen months of strenuous endeavours to heal the sore and get the contention out of the way, I said to the Lord, 'Thou hast put me here, and Thou art bound by Thy promise to stand by me. Now, I have sought to remedy this difficulty and I cannot, and I find this conflict facing me every way, and the antagonists have arrayed themselves against each other like hostile forces; now, Lord, either heal the breach or remove out of the way the real offenders.' And from the day that I offered that prayer not one of these offenders ever darkened that church door. I speak of it with solemnity. I feel very solemn about it; but I want the witness to go to your hearts to-day that the mighty God is on the side of any man who seeks to be filled with the Holy Ghost, to cultivate insight into the word and the instincts of a spiritual man, and so to administer everything in the interests of God."

THE RUNAWAY CONGO BOY.

Mr Whytock, writing from Africa, says:—"One day I had to chastise my boy for misconduct, and after it he fled to a town called Nsongo. He had once been a slave, and took this opportunity of going back to his people. On Sabbath morning Mr E. and I proposed to go to this town to get him, and at the same time preach to the people. On the way we met men from Nsongo, who said that the boy's friends were waiting to give him up. After going through the bush a considerable way we saw that the town was too far distant for us to reach that day, so we allowed two men who volunteered to go on themselves. We intended to keep the others by us, but in a short time I missed the rest, and found that all except two had gone on to Nsongo. We returned to Basankusa and waited a long time for them, preaching to the people meanwhile. The men had not returned by sunset, so we got into our canoe, and had just started when they arrived, and breathlessly told us that after talking to the boy's friends the latter had attacked them. They captured one, who had been taken back to the town, while a second man was lost in the bush. We both felt very distressed at this, though it was their own blame, as the men had been told to stay with us. The father and mother of the man who was captured came crying to us, and we told them we would ask God to deliver their son, as we felt sure that He would. The matter sent us both very frequently to our knees that night and the whole of the next day. The following morning, when we had assembled our workmen and the father and mother of the captured man, whom they feared might be killed and eaten too (for these forest backenders are reputed cannibals), I gave them the promise I had been specially led to plead—'Call upon Me in the day of trouble; I will deliver thee and thou shalt glorify Me.' (Psa. i. 15.) We then proceeded to Basankusa to consult with the state officer. I was afraid lest this affair should render a visit of the state officials to Nsongo necessary, and perhaps be the means of closing a large district to us and the Gospel. But God graciously answered prayer in this also. The state officer happened to have two prisoners from this very town, and he sent a chief to Nsongo, who brought back both our man and boy—I suppose liberating his prisoners in their stead. We did not forget to glorify God who had so wonderfully succoured us. We had a special praise meeting, and I urged all to trust such a God and Saviour. The man who was lost in the bush had by this time returned, and said that he hid behind bushes while his pursuers passed close by, and he heard them threaten to kill anyone they caught. He said that he prayed to God to save him. I asked, 'What did you tell God?' He replied, 'I said, "Oh God, forgive me my sin. It is night, and they want to kill me. Oh Father, Thou knowest I came with the white man, and he was to preach Thy Word. Oh Father, bring me back to my home again, for Jesus' sake."' These were, as nearly as I can put them, the simple petitions of this dear dark-skinned lad. We love him very much, and believe that if he is not in, he is not far from, the Kingdom of God."

PRAYER AND MISSIONS.

<table>
<tr><td>SCRIPTURE TESTIMONY</td></tr>
<tr><td>God's work will not lack God's supply</td></tr>
<tr><td>PHILIPPIANS 4:19</td></tr>
</table>

Dr A. J. Gordon, in *The Missionary Review of the World*, says:—"Pastor Fliedner, of Kaiserwerth, gives us an inventory of his vast work— orphanage, seminary, deaconess' house, asylum, &c.—and when we ask how he manages to support it all, his answer is, 'We live by grace, and the gracious Lord of the heavenly treasury knows how to furnish us every year with so many under-treasurers of every rank and age, that to the question, 'Have you ever wanted?' we must joyfully answer, 'Never.'"

"Pastor Gossner, single-handed, sent into the field 144 missionaries; including the wives of those married, 200. Besides providing outfit and passage he had never less than twenty missionaries depending directly on him for support. How did he raise the necessary funds? Read his life and learn. The answer can be best given in a sentence from the funeral address over his open grave:—'He prayed up the walls of an hospital; he prayed mission stations into being and missionaries into faith; he prayed open the hearts of the rich, and gold from the most distant lands.'"

"Pastor Harms and his single church of poor peasants at Hermansburg did a foreign missionary work almost equal to that of any of our largest societies, sending out and supporting 357 missionaries in thirty years. We read the story with astonishment and ask again, 'Where did you get the money for all this?' His reply tells us only that the Divine draft, 'My God shall supply all your need according to His riches in glory,' was promptly cashed when presented. It is so artless the way in which he jots down his business transactions with the Lord. 'Last year,' he wrote in 1858, 'I needed for the mission 15,000 crowns, and the Lord gave me that and 60 over. This year I needed double, and the Lord gave me double and 140 over.' '*I needed*' and *my God shall supply all your need.'* No mention of what he had as a basis for his enlarged undertaking, but only of what he *must have*, making that the schedule of his expectation from God."

"These noble lives constitute a kind of latter-day- exposition of those memorable words, 'When I sent you without purse and scrip and shoes, lacked ye anything? And they said 'Nothing.' (Luke xxii. 35.)"

"MORE PRECIOUS THAN MONEY."

Rev. Jonathan Lees, Tientsin, says:—"It is very significant that there is a growing disposition to link success here with prayer at home. It is known that at least one large gathering of poor women in England are praying constantly for their yet poorer sisters in Tientsin. And there is a great deal to be thankful for in the present state of the work here. There has been a very interesting development of life at the City Chapel, where things have long been at a low ebb. Mainly through the devotedness of the young preacher, and his success in getting the voluntary help of some of the members, there have been quite a number of inquirers lately, of whom a dozen or more have been baptised, and the meetings of the church have been well attended. The like is true of the work in the hospital this autumn. We have had some extremely interesting cases of hopeful conversion, and there has been, the brethren say, a very marked willingness to learn among the patients generally. From Miss Winterbotham's class of women some have recently been received, and hardly a week passes without some incident being reported which shows that in many ways the Gospel is making its way among the people. Dr Roberts connects the conversions in the hospital with special meetings for prayer on its behalf held among some Welsh colliers. And there seems reason to trace the revival in our Ku-lou-hsi Chapel to the daily prayers of a friend who, having been here, knows the peculiar difficulties of the place, but who is now far away. There is a solidarity in the work of the church which we too faintly recognise. The share of those in mission work who cannot themselves leave home is much larger than many imagine. We depend on them for what is far more precious than money."—*Missionary Chronicle.*

SENT BY THE LORD.

In giving an account in Exeter Hall of the formation of the Canadian Council of the China Inland Mission, Mr H. W. Frost said:—"Mr Taylor went over to Toronto on his way to China, and one meeting there I shall never forget. The place was thronged inside and outside, so that the speakers could scarcely get into the building. Next morning Mr Taylor was closeted with Mr Sandham and myself, seeking the Lord's guidance as to the steps to be taken. After prayer and conference, he concluded to form a temporary Council to assist us in the various cases dealt with. I must tell you a little about the formation of that Council, and I think you will see that the Lord had undertaken for us in reality.

"We were sitting together in the building known as The Christian Institute in Toronto, and Mr Taylor asked if we would suggest the names of any persons in sympathy with us who might be asked to serve upon the proposed Council. We suggested three names——Dr Parsons, Mr Gooderhain, and Mr Nasmith —and as it was impracticable for Mr Taylor to call on them, he said, 'I must leave it with you to invite them.' We very gladly agreed to see the friends and invite them. What was our surprise when one of the very gentlemen—I think it was Mr Gooderham— came up to us! Mr Taylor seized the opportunity, and asked him if he would serve, and he gladly consented. A few minutes afterwards another of those named presented himself; and in a like manner the third came in very shortly afterwards, and each agreed to serve upon the Council. It was not a little encouraging to see these men coming up one after the other. Two of them had not been in that building for months, and at the time of coming they had no idea that Mr Taylor was there; but they were truly sent by the Lord. And we were not disappointed in God's choice; one of them has gone to glory, and his service is before the King; the others are helping still."

A JAPANESE CONVERT.

Mr William Wynd, Japan, sends the following:— "Our landlord's son, a young man of twenty, came to our meetings and showed us great kindness, but for a long time he manifested little interest in spiritual things. Our native evangelist talked with him and prayed for him, and as soon as I could make myself understood I talked with him too; but he showed only indifference, so we were obliged to let him alone and have recourse to prayer. After Mr Scott came he too got interested, and often talked with him; but although he understood he was still hardened. In our weekly mission prayer meeting we made united supplication for him. Soon after that he appeared one morning at the house of Miss Phillips, one of our lady workers, with a bright face, and, when she was introducing him to her teacher, she said we were all praying that he would speedily be converted, to which he replied, 'But I am already a Christian.' 'How? When?' she asked, in surprise. 'Last night the Kingdom of God came very near to me, and I stepped in at the door, which I saw had been opened for me.' He seems greatly changed; takes part in the meetings, and teaches in Sunday School; and has begun to pray for his family, some of whom are very much troubled about his conversion."

REV. E. BASSIN.
I.—*Relieved of the Rifle.*

Rev. E. Bassin, speaking of his early trials in Russia, says:—"My prayers were answered above my expectations many years ago, when, after my conversion, my persecutors succeeded in illegally putting me

SCRIPTURE TESTIMONY
Whatever you ask in prayer, in faith, abiding, you will receive
MATTHEW 21:22 · MARK 11:24 · JOHN 15:7 · I JOHN 5:14-15

into the Russian army. During the six months in which I was drilled and prepared for active service I prayed earnestly to be relieved of the rifle, so that I should not be compelled to shed the blood of men. My Christian friends used every means in their power to obtain my release, but in vain. Several months passed, in which I expected day by day to be set free, but Jewish bribery prolonged it; and at the end of the summer of 1870, when the drilling battalion was dissolved, and the young soldiers were appointed to active service in different regiments, I was appointed to the 24th Regiment of Infantry, whose headquarters were in Russian Poland. The day after my arrival I was chosen as clerk of the company; and when I had been a fortnight in that position I was taken as clerk to the office of the regiment. I was not there long till I was sent as student to the Military Medical College, where I attended the full curriculum of three years, and passed my examinations. I was then appointed as Medical Officer to the Military Hospital in Warsaw, and afterwards in St Petersburg. Here, then, in God's own time, was the answer to my prayer, so wonderfully above my asking or even thinking; for instead of being compelled to shed the blood of men, from which I prayed to be released, I became a healer of the wounded. Yes, He will answer your prayers above your expectation."

II.— *Terrible Persecutions.*

SCRIPTURE TESTIMONY
Nothing can separate us from the love of God
ROMANS 8:31-39

Speaking further of his persecutions, Mr Bassin says:—"It was when living in Constantinople, in the year 1869, after my conversion to Christianity, that I began to endure terrible persecutions. My over- zealous relations and Jewish friends, thinking that by becoming a Christian I was lost for eternity, and desiring of saving me from such a doom, spared no pains to convince me that I was in error. Not succeeding in this, however, they richly bribed the Russian Consul to have me seized in a most unlawful and violent way and shipped off to Russia. My seizure took place on the 2nd October, and the vessel left on the 5th, the intervening time I spent in a dark dungeon in the Russian Consulate. All my representations to the Consul, as well as those of my Christian friends, were of no avail to secure my liberty, for Jewish gold was very potent. Much prayer was therefore made on my behalf in Constantinople, and I can only look upon my deliverance from great temptation on the night of the 5th October as a direct answer to those prayers, combined with my own. Before leaving for Odessa my Christian friends came on board to take leave of me, and a little before the time of separation some of my persecutors came on the steamer to accompany me to Odessa, with great triumph at having got me in their power. When they boasted of this to me I said, 'The reason why my Saviour permitted me to fall into your hands is that He has some wise purpose which I do not yet know; but He has not forsaken me, and in due time will deliver me from your cruelty.' The night was coming on, and my persecutors, finding they could make no impression upon me, retired to their berths. But another and greater tempter attacked me. As I paced the deck, hardly knowing what I was doing, my past life rushed before my mind; the thought of my large circle of relatives and friends whom I had given up; of the torments and indignities to which I had been subjected by my Jewish brethren; and of the separation from my Christian friends—all came upon me with such force that I was overwhelmed with anguish of mind and bitter sorrow. Whilst thus reflecting, I seemed to hear the voice of an unseen tempter whispering in my ear:—'Unhappy man! Unhappy man! Bethink thyself of thy position; thou art entirely in the hands of the Jews. They will conduct thee to thy native place; and as thou art a too sincere follower of Christ thou wilt but excite the anger and contempt of thy relations and former co-religionists, so that thy life will be in danger. There is nothing better for thee than to get rid of thy present miserable condition by casting thyself into the sea, leaving the consequences of it in faith to thy Master. Either He will miraculously rescue thee, as in olden times He did the prophet Jonah, or He will take thy spirit to dwell with Him for ever. The Jews, with their miracle-performing rabbi, will be filled with shame and remorse, for the world will be loud in condemning the conduct of those Jews who are triumphing over thee.' One can imagine how I was half maddened by this suggestion, and, indeed, was about to jump into the roaring waters, when an invisible hand restrained me, and a passage which I had read on the 2nd October with the Rev. Mr Tomory a few hours before my seizure, came to my mind, and brought me light. The words are in the Epistle to the Romans, viii. 35-39 — 'Who shall separate us from the love of Christ?' &c. Immediately I threw myself on my knees and thanked the Lord for the light He had sent me, and I implored Him not to leave me alone for a moment, for I was not able to fight with the tempter of souls. My prayer was heard, and I rose from my knees strong in His grace, and filled with His praise."

DR A. A. BONAR.

The following answers to prayer are taken from the "Memoir of the Rev. Andrew A. Bonar, D.D.":—

Monday, December 7th, 1835.—"Greatly encouraged to-night, and see it an answer to Saturday's prayer. A woman came to Mr Purves, and he brought her to me. She has long been awakened to feel that she needed something better than this world. She had often thought of coming, but it was my sermon yesterday which kindled her desire still more, so that she came at last. My sermon was upon 'All things are now ready, come to the marriage,' and I never felt more assisted than yesterday."

***

Monday, March 5th, 1838.—"Resolved to pray three times every day this week for the following things:— Revival in our prayer meeting, and that my heart may be knit together with the person praying; reading of the Scriptures more profitable to me; opening and enlarging to Mr Candlish, Moody, and John Thomson in regard to those things they seem to me specially to need; myself to get nearer to God in common prayer; higher tone in family and in family prayer; blessing upon reading the Scriptures to others; and if God sees good that I may hear of some conversions by this means."

Saturday, 10th.—"The Lord through the week has shown me much favour. Many of my special prayers begin to be answered. The Scripture has been much more profitable to me this week. In the case of all the persons I prayed for, in regard to enlarging of soul, I have seen something that seems cheering."

***

Monday, March 4th, 1844.—"The 'Memoir of Robert M'Cheyne' is now just about to appear. O that it may be blessed. Several of us are to observe Monday as a season of special prayer and fasting to ask blessing on the 'Memoir' and the raising up of holy men."

Friday, March 27th, 1846.—"Received a letter to-day telling me of the blessed effects of 'Robert M'Cheyne's Memoir' on one in London. Many tokens have I received of the Lord blessing that book. It roused me to thanksgiving, and I began to think that if I oftener thanked God at the moment I might oftener hear of his blessing upon my labours."

Wednesday, 31st December 1856.—"Encouraged by hearing of a soul awakened by reading 'M'Cheyne's Memoir' in Guernsey."

***

Saturday, 6th January 1848.—"Tried to keep this day with the brethren for special prayer. Prayed for my tract for young men, 'Real Joy,' of which 13,000 are to be distributed in and about London."

Saturday, July 24th.—"A week of mercies. I heard of some good from my tract, 'Real Joy.'"

***

Saturday, October 8th, 1853.—"One thing to-day has struck me. I should seek to be earnest and warm in family worship as well as in public. Prayer, prayer, prayer, must be more a business than it has been."

Saturday, Dec. 31st.—"I have been helped in family prayer remarkably ever since that day in October when I sought special assistance in this matter."

***

Saturday, March 1st, 1856.—"Yesterday got a day to myself for prayer. With me every time of prayer, or almost every time, begins with a conflict, and often it is when I have been long done, and am at my usual study, that the tide seems to set in by way of answer, or earnest of an answer. For I scarcely ever have set apart special times for prayer and waiting upon the Lord without getting some such token of acceptance soon. O, the folly of not praying more."

***

Saturday, 22nd March 1856.—"Much, very much struck with the hope there is of the conversion of Mrs L. Indeed, she seems to have really received salvation. Many years ago I remember, in passing through the wood near Dunsinane, to have knelt down upon the grass, with the clear sky and bright stars above, and to have prayed—'Lord, Thou canst turn back the course of those stars, and Thou canst change the heart of that family;' and now it seems as if it were answered when I was forgetting my own prayer."

***

Saturday, May 12th, 1860.—"Last week remarkable awakening in my old neighbourhood, St Martins, Cargill, &c. I think I distinctly see the answer to prayer in former days in what is now taking place at Cargill; it is God giving what He enabled us to plead before I left.—Jer. xxxiii. 3."

Monday, 15th April 1861.—"Spent some time in prayer with our missionary for the district and congregation."

Thursday, 18th.—"Every night this week some blessing, and to-night very remarkable. About twenty people remained in anxiety."

***

Saturday, January 15th, 1881.—"Most unexpectedly a few friends in Edinburgh have kindly sent £1,000 to help us as a congregation to clear off our debt. This is the beginning of the answer to many, prayers on this matter. We have on hand a scheme which extends over some years, and which has been prayed over much. 'Cast thy burden upon the Lord' applies to a congregation. I myself have every day been praying about this for some months past, and now the Lord has begun to own the prayers."

FROM THE "LIFE OF REV. C. H. SPURGEON,"
By Rev. J. J. Ellis.

I.—*The Orphanage.*

August 1867.—"Let the facts, which with deep gratitude we record, strengthen the faith of believers. In answer to many fervent prayers the Lord has moved His people to send within a month in different amounts towards the Orphanage the sum of £1,075, for which we give thanks unto the name of the Lord. More especially do we see the gracious hand of God in the following incidents:—A lady (Mrs Tyson) who has often aided us in the work of the College, having been spared to see the twenty-fifth anniversary of her marriage day, her beloved husband presented her with £500 as a token of his ever growing love to her. Our sister called upon us, and dedicated the £500 to the building of one of the houses to be called

'The Silver-Wedding House.' The Lord had, however, another substantial gift in store to encourage us in our work; for a day or two ago a brother believer in the Lord called upon us on certain business, and when he had retired he left in a sealed envelope the sum of £600, which is to be expended in building another house. This donation was as little expected as the first, except that our faith expects that all our needs will be supplied in the Lord's own way. The next day, while preaching in the open-air, an unknown sister put an envelope in my hand enclosing £20 for the College, and another £20 for the Orphanage. What hath God wrought?"

II.— *"My Father's Child!"*

One year at the Mildmay Conference Mr Spurgeon made the following references to himself:—"After a period of continued pain, with little sleep, I sat up as best I could one morning in my bed in an agony of pain, and cried to the Lord for deliverance. I believed fully that He could deliver me there and then, and I pleaded my sonship and His fatherhood. I went the length of pleading that He was my Father, and I said, 'If it were my child that suffered so, I would not let him suffer any longer if I could help him. Thou canst help, and by Thy Fatherly love I plead with Thee to give me rest.' I felt that I could add, 'Nevertheless not as I will, but as Thou wilt.' But I did the first thing first. I pleaded with my Father, and went first where Christ went first, saying, 'Father, if it be possible let this cup pass from me.' I shall never forget my success in my appeal. In real earnest I believed God to be my Father, and threw myself upon Him, and within a few moments I dropped back upon the pillow, the pain subsided, and very soon I slept most peacefully."

III. — *"A Praying People!"*

Of his early ministry, when speaking of his astonishing success, Mr Spurgeon says:—"I recollect when I first went to preach to a mere hand-ful of people in London—such a handful; but, oh! how they could pray. How we sometimes seemed to plead as though we could see the angel present, and must have a blessing; but we were all so awestruck with the solemnity of prayer that we said, 'Let us be quiet.' And we sat for some moments silent, while the Lord's power seemed to overshadow us, and all the minister could do was to pronounce the blessing, and say, 'Dear friends, we have had the Spirit here to-night; let us go hence, and not lose His blessed influences.' Then down came the blessing; the house was filled with hearers, and many souls were converted; and I always give the honour to God first, and then to a praying people."

IV.— *The Pastors' College.*

SCRIPTURE TESTIMONY
God's work will not lack God's supply
PHILIPPIANS 4:19

From the first the financial burden of the Pastors' College rested entirely on Mr Spurgeon. Two friends indeed generously assisted him to support the first student, but as the one student grew to many, the whole of the increased expense fell on Mr Spurgeon, and hence lessened his income. He has often related how he came to his last pound, and knew not where to find the money that was absolutely necessary for the continuation of the work. He mentioned his need to a friend, who reminded him that he had a good Banker. "Yes, and I should like to draw upon Him now, for I have nothing," replied Mr Spurgeon. "Have you prayed about it?" "Yes, I have." "Well, then, leave it with Him. Have you opened your letters?" "No, I don't open my letters on Sundays." "Well, open them for once." He did so, and in the first one there was a banker's letter to this effect:— "Dear Sir,—We beg to inform you that a lady, totally unknown to us, has left with us £200 for you to use in the education of young men."

V.— *The Tabernacle.*

With regard to the building of the Metropolitan Tabernacle, Mr Spurgeon fully realised the immensity of the design, and therefore he trusted God for strength to accomplish it. He says somewhere that if it had been a small undertaking he might perhaps have attempted it in his own strength; but because it was so vast he cast it all upon God. Hence the Tabernacle is a proof both of the power of prayer and of the consequences of fervent faith. Mr Spurgeon tells us that he and a friend especially prayed one evening amidst the planks, bricks, and stone that not only might the work prosper, but that not one of the workmen might be injured—a prayer which was most minutely answered. Why should it be thought a strange thing for God to hear the prayer of faith?

"THE STORY OF THE CHINA INLAND MISSION."

In the two volumes of "The Story of the China Inland Mission" the following answers to prayer are told by Mr Hudson Taylor and others:—"Often as our faith has been tried with regard to funds, the Lord has ever proved faithful. Beloved brethren and sisters have been marvellously helped when brought very low. One brother, in the absence of funds, was sustained for days (if not weeks) by presents of food from the heathen around him. Another brother and sister were tided over a difficulty by a birthday present made to their child from one of the native Christians. A third was sustained for a time through money given him by a native helper, who had raised it by pawning his own clothes. A fourth, in great need, received a present in money from a native sister, who in a dream had been directed to aid him, and was helped on several other occasions in ways equally marked."

I.— *The Answer at Home for Extension Abroad.*

"During November, December, and the first part of January I asked the Lord to make it unmistakably clear whether He would have us prepare to commence work in some of the totally unreached provinces or not; and also whether we should seek to occupy more stations in Cheh-kiang. My mind was assured that we ought to do both, and I felt constrained in prayer to ask the Lord to give us labourers to extend the work into every unoccupied county of Cheh-kiang— of which there were fifty—and also men and means to commence operations in the nine unevangelised provinces as well. While we were thus waiting upon the Lord in China, He was putting it into the heart of one of His stewards at home to devise and execute liberal things for the spread of the Gospel. A letter was received by Mr Hill, one of the Honorary Secretaries, dated December 5th, 1873, in which the writer said, 'In two months I hope to place in the hands of your Council the sum of £800 for the further extension of Inland China Mission work. Please remember that it is for fresh provinces.' Need I say that when a copy of this letter reached me in China it caused our hearts to sing for joy."

II.—*How Prayer Saved Ning Sien-seng.*

Ning Sien-seng was a man of considerable influence and standing in Ching-hien, an able and literary man, holding the B.A. degree. He had seen something of Christian literature, but finding the Scriptures dry and unintelligible, he had given up reading them. Careless and sceptical as to spiritual things, he considered prayer absurd. "If there be any God," he would say, "which is more than doubtful, of course He must be far too great a Being to take any interest in the little affairs of our daily life."

One summer day he met Mr Stevenson, who, at the close of a long and serious conversation, felt greatly drawn to the man, and yet pained at his open infidelity. "Let me freely confess it, teacher," concluded Ning Sien-seng, "I do not believe the doctrines taught by you foreigners." With an earnestness which surprised the Confucianist, the missionary replied, "I shall remember you constantly in prayer to the true and living God."

Ning Sien-seng went away, but could not forget the sentence. "Here," thought he, "is a foreigner, a perfect stranger to me, and yet so concerned about my soul that he will pray for me, and I do not even pray for myself. What if I should begin?" Then doubtfully, but earnestly, a cry went up from that heathen heart to the unknown, "O God (if there be a God), give me light, if light is to be had." Again he turned to the Bible, and this time it seemed an entirely new revelation, while the scholar, to his surprise, found in himself a change for which he could not account. The Book so interested him that he read far on into the night. The study of the Word became his great delight. He was led to believe its truths, and to trust the Lord Jesus as his personal Saviour. "Prayer has saved me," said Ning Sien- seng.

III.— *Mrs. Hudson Taylors Mission and Means.*

SCRIPTURE TESTIMONY
God provides exactly what is needed
2 CORINTHIANS 8:15 · PHILIPPIANS 4:19

It was the terrible famine time of 1878. Tidings of the distress in Shansi had reached Shanghai, and relief work was started; but who could be spared for the responsible undertaking? No foreign lady had ever been seen within its borders; yet ladies were unspeakably needed to care for the hundreds of orphan children left destitute, and to seize the opportunity of gaining access to the women in their desolate homes, no longer closed against the Gospel. Mrs Hudson Taylor felt it laid upon her to leave her husband and children and undertake the long journey and the arduous work; but as some much-valued friends questioned the wisdom of the step, she felt for their sakes as well as for her own the need of some sign that this step was indeed of the Lord's ordering. Her prayer was twofold. She asked the Lord graciously to confirm His guidance by sending her a sufficient sum to meet the expense of a small outfit, and also to add a special gift of £50—neither more nor less, but exactly £50—to be appropriated to another purpose. More willing to give and to guide than we can be to follow, the Lord did not long keep His child waiting. That very day a gentleman called at Pyrland Road, London, asking for Mrs Taylor, and after conversation, inquired whether it was really a fact that she intended starting shortly for China. Upon being told that she was preparing to do so unless the Lord hindered, he took from his purse a cheque, which he said he had brought towards any necessary expenses of outfit, and that he would like it to be reserved exclusively for that purpose. The amount thus provided was exactly the sum usually given by the Mission for the outfit of candidates. With an expectant heart she waited, still saying nothing of her other special prayer. Half a week later the morning post brought a letter containing a cheque for £50, with permission to appropriate it to the very purpose for which it had been asked of God.

IV. — *The Poor and Needy.*

Mr Hudson Taylor writes:—"On Saturday our regular home mail arrived. That morning we supplied, as usual, a breakfast to the destitute poor, who came to the number of

> **SCRIPTURE TESTIMONY**
>
> *God's work will not lack God's supply*
>
> PHILIPPIANS 4:19

seventy. They come to us every day, Lord's Day excepted, for then we cannot manage to attend to them and get through all our duties too. Well, on that Saturday morning we paid all expenses and provided ourselves for the morrow, after which we had not a single dollar left among us. How the

Lord was going to provide for Monday we knew not: but over our mantel-piece hang two scrolls in the China character—Ebenezer, 'Hitherto hath the Lord helped us;' Jehovah-Jireh, 'The Lord will provide.' And He kept us from doubting for a moment. That very day the mail came in, a week sooner than was expected, and Mr Jones received a bill for two hundred and fourteen dollars. We thanked God and took courage. The bill was taken to a merchant, and although there is usually a delay of several days in getting the change, this time he said, 'Send down on Monday.' We sent, and though he had not been able to buy all the dollars he let us have seventy on account; so all was well. Oh, it is sweet to live thus directly upon the Lord, who never fails us! On Monday the poor had their breakfast as usual, for we had not told them not to come, being assured that it was the Lord's work and that the Lord would provide. We could not help our eyes filling with tears of Prayers of gratitude when we saw not only our own needs supplied, but the widow and the orphan, the blind and the lame, the friendless and the destitute, together provided for by the bounty of Him who feeds the ravens."

SENT TO PO-YANG LAKE.

"Before the way had opened for me actually becoming a missionary," Mr Cardwell says, "I met with a gentleman who, knowing my heart's desire, forwarded the matter as far as possible. One day, while talking with me about it, happening to have a map of China in his room, he said, 'Dear brother, look at that map; you see the province of Kiangsi; you see the Po-yang Lake and rivers in all directions by which one might reach almost every city. Shall we pray that, if it be the Lord's will, you may be sent there, to labour on that lake without a missionary?' We did pray over the matter, and at the end of seven years I went to China—not to the Po-yang Lake, however, but to a city a long distance away from the province for which we had been praying. I had only been in this place about three months when I was laid low by illness, which continued for a year and a half. My friends in Ningpo said regretfully, 'You must return to England.' 'Return to England?' I exclaimed, 'after seven years of prayer for this work' No, I could not think of it. The Po-yang Lake and the needs of that large province were continually upon my heart; I felt I must go there before thinking of returning home." Remarkable to say, Mr Cardwell had not been in Kiangsi more than a week, when, to his great joy and thankfulness, the trying complaint from which he had so long suffered took a decided turn, and without a single relapse rapid recovery proceeded. From that time he devoted himself to evangelistic labours on the very lake and down the course of the very rivers about which he had so long before commenced to pray."

BISHOP HANNINGTON'S CONVERSION.

The following account of the conversion of Bishop Hannington is taken, in a condensed form, from his *Life*, by E. C. Dawson, M.A. Extract from diary: "--- (an old college companion) opened a correspondence with me, which I speak of as delightful, as it led to my conversion." The answer returned by Hannington to this letter, though written lightly enough, had a touch of seriousness which induced his friend to write again; so with prayer for guidance he wrote a simple, unvarnished account of his own conversion, and urged Hannington as he valued his soul to make a definite surrender of himself to the Saviour of the world. For thirteen months no answer was returned. Prayer was made for him without ceasing by his friend, but there was no response, and he concluded that his letter had been consigned to the oblivion of the waste-paper basket. He was, however, wrong. Hannington's own words will best describe the phase of his mind during this important period of his career. "And now," he says, "comes a tale of surpassing interest to me. More than a year ago --- wrote me a letter. I did not answer it, though the impression it made never left me. Time passed on, and I knew that I was not right. I sought, and sought most earnestly, at times being in terrible bondage of spirit and doubts and fears. I began to despair of ever coming to a knowledge of the truth. At length I again wrote to --- and begged him to come and pay me a visit. Most earnestly did I pray that he might come and bring me light, as Ananias did to St Paul." Alas, his friend was not master of his own time. He was strangely moved by this marvellous response to his prayer. He now understood how it was that the burden of that soul had never ceased to press upon him during all that time. He at once did what he was able. He wrote what he thought might be helpful to one in spiritual darkness and distress. He invited Hannington to come and see him, and laying his hand on the only suitable book he then had by him, he sent it with the letter. The book was "Grace and Truth," by the late Dr Mackay, of Hull. Hannington was dreadfully disappointed. He writes:—"I was in despair. It seemed to sound my death-knell. I thought the Lord would not answer me." His heart was sore that he could not have his friend, and the book lay in a corner unread for some little time. He shall himself narrate what followed:—"When I left on the 16th September for Exeter I spied the book, and said, '--- is sure to ask if I have read it. I suppose I must wade through it,' and so stuffed it into my portmanteau. At Petherwyn I took it out and read the first chapter. I disliked it so much that I determined not to touch it again. So back to the portmanteau it went and remained until my visit to Hurst, when I saw it and thought I might as well read it so as to be able to tell --- about it. So once more I took it up and read straight on for three chapters or so, until at last I came to that one, 'Do you feel your sins forgiven?' By means of this my eyes were opened."

His anxiety had been great. His search for the hidden treasure had been long, continuous, and painful. His joy was now correspondingly great. His pent-up feelings rushed forth in a torrent of thanksgiving. He says—"I was in bed at the time reading. I sprang out of bed and leaped about the room, rejoicing and praising God that Jesus died for me. From that day to this I have lived under the shadow of His wings, in the assurance of faith that I am His, and He is mine."

These words were written just before his second missionary journey to Africa, where he was so soon to win the martyr's crown.

THE LORD'S FAITHFULNESS.

Mr David Barron, of the "Hebrew Christian Testimony to Israel," in an open letter to friends, writes:—"I had a great desire that the Lord might give me the joy of serving Him in the gospel untrammelled and without being the paid agent of this or that Society or Mission, believing that my liberty for Christ and usefulness would thereby be enlarged. For about ten years I made this a subject of daily prayer. I told no one, but felt all the time that, though perhaps by a way I knew not, the answer would come. I had been for nearly fifteen years associated with a Mission, into which, in the first instance, the Lord Himself had undoubtedly led me, and in which He condescended to bless me, and was therefore loth to move one step without very clear guidance. When I withdrew from that Mission in obedience, as I believe, to the clear guidance of God, I stepped out into the dark, not knowing whither I went, except that the Lord was with me, and was going before me, and that if I sought His glory He Himself would maintain my cause. I gave up a stated income, my sphere of work, and friendships and associations of many years, but, blessed be the name of Jehovah, I can testify to His faithfulness, and that He is indeed a very present help in time of trouble. We never know what our God can do for us until the day of need, and until He is put to the test of an obedient, simple faith. My personal needs have for these past few months been most bountifully supplied, and in ways truly wonderful and unforeseen I have experienced the truth of His Word that 'it is better to trust in Jehovah than to put confidence in man,' yea, that it is 'better to trust in Jehovah than to put confidence in princes.'"

MRS AMANDA SMITH.

I.—*Proof of Blessing.*

The following answers are taken from the autobiography of Mrs Amanda Smith, the coloured evangelist. She gives a graphic account of how she entered on the life of full consecration and sanctification, and proceeds— "Just as I got fairly on my feet they struck the last verse of the hymn—

'Oh, bear my longing heart to Him
Who bled and died for me,
Whose blood now cleanseth from all sin,
And gives me victory.'

And when they sang these words, 'Whose blood now cleanseth from all sin,' oh, what a wave of glory swept over my soul. I shouted, 'Glory to Jesus.' I afterwards told a dear sister that the Lord had sanctified me, and I thought she would be so glad, for she had told me that years before in Canada she had got the blessing, though she had never spoken definitely and clearly about it; but, to my surprise, she very coolly said, 'Well, I hope you will keep it,' and said not another word. Oh, what a shock. 'O Lord,' I said, 'can it be that I am mistaken, and will have to go back and go over all the same ground?'

"Then the devil tempted me, and said, 'You have no witness that you are sanctified.' 'Well,' I said, 'I will have it, God helping me, right now.'

"It was Friday—I was ironing. I set down my iron and went and told Jesus. I said, 'Lord, I believe Thou hast sanctified my soul, but Satan says I have no witness. Now, Lord, I don't know what to ask as a direct witness to this blessing, but give me something that shall be so clear and distinct that the devil will never attack me again on that point while I live.'

"After a short prayer, I waited a short time in silence, and said, 'Now, Lord, I wait till Thou shalt speak to me Thyself.' A moment passed and these words came, 'Ask for the conversion of Miss C.' I said, 'Lord, for a real evidence that Thou hast sanctified my soul, I ask that Thou wilt convert Miss C. between now and Sunday morning.'

"Miss C. was a very nice young woman though not a Christian. She was an upright, moral person. She was taken ill, and her sister had asked me to come and pray with her. One day I went and sang and prayed with her. And now a week had passed and I had not heard from her. I had thought that was why the enemy had attacked me so fiercely on Friday. Sunday morning came, and I went to church. Afterwards Sister J. came over to me, saying, 'Miss C. has got the blessing.' I said, 'Praise the Lord; when did she get it?' 'Yesterday afternoon,' was the reply. Then these words were spoken to my heart in power —'Now that is your evidence.' I said, 'O Lord, I do thank Thee, Thou hast answered my prayer.'

"Many times since then my faith has been tried sorely. I have had much to contend with, and the fiery darts of Satan have at times been sore; but he has never from that day had the impudence to tell me that God had not done this blessed work. Hallelujah! what a Saviour!"

II.— *The Lord Provides.*

Mrs Smith, when on a mission to Salem, writes:— "Oh, how I was tested to the core in every way. My rent was five dollars a month, and I wanted to pay two months' before I went. I prayed and asked the Lord

SCRIPTURE TESTIMONY
Whatever you ask in prayer, in faith, abiding, you will receive
MATTHEW 21:22 · MARK 11:24 · JOHN 15:7 · I JOHN 5:14-15

to help me to do this. It was wonderful how He did. I needed a pair of shoes. I told the Lord I was willing to go with the shoes I had if He wanted me to, but they were broken in the sole. I said, 'Lord, Thou knowest if I get my feet wet I will be sick. Now, if it is Thy will to get the shoes, either give me some work to do or put it in the heart of some-body to give me the money to get the shoes.' These words came to my heart, 'If thou canst believe, all things are possible to him that believeth.' I said, 'Lord, the shoes are mine, and I put them on as really as I ever put on a pair of shoes in my life!' Oh, how real it was! Some three days after I said to a friend, 'I want to go to Seventh Street before I go away, for I promised, and I have never had the chance to go.' We had a good prayer and testimony meeting. The Lord helped me to speak, and I told them the Lord was sending me to Salem. At the close friends gathered round me, and as old Father B. passed out he said, 'Good-bye, Sister Smith.' He shook my hand and put something in it. I thanked him, put it in my pocket, and went home. As I sat by the fire thinking about the meeting, I began to get very drowsy. 'Well,' I thought, 'I must get off to bed.' Then the thought came to me, 'You had better see what that money is Father B. gave you.' 'Yes,' I said, 'I had forgotten that.' I took it from my pocket. There was one two-dollar bill and three one- dollar bills. It was the first time I had ever had so much money given me in my life, just for nothing, like, and I thought I must have made a mistake in counting it, so I counted it again. Yes, it was really five dollars. Just then a voice whispered, 'You know you prayed about your shoes.' 'Oh,' I shouted, 'yes, Lord; I remember now. Praise the Lord.' I was so happy I could hardly go to sleep. It was the Lord's doing, and it was marvellous."

III.—*"The Winds Obey Him!"*

SCRIPTURE TESTIMONY
Ask Me anything in My name
MATTHEW 18:19 · JOHN 14:13-14 · JOHN 16:23-24

"Thursday was a beautiful bright day, but oh! cold, bitterly cold! So I got down, and prayed, and said, 'Lord, Thou has sent me to Salem, and hast given me the message. Now, for an evidence that Thou hast indeed sent me, cause the wind to cease blowing at this fearful rate. Thou knowest, Lord, that I want people to hear Thy message that Thou hast given me. They will not mind the cold, but the wind is so terrible. Now, cause the wind to cease to blow, and make the people come out.' The wind blew all morning and all afternoon. I started to go across a field to talk and pray with a friend. On my way back, about five o'clock, as I was crossing a ditch on a little plank, the wind wrapped me round and took me down into the ditch. I could not hold on, I expected to be thrown up against the trees, and I cried out to Him all alone, 'O Lord, Thou that didst command the wind to cease on the Sea of Galilee, cause this wind to cease, and let me get home.' Just then there came a great calm, and I got up out of that ditch, and ran along to the house. By the time we went to church it was as calm as a summer evening. It was cold, but not a bit windy—a beautiful moonlight night. The church was packed and crowded. I had gone on but a little way when I felt the Spirit of the Lord come upon me mightily. Oh, how He helped me! The Lord convicted sinners, and when I asked for persons to come to the communion rail it was filled in a little while. A revival broke out, and spread for twenty miles around."

IV.—*How I got to Knoxville.*

SCRIPTURE TESTIMONY
God using an inner voice to communicate
JOHN 14:26 · ACTS 10:19-20 · ACTS 11:12

Mrs Smith believed that the Lord wanted her to go to a camp-meeting held at Knoxville, but was not sure. "The rest of the people who were invited to go to help in the work had their expenses paid," she says, "but they did not provide any for me, so I thought I would ask the Lord for fifty dollars, which seemed to me a great sum. I said, 'Now, Lord, I ask Thee for this evidence. If it is Thy will for me to go, put it into somebody's heart to get me fifty dollars;' but I did not say a word to anyone. On Sunday morning, at the eight o'clock meeting, which was always a good one, the Lord led me to relate my experience. And the Spirit said to one lady, 'Get Amanda Smith fifty dollars to go to Knoxville.' This lady was the wife of a minister, and she told the Lord when she was consecrating herself to Him that she would do anything He told her. So, when the Spirit suggested this to her, she said, 'I'll do it.' This she told me afterwards. Next day a number of us had been invited to a friend's tent to tea. I was a little late, and when I went into the tent, a gentleman rose and said, 'Well, Sister Smith, Sister Gardiner and some other ladies have got a little purse for you, and they want me to present it to you, for you to go to Knoxville. Then handing it over to me he presented me with fifty dollars and fifty-five cents. Well, there was my money for Knoxville! Mrs Gardiner told me she could have got a hundred dollars just as easily as she got the fifty; but the word of the Lord to her was, 'Get Amanda Smith fifty dollars to go to Knoxville.'"

V.—How the Answer came in Africa.

"When at Monrovia, Africa, I saw a great need among the native boys that lived in Liberian families. I thought if I had a place of my own I might do something for them. There

SCRIPTURE TESTIMONY
Don't be anxious, for He cares for us
MATTHEW 6:25-34 · I PETER 5:6-7

was an old seminary with a large garden, that was all grown up with weeds. It would take some money to put the place right, so I began to pray the Lord to put it in the hearts of some of my friends at home to send me money. I had been all around in America to so many camp meetings, and everybody seemed to know Amanda Smith, and so many had helped me while there, and they would remember me now in Africa, and so help me here. So now in good faith I began to pray as I had always done. I prayed the Lord to put it into the hearts of some of my friends to send the needed money for this work. Week after week passed, and no money came. I still prayed on, remembering how often in the past God had heard my prayer for temporal things. I told Him He knew I was not asking for myself. The steamers arrived and went; letters came, but no money. Sabbath after Sabbath passed; there were the native boys I wanted to help, and still it did not come. So one day I went to the Lord and asked what it meant, and He seemed to say to me, 'You are not trusting in Me—you are trusting in America; you are looking to America for help more than to Me.' I saw it in a moment; yes, it was true; I really was leaning on America. 'Lord,' I said, 'forgive me, and help me to give up every hope in America, and trust in Thee, the living God and I rose, praising the Lord for showing me my mistake. About two weeks after this a letter came from my good friend Mrs D---, of Ireland, and in it was a five-pound note. So God in His own way began to help me. Then shortly after this a friend in India sent me five pounds; then, after I had learned my lesson well, a letter from America came with five dollars in it. So God showed me when I had learned to let go all human help and expectation, and trust in Him alone, that He could take care of me without America if He wanted to, for He had sent me to Africa Himself, and I must trust Him to see me through."

MRS C. H. SPURGEON'S EXTREM-
ITY THE LORD'S OPPORTUNITY.

By kind permission of Mrs C. H. Spurgeon we give the following answer to prayer which appeared in *The Sword and the Trowel* (Passmore & Alabaster).

Mrs Spurgeon says:—

SCRIPTURE TESTIMONY
God's work will not lack God's supply
PHILIPPIANS 4:19

"As my dear friends will remember, I was led to protest against bazaars and similar worldly means of obtaining money for the Lord's cause, and I earnestly recommended the 'more excellent way' of waiting upon God in prayer when funds were needed to carry on His work. Very quickly the Lord sent a testing time, and gave me the opportunity to 'practice what I preached' by permitting a trial of faith in connection with my own special work—the Book Fund. The Magazine, with the 'Personal Note' on bazaars, had not long been published *when my quarterly invoice for books came in, and, to my dismay, I found there was not enough money in the bank to pay it.*

"Now, thought I, I am in much the same position as some of those dear people with whom I pleaded so recently, and the Lord is just trying me to see whether I possess the faith which I counselled them to exercise. So I betook myself to prayer, laid my needs before God, pleaded my entire dependence on him, reminded Him of His many precious promises, paid the lacking money for the bill as a thankoffering for all His past mercy and faithfulness, and then waited for His answer to my supplication.

"This was on *October 3rd*, and in the evening of that day I noted down the facts, and wrote the following words *to you*, my dear sympathising readers:—

"'I am anxious to tell you *at once* of the dealings of God with me, that you may rejoice and take courage when He delivers me from the present "dark place." I have put the matter wholly into His hands, earnestly asking Him to provide the necessary means to carry on my work; and, in sure confidence in His power alone, I am now expectantly waiting for the fulfilment of my heart's desires. I ask those who believe in the power of prayer to *pray with me* for the outpouring of the riches which are His. He has said, "I will fill their treasures," and I believe His Word. He sees my empty coffers, and I look to Him to make them overflow once more. Before the time comes for the November Magazine to go to press, *I believe I shall have a joyful postscript to add to these words.*'

"This was my 'confession of faith' in my God, dear friends; and how long do you think it was before He sent an answer to my begging petitions? *The next morning* I received 10s., not from old friends, who are in the habit of sending to me, and who know of my constant necessities, but from new ones—strangers—whose hearts the Lord had evidently touched and inclined to give me help just at the very time of need. Moreover, the kind donor of £50 generously hinted at 'more to follow,' and thus made my debt of gratitude the greater. Oh, what a glorious God is ours!

'My heart trusted in Him, and I am helped: therefore my heart greatly rejoiceth; and with my song will I praise Him.' This we literally did; for I called several of the inmates of the house together, and in my beloved's sacred study we sang with joyful lips, 'Praise God, from whom all blessings flow.'

"Full often, in the many Reports I have written of my work, have I made my 'boast in the Lord' that from Him alone is derived the sustenance of the Book Fund. I ask of God only, and I glory in the privileged position of being wholly dependent on His bounty for the carrying on of the service in His Name. I cherish an absolute certainty that He will not forsake the work of His own hands. *He may try me, but He will not fail me; and though he does increase my needs, He will not forget to supply them also.* 'Cast thyself on Him,' said dear Mr Spurgeon in the Evening Portion to-night, 'and perseveringly depend, even when thou canst not rejoicingly hope.'

"Very earnestly do I pray that some who read these lines will make a like trial of the love and faithfulness of the Heavenly Father. Want of money for His service will then become a means of grace; and to go begging to God will not only bring glory to Him, but plenteous gifts to the suppliants."

A HOME PROVIDED.

SCRIPTURE TESTIMONY
God's work will not lack God's supply
PHILIPPIANS 4:19

Prediger C. T. Lipshytz, of the London Barbican Mission to the Jews, says:—"In writing these lines it is my special desire to show forth the Lord's goodness in answering the prayers of those who believe that He is a prayer-hearing and answering God. About seventeen years ago, by the grace of God, my eyes were opened to see Him in Whom is life eternal. To tell of my wanderings since then would occupy a good deal more space than I have now at my disposal. About seven years and a half ago I came to England, and in December 1887 God called me to work in the Barbican Mission to the Jews, under the Rev. P. Warschawski. After eighteen months my chief wrote me that broken health compelled him to give up the work, and he therefore thought it well to ask me to look for another sphere of labour. Friends met in the house of the late President of the Mission to consider what should be done, and unanimously asked me to undertake the task of reorganising the Mission. After waiting on the Lord for guidance, I accepted it as a call from Him. Since then it has been my duty and joy to preach Christ crucified to Jew and Gentile, although I regard it as my chief office to be an ambassador of God's grace among my Jewish brethren. For nearly two years I felt the need of better accommodation and a more suitable location than the second floor of Albion Hall, London Wall, which we then occupied, where, however, many a precious soul has found peace and joy in Christ. We wanted a home for converts, a reading and class-room for passers-by, and a hall for preaching the Gospel. The adversary often sought to discourage us from prayer; but, after two years' supplication, we realised God's faithfulness to the promises which we had pleaded. It seemed that we could not afford to rent a suitable house; but in June of 1891 a gentleman who had called at my house in my absence wrote inviting me to call upon him, which I did. He said he had read about my work, and wished to know what he could do to help it. I told him that it was a difficult question, as I did not know anything of his ability, and it was not my custom to ask support for the work from man. He referred to the uninviting approach to our mission room, and I said that so long as the Lord was not pleased to make better provision I was quite satisfied. I then left him. After some time he invited me to dinner, and gave me £5 for the work. On another visit he wished me to accompany him in search of fresh mission premises, and I took him to the present headquarters of the mission, 33 Finsbury Square. (I had previously remarked to a friend that it was the very house we needed. That friend laughed, and said — 'Now, Lipshytz, you are becoming high-minded. That house will cost about £250 a year, in addition to rates and taxes. You cannot pay that out of your annual income.' I said, 'I am sure if the Lord will, it would be an easy thing for Him to give it to us.') The friend, after inspecting the house in question, announced his intention of taking the house for seven years, and suggested an immediate visit to the landlord; but I asked for time, that I might see whether the thing was of the Lord, and that my new friend might not take a step which he would afterwards regret. On a later day, after having prayer together, we visited the landlord, and the result was that my friend arranged to take the house for us, his gift covering the expenses of rent, rates, and taxes for seven years, together with the furnishing of the house. This good man takes a great interest in the Jewish cause, as he has shown in a very practical way, and I am sure we all wish him a realisation of God's promise, 'I will bless them that bless thee.' It only remains for me to say, for myself and helpers, that we are determined, by God's grace, to fight the good fight of faith as long as it pleases Him to call us to do so; and we shall be thankful for and value your earnest prayers that the Lord may fit us more and more to be effective instruments in His hands for the glory of His name and the salvation of many precious souls among our nation. My desire and prayer is for increasing unity among all who labour for God. May He find us faithful in His service, so that His name may be glorified in Israel's realising His salvation. Friends, pray for us."

THE COLONEL'S PACKET.

SCRIPTURE TESTIMONY
God's work will not lack God's supply
PHILIPPIANS 4:19

Dr Barnardo relates the following:— "I well remember a case which occurred a few years ago, when the work in my hands was very much smaller. Some heavy payments, one of them for the clearance of a mortgage which had been entered into in error, and which was threatened with foreclosure, were to be made upon a certain date, I think June 24. The total amount required for this urgent purpose was £500—in those days an enormous sum. I had a month before me in which to get it, and of course during that month the current daily payments had also to be met.

"We used to have a little meeting every day at twelve o'clock for prayer, when all the wants and difficulties of the work were brought before our Father, and when I and my colleagues entreated God's blessing and guidance. Among other matters, this urgent need was borne in mind daily, and we pleaded with God that He would remove the difficulty. But when the 15th of June arrived, and there was still absolutely no money in hand, and when, as is usual at that time of the year, the donations began to slacken, I confess that I was greatly alarmed.

"I had then two special friends of large means to whom I occasionally communicated my anxieties; generous friends, each of whom had written to me and said, 'Whenever you are in great difficulty apply to me.' So I wrote to them under these stringent conditions, setting forth our position. To my dismay I learned that *one of them was out of town*, and that it was not known when he would return, and that *the other was seriously ill* and unable to attend to any matters.

"By the 20th of the month I not only had not any money to meet the claim, but a positive additional debt of £50 had been created in discharging the cost of daily necessaries. I continued to earnestly beseech the Lord for help, and in some poor manner—I cannot say with any real or strong faith, but in a halting fashion like that of Jacob of old, I laid hold of God's strong arm. The day before the money was due, the donations *were lower even than they usually were*. But on the morning of the day when this urgent claim must be met I reached the climax. The donations on that day amounted to about 15s., in addition to which were two halves of single £1 Irish notes from a good friend in Dublin, who said he would send the other two halves when these were acknowledged. That was all! Yet that very day the claim had to be met!

"The money which I needed to discharge this mortgage had to be paid in at a West End office. I looked the matter boldly in the face. It was perhaps, I thought, God's will that this heavy additional load should be borne by me, and the debt, for which I was not really responsible, added to my other burdens. I felt that perhaps I could obtain a postponement if I saw the solicitors who had the matter in hand, and I made my way west at about one o'clock in the afternoon bound for their office. Passing down Pall Mall, I noticed standing on the steps of one of the large clubs a military-looking man, who stared intently at me as I came along. I glanced instinctively at him, and then resumed my way.

"In a moment or two I felt someone patting me on the shoulder. 'I beg your pardon,' said my interlocutor, as he raised his hat, 'I think your name is Barnado?' I said, 'Yes, that is so; but you have the advantage of me.' 'Oh!' he said, 'you do not know me, but I recognise you. A brother officer of mine in India had your photograph, and was deeply interested in your work, and he and I have often talked of it. I recognised you immediately. The fact of it is,' he continued, 'I have a commission to discharge. I left India about two months ago, and Colonel gave me a packet for you. It contains money, I believe; for he is a great enthusiast for your work, and he made a large collection for you after a bazaar that his wife held. But I have not been long in London, and have not had time to go down and see you. Only this very morning, however, I was thinking that I must make time to call upon you, when, curiously enough, I saw you coming along. Do you mind waiting a moment until I fetch the packet?'

"I gladly acceded to his request, and returned with him to the club. He ran up the stairs, and presently brought me down a large envelope addressed to me, carefully tied tip with silk, and sealed. I opened it in his presence. Imagine my astonishment and my delight when I found in it a bank draft to the value of £650! This had been sent from India *rather more than three months previously, before I myself realised that I would have to make the special payment which was that day due.*

"I cannot doubt that in the providence of God the bearer of the message was allowed to retain the package until almost the last minute, so that faith might be tested and prayer drawn out unceasingly. And then, just when I was in the greatest extremity, the mighty hand of God was thus held out in assistance to His servant.

"Need I say I went at once to the office of the solicitors: not to postpone the payment, but to make it, and then I returned with a grateful heart to discharge the liabilities that had arisen within the past three weeks of short supplies. I found that when all had been done *I still had in hand some £90 over and above my requirements.* I think any one of my readers to whom such an experience had occurred would no doubt have said, as I did: 'This is the Lord's doing, and it is marvellous in our eyes.' And as he went on his way rejoicing he would then, as I did at the time, feel assuredly that never again would he distrust his Heavenly Father; and that, whatever the trial be, he would meet it with unquestioning and child-like faith."

THE MIRACLE OF THE COTTAGE HOMES.

When Dr Barnardo conceived the idea of putting orphan children in cottage homes instead of in houses like barracks, as was the custom at the time, he got little sympathy, and

SCRIPTURE TESTIMONY
God answers prayer
LUKE 18:7 · JOHN 15:7 · ACTS 12:5 · JAMES 5:15

no response to the appeal for money. He began to doubt, even after much prayer, if the scheme were according to the Lord's will. He thus relates how the Lord answered two prayers:— Just then some remarkable conferences of devout and experienced Christians were being held at Oxford, and I felt strongly disposed to venture thither in search of rest and cheer. At Paddington Station, while waiting for the train, I met a Christian brother in a humble sphere of life, whom I knew as one of the godliest men it was ever my privilege to meet—a man of prayer, a man of faith, a man whose very face told you something of the peace of God which reigned within. While walking up and down the platform he told me he was going to Oxford too. We talked together, walking up and down, and then in the carriage, where we were alone. I had many burdens on my mind just then, and was feeling sad and downcast about them. I suppose I showed my thoughts by the expression of my face, for he said to me, in a tone of very sincere sympathy, when we were in the railway carriage alone, "How is your work going on?"

Upon this I opened my heart to him, and beginning at the beginning told him of my experiences and resolves, of the scheme for cottage building, of the articles in the press, the letters of discouragement, the lack of help, and then, with some shamefacedness, of the doubts which had grown up in my mind, and of the anxiety and darkness- which had fallen upon me. We were, as I have said, alone. This man of God thought for a moment, and then, like a true physician of souls, he laid his finger at once as it were on the sore spot, and looking in my face tenderly, he said, "My dear brother, if God were to show you that your proposed scheme is too large or too ambitious, or that, although good, you are not the person to carry it out, or that this is not His time for doing it, are you prepared at once to give it up, or to wait His time, and if need be to announce this change of plans as publicly as first you set forth your scheme?"

The very question was a revelation to me. It was a revelation of myself! I saw as in a moment my folly and my impatience, and I blessed God in my thoughts that He had not suffered me to go on alone. It took me but a moment to feel convinced that if God's approval and blessing were not with me, it were better I did not succeed from an earthly point of view. So I said, slowly and solemnly—"Yes; I am quite prepared." He replied, after a moment's pause—"We are going down to Oxford for a special purpose, for rest and spiritual refreshment. Let us here, in this carriage alone, kneel down and commit your case to God, and let us ask Him, if it be His will, to show you clearly, before you leave Oxford, whether you should go on or turn back, and to give you grace to be content to follow His guidance utterly."

We knelt down together in that carriage. We committed the cause of the children to God. We rose up after prayer, lightened and refreshed. On reaching our journey's end I went to my hotel. My friend said "Good-bye." He was stopping somewhere else, but he arranged to breakfast with me at the hotel at eight o'clock the next morning.

Already my mind was at peace. The following morning, while I was dressing, a knock came to my door. I thought it was the servant bringing up hot water, so I said, "Come in." The door was opened just wide enough for a man to thrust his head in, but so that I could hardly see who the owner of it was. His hair was all dishevelled, and he was evidently not yet fully dressed. "Is your name Barnardo?" he asked abruptly. Somewhat surprised, I answered "Yes." "You are thinking of building a village for little girls at Ilford, are you not? You want some cottages?" I was scarcely able to reply to him. But I said, "Yes, yes." He asked, "Have you got any?" —never coming in beyond putting his head through the door. I replied, "No—not yet." "Well," he cried, "put me down for the first cottage! Good morning!" And away he went, closing the door behind him!

I was literally staggered, and for a moment knew not what to say or think. As to putting an unknown man's name down as a contributor of the first cottage it was almost too ridiculous. Moreover, I had not even seen his face properly, and would not recognise him again. But in an instant I had opened the door, rushed down the corridor after his retreating form, caught him as he reached his room, and compelled him to return at once with me to mine. There, with the door shut on us both, I begged him for an explanation of his wonderful announcement, and received the following brief but deeply instructive narrative.

My unexpected visitor's name was AE---D---. He had for some years been an occasional contributor to my work, although we had never met before, and there had grown up in his heart a strong desire to assist that work in some permanent fashion, but the way to do so was not for a while made manifest. This desire was strengthened by the lingering illness and death of his only daughter, which had taken place some months before, and his intention was to link on the name and memory of his dear child with the gift he purposed to bestow. While these thoughts were in his mind, my articles in *The Christian* describing my new scheme came before him and his wife, and they said to each other, "This is what we will do; we can afford that amount. We will build one of these cottages for little destitute girls in memory of our dear child." He being, however, much occupied and perplexed with business anxieties just then, had postponed his announcement to me, and so I had not the least intimation of his desire. May it not have been that I was designedly suffered to remain so long without the comfort which a knowledge of his intention would have given me in order that I might learn to submit myself more completely to God's will, and to wait patiently for His time?

That very morning, while engaged in dressing, my friend had inquired of the boots as to who had lately arrived? The man replied, "I will get you the book, and you can see." He went down and got him the book of arrivals. Among these was my name, and the number of my room! Suddenly recalling his intention; and fearing he might again postpone his act, he, on the spur of the moment, in his impulsive manner, dashed away, and, without finishing his dressing, reached my room, just opened the door and made his announcement in the manner I have related. I told him at once of my anxieties and of the previous day's resolution, and how I regarded his unexpected announcement a special answer to prayer. We then both joined in thankful praise for the door thus thrown so widely open for the relief of my little waif girls!

I went presently down to the breakfast-room. My poor-rich friend of the previous night was awaiting me there by appointment. When I came up to him I suppose he saw in my face an expression very different to that of the previous evening, for he just looked at me, and then quietly said, *"It shall come to pass that, before they call, I will answer; and while they are yet speaking I will hear!"* And we together there and then gave God thanks for that wonderful answer to prayer, an answer which had been on the way for many months, but which for some wise purpose had been prevented for a time from reaching me, so that I might not lean on my own understanding."

MRS SHIPTON.

In her book, entitled "The Upper and Nether Springs," Mrs Shipton narrates the following remarkable instances of answered prayer:—

I.— *The Vicars Conversion.*

"Many who are laid by for a time will learn that waiting is preparation. I knew a farmer's wife who, like many other hidden ones of God, was little accounted of in the village where she was born, and where she had dwelt from childhood, externally one of the loveliest, and internally one of the darkest, valleys in England. She was always feeble and sickly, and unable to enter into the active duties that devolved on a farmer's wife. Perhaps had it been otherwise with her, the service to which the Lord had designed her might not have been so fully accomplished. Years had gone by without any faithful messenger of God sending forth the invitation of the Heavenly Father to His prodigals, or telling forth the joys of salvation in that remote village. It was not then as now, when the good news of salvation sounds forth in every hamlet in our island."

"The death of an aged clergyman, who had left the people in the same dead calm in which he had found them in his youth, made way for a young and accomplished student to the vacant cure. His thoughts were absorbed in his studies and literary pursuits, and in the calm retreat allotted to him Greek and Hebrew and botanical researches occupied his time. His Sunday service once concluded, his days were spent in theological discussions or the current literature of the day; and as he had no experimental knowledge of that which he had been sent to teach, the Gospel of Jesus Christ was only presented in eloquent words in the pulpit, but sufficed not to reach a scattered and very poor and ignorant neighbourhood, called a parish. So time went on. One day, as the young man stood at his door, hat in hand, to proceed on an excursion, he was confronted by a pale, bowed-down woman, whom he supposed to be an applicant for some pecuniary assistance. He politely accosted her, and inquired what he could do for her. With a quiet smile she replied, 'Nay, sir, I know not what you can do for me; but I thought as the shepherd did not look after his sheep, that it was time at least for the sheep to look after the shepherd.' "Then followed the faithful rebuke and warning; and accompanying him to his study, the message the Lord had sent was told forth by His messenger in simplicity and power. That day was the turning- point in the young vicar's life. None knew whence that great transformation arose, and he who went to teach remained to learn. He was a slow learner in comparison to one who had been taught of God; however, he became the instrument of the faith and prayer of this faithful woman."

II.—*Healed by Faith.*

"This woman told me of the peculiar blessing bestowed on her the morning she went forth to do her Master's bidding, to preach the Gospel to the new incumbent.

> SCRIPTURE TESTIMONY
>
> *I can do all things through him who strengthens me*
>
> PHILIPPIANS 4:13

Unasked, the Lord gave her a promise of healing from a disease pronounced incurable, which for many years had prevented her from walking beyond the precincts of the farm, and which had rendered the journey from the hamlet to the vicarage almost impossible; and though in faith she commenced it, she shrank in dismay from the painful and distressing undertaking.

"She had not proceeded above a quarter of the distance, when, asking for strength to accomplish her task, immediate healing was promised her, and this not as an answer to prayer, but gratuitously offered by the

Great Healer, as if to seal her commission on the important errand, and enable her to accomplish the service to which she was ordained. She was never anything more than a feeble, ailing woman, but from that day she could undertake many duties hitherto impossible, and she was healed of her infirmity. She told me that the promise was given with such distinct power, that she looked around to see if anyone had overheard her groan and prayer, but the birds on the hedgerow were the only witnesses; and when it was a second time repeated, she walked on and found she was healed."

III.— *The Sweet Cheese.*

SCRIPTURE TESTIMONY
God answers prayer
LUKE 18:7 · JOHN 15:7 · ACTS 12:5 · JAMES 5:15

"At one time things had gone very sadly at the farm, and faith was tried to the utmost. The hidden witness knew not then that this was the answer to her prayers for a more practical faith to her husband. At last the day came when faith was to be proved to the uttermost; even bread for their daily need failed, and at the breakfast hour, when the farmer returned from the fields for his early meal, the table was certainly spread, but without any bread. While he was labouring in his field, she was labouring at the throne of grace; and she strove to share with him the hope which now animated her, that, though they had not bread, the Lord had surely heard her cry and would answer it. With all their losses and trouble they had never been in debt, and never so low before; but now, what was to be done? The dairy had a few cheeses, but the fair was now at hand, and not one could be touched without loss.

"'If Johnston would only pay me what he owes 'me,' said the farmer, 'we should get along until fair-day, for we are safe for the sale of our cheese; but it's all in vain. I have left off asking for the money. There's nothing for it,' he continued sadly as he sat down to the table. 'Fetch the cheese; we must cut it.' She did not move towards the dairy. 'Wait,' said the woman who watched unto prayer, 'wait; let me tell the Lord that no help has come,' and she again entered into her closet. When she left it the cheese was on the table—the cheese, the pride of her dairy — but as yet untouched. She stayed her husband's hand raised to cut it, saying, 'Wait; I see a man in the barley field yonder; I am sure he is bringing us help.' The little homestead lay on the outskirts of the hamlet, where no one would come save to and from the house. The farmer rose from his chair, and looking in the direction that his wife pointed, he exclaimed 'It is Johnston!'

"So it was. Breathing hard from his hurried walk, the man made his way through the yard, as if on some desperate errand, and, almost speechless, laid thirty shillings on the table. Yes, it was Johnston; prayed out of his house, and brought miles at that early hour, with his conscience touched to the quick. He looked on the empty plates and the uncut cheese, and confusion covered his face while he said, 'I know how long I have owed you this money. I have been using it instead of giving it to you. Some days since I could well have repaid it, but I did not intend to give it to you yet. I hired a horse yesterday to put in our car to take my wife and children to the sea-coast for a few days. In the night the horse fell sick and we feared he would die before morning; I had to send him back, and I have been so miserable ever since dawn about the money. I could not rest till fair-day, when I meant to give it back to you, but I have brought it over myself, and there it is.'

"Sometimes these tangible answers are sent for our own weak faith, or the unbelief of others, while long waiting in patience and hope is called for in the reception of the spiritual blessing invisible to our natural sense."

"SOUTH AFRICAN MISSIONS."

Major Malan, in his book, "South African Missions," says:—

I.—*Among the Kaffirs.*

"I went forth, weary in body, to seek a place for a mission station among the Galeka Kaffirs, near the Bashee River. I did not know the country, and I had no idea what to do. But I had given some days to

SCRIPTURE TESTIMONY
Reading and studying essential for believers
ACTS 17:10-12 · ACTS 18:24-28 · 2 TIMOTHY 2:15

earnest prayer concerning this journey. Three Kaffir brethren accompanied me. We had off-saddled for the first time, and I gathered them round me to hear the Word. Opening it at the place of my daily meditation, what was my joy to find in the portion for the day these words, 'And as they went, Jesus met them, saying, All hail!' How it cheered me. It seemed as if the Lord had met me and my companions, and had saluted us with His own voice, saying, 'All hail!' The next verse was yet more assuring: 'Then said Jesus : Go tell my brethren that they go into Galilee and there shall they see Me.' My heart was full. We shall find Galilee somewhere near the Bashee, and there shall we see Him. This was all my comment. We prayed and went on. If ever the Lord manifested His presence by His works in behalf of His servants, He was seen by us at the Bashee. He made Kreli and his chiefs choose the station, and all was settled without trouble in one day! I record this as it may encourage some brother or sister going forth in the Lord's name to difficult work in an unknown place."

II.—*Streams in the Valley.*

"It is good that Christians should believe that the Lord careth for them. We do not half believe it. The Lord forgive us. That evening, after arriving at a brother missionary's hut, my hands felt very hot and dry. There is no refreshing basin for the African evangelist. I felt inclined to ask for some water in a dish, but it was dark and drizzling, and the stream was at some distance. I was consoled by thinking how often the Lord Jesus must have lacked such comforts in His earthly pilgrimage. I had just given up all thought of relieving my hot hands, when a tremendous storm of rain burst over the valley. There happened to be one small hole in the thatch of Maliwa's hut, just over the table. Heavy drops of rain fell through this. His wife came in at that moment and put a tin dish to catch the rain. She went out. When the dish was half full I washed my hands and praised the Lord. The rain ceased as soon as there was enough water for me to wash my hands. 'Delight thyself in the Lord, and He shall give thee the desires of thine heart.'"

III.—*God in the Storm.*

"A storm came on at sunset, with thunder and lightning. There was every appearance of my being stopped in my journey. I prayed the Lord it might not be so. Awoke at 2

SCRIPTURE TESTIMONY
Elijah, a normal human being, prayed for rain
JAMES 5:17

a.m. and the thunder and lightning were very heavy. Nevertheless I knelt up in my bed and prayed, 'Lord Jesus, Lord of the thunder and lightning and rain, I pray Thee drive it away, that I may go on my journey in Thy Gospel to-day.' The storm ceased almost instantly. In half an hour the moon came out. I got up at 3.30, called Solomon, and prepared to start. The Lord sent 'an exceeding strong wind' as soon as the storm ceased, to dry the roads. If an infidel asks, 'Do you suppose this was all in answer to your prayer?' I reply, 'Yes.'

"There had been a long drought in the Transkei and throughout the country. 'I hope we shall soon have rain,' a lady had remarked to me some days previously. I replied that I believed the Lord was holding off the rain until I had passed the Orange River. She laughed and asked when that would be. I told her. My faith was verified. I crossed the Orange River at about 11 a.m. to-day. Another hour and it began to rain, and by night it was impassable for the first time this summer. Whatever infidels may write or think, I believe in prayer, for I always find that my prayers are answered."

IV.— *The Praying Basutos.*

"Let us praise the Lord, who is ever the same. As in Madagascar, so in Basutoland; when the missionaries were driven out, when war, famine, and misery prevailed, the Church most thrived. The three years from 1865 to 1868 was the period of a marvellous revival throughout all the churches in Basutoland. The Lord raised up in the native churches evangelists and pastors, who fed the scattered flocks and preached His Gospel to their fellow-countrymen. The result was that at the end of the war all the churches had largely increased. When the missionaries were able to return, one evangelist brought, as a present to his minister, 100 souls he had gathered and taught while taking refuge in the mountains from the enemies of his country. Prayer was maintained daily by the Christians throughout all that time of trial; and as an old soldier, who has studied the history of war from my youth, I can only account for the marvellous deliverance which God vouchsafed to the Basutos, and the fact that they are still a people, and flourishing under the British Government, as direct answers to the prayers of the Basuto Church."

MISSION WORK IN PERSIA.

In the "Life of Fidelia Fiske," that devoted missionary to the women of Persia, we have the account of a deep work of grace among the girls attending her school—a revival that was begun and continued in much earnest prayer. The story is told in her own words.

"The first Monday of the New Year was observed by our school as a day of fasting and prayer. We had spoken of passing the day in 'wrestling for souls,' but we had only begun to *seek*, not to *wrestle*, when we learned that souls were pleading for themselves. I went into the school as usual at nine o'clock, and after telling the pupils that many prayers would that day be offered for them by friends far away, I prayed with them, and then asked them to retire to another room, where they would study with a native teacher. All but two passed out. As these two lingered, I said, 'Do you understand me?' They came nearer, and I saw that they were in tears, and one whispered, 'Can we have to-day to care for our souls?' I had no private room or closet to give them, but the dear children would find a place. They went to the wood cellar, and taking sticks of wood, made their own closets, and there they spent that cold day seeking the forgiveness of sin. Nor did they seek in vain. They were soon trusting in Christ, and we were led to hope for still greater blessings.

"I cannot well describe the scenes of that week. One after another bowed under a sense of sin. Every place was occupied for prayer. We could hardly command our own rooms long enough to bend the knee therein, while we were glad to write on all around us, 'Immanuel!' For three weeks after the revival commenced we had but little company. The time seemed to be given us to labour expressly for our pupils, and it was to us like one continued Sabbath. Every place in our house was consecrated by prayer, and all our work was for souls. At the end of three weeks Nestorians from without began to flock around us, and now our dear converted pupils were true helpers. I sometimes had as many as ten or fifteen women to pass the night with us. I often stayed with them till midnight, and then from my room I heard them pray all night. I love to remember these nights of watching with the Lord Jesus for those precious souls. Oh, how easy it is to watch when He is with us."

There were many such seasons of awakening and revival during Miss Fiske's ministry amongst them.

Of another occasion she thus speaks:—"As usual, the first Monday of the year was set apart as a season of fasting and prayer. It was a day of interest and of more than usual prayer, yet we saw not that agonising wrestling which preceded the revival of last year. During the week that followed there was more than usual tenderness in the boys' seminary, and the same was also true among our girls. There was a solemn quiet pervading the whole school, which seemed like that which precedes the breaking up of the deepest fountains. Nothing, however, very special occurred till Sabbath evening, January 13th. I was not able to attend the prayer meeting of that evening, and was left quite alone while all the school were absent. I was apprised of their return by the gentle opening of my door; and immediately saw a little group with silent and almost breathless haste pass through my room to apartments beyond. I rose at once to follow the little company, but had scarcely reached the door when I heard some half-dozen voices going up to heaven in earnest supplication. I turned to the stairway which leads to the lower apartments, and there a sound as of many waters fell on my ear. I found that every closet had its occupant. I stood silently for a few minutes, asking, not what meant the sound of many voices in prayer, but what meant such a simultaneous rushing to the throne of grace. I soon learned that there had been nothing particularly exciting in the meeting, and I sat down with the sweet belief that we were about to be visited by the Heavenly Dove, and that too before we had asked. It was a late hour before these young disciples were ready to leave their pleading, and then they retired in perfect silence. What was our joy in hearing from Seir, to learn that at the same hour in which such a spirit of prayer seemed to pervade our little circle the previous night, the Holy Spirit came in a far more powerful manner among the pupils there, and the hopefully pious spent the whole night in strong cryings and tears. In the girls' school, the week succeeding January 13th was one of deep solemnity. Our older girls spent every leisure hour, yes, and moment too, in prayer. You will not be surprised to know that we had a blessed Sabbath after such a week of prayer. Two months have passed since then, and each day has given us increasing evidence that the prayers then offered were armed by a faith which moved a heavenly hand full of blessings. We look upon no past season of revival with deeper interest than the present one. There has been less tendency to excitement than formerly, but, we believe, no less deep feeling. We saw no diminution of interest to the last day of our term, which occurred about a week since."

The two teachers of this Nestorian School, Miss Fiske and Miss Rice, were women singularly calm and wise. The method they adopted was not so much acting on the girls, as maintaining an expectant attitude that looked alone for blessing from God. And the Lord could use them, for they gave back the glory to Him.

ENGAGEMENTS KEPT.

> SCRIPTURE TESTIMONY
>
> *Ask Me anything in My name*
>
> MATTHEW 18:19 · JOHN 14:13-14 · JOHN 16:23-24

A well-known Christian worker in London, who is also a valued speaker at Prophetic Conferences, once related the following answers to prayer at the monthly prayer meeting of the Mission with which he is identified. He said that a few months previously he had received a letter from his sister in the country telling him that their aged mother, who resided with her, and who had long been in failing health, had now taken to her bed, so that he must hold himself prepared to be summoned to her side at any moment. He had already promised to speak at three successive Conferences, and knew that his withdrawal would cause both inconvenience and disappointment, he therefore at once spread the letter before the Lord, and prayed that he might not be needed by his mother until these engagements in the Lord's work had been fulfilled. Two of the Conferences came and passed, the date of the third arrived, at which our friend was the first speaker, and as he descended from the platform after giving his address a telegram was handed to him, which proved to be from his sister requesting his immediate presence. He set out at once for the station, with his Bible, but without any luggage, and as the train started, being alone in the railway carriage, he knelt down to thank God for this exact and definite answer to prayer, and further prayed that he might find his dear mother still living and conscious. This prayer was also abundantly answered, for his mother was not only able to greet him on his arrival, but the following day partook of the Lord's Supper with him, after which she gave him full and clear directions for the settlement of her affairs. She lived three days longer, and then departed joyfully to be with Christ. How true are the words of the old hymn:—

> "Make you His service your delight,
> Your wants shall be His care."

E. R. V.

EIGHT HOURS OF PRAYER.

In his volume, "The Pilgrim Fathers of New England," the Rev. Dr John Brown, in recounting the hardships of the first settlers in New England, relates the following

SCRIPTURE TESTIMONY
Elijah, a normal human being, prayed for rain
JAMES 5:17

answer to prayer "This time of stress and suffering was further darkened by the setting in of a disastrous drought of seven weeks in the early days of June. The young maize plants began to wither, and the older to mature abortively. Even before the time of harvest, famine began to play havoc among the pilgrims, and Winslow tells us that he saw men staggering at noonday for want of food. We read, too, of William Brewster sitting down to table with a meagre wooden platter of boiled clams and a pot of water before him. Nevertheless the grand old spirit was in him still, for over this lenten fare he gave thanks to God that he and his were permitted to 'suck of the abundance of the seas and of the treasures hid in the sand.'

One memorable scene belonging to this time of trial has been preserved to us. As day after day the burning sun of July glared down upon their fields, they thought it good that not only should every man privately examine his own estate between God and his conscience, but that also publicly and solemnly they should together humble themselves before the Lord by fasting and prayer. Weaklings neither in work nor worship, these religious exercises continued for eight or nine hours without intermission. In succession they recalled the promises of God, wrestled in prayer, and exhorted each other to steadfastness. They pleaded that the Lord would grant the request of their troubled souls. They have left it on grateful record that God was as ready to hear as they were to ask. For though when they met in the morning the heavens were still cloudless, and the drought as likely as ever to continue, when they came out after those hours of pleading supplication, they began to look at each other as only men can look who have been nigh to perishing, and who now at last see that rescue is near. For as they wended their way down the hillside the clouds were steadily gathering along the face of the sky, and before many hours were past the rain began to fall in softening showers upon the parched fields. Day after day it continued to fall, till 'it was hard to say whether their withered corn or their drooping affections were most revived.' Winslow goes on to say, 'Having these many signs of God's favour, we thought it would be great ingratitude if secretly we should smother up the same, or content ourselves with private thanksgiving for that which by private prayer could not be obtained. And therefore another solemn day was set apart and appointed for that end; wherein we returned glory, honour, and praise with all thankfulness to our good God who dealt so graciously with us.'"

REV. DR C. L. MACKAY.

Rev. C. L. Mackay, D.D., in his book entitled "From Far Formosa," tells the story of his Mission work in that beautiful island, a work carried on from beginning to end in expectant prayer. Of his outgoing he thus writes:—

I.—*"Lo, I am with you always!"*

"The signal was given, the guns were fired, the stately ship weighed anchor, slowly steamed out through the 'Golden Gate,' and I was at last alone. Such experiences are common

SCRIPTURE TESTIMONY
God will never leave nor forsake us
HEBREWS 13:5

enough now, but then they were new and strange. I did not feel afraid, nor sorry, nor glad. Thoughts of home came, thoughts of the loved ones more than three thousand miles behind, and thoughts of what might be before. The sea was wide. The regions beyond were dark with the night of heathenism, and cruel with the hate of sin. Would I ever return to my native land? Could it be that I had made a mistake? Such hours come to us all. They came to our Lord. They are hours of testing and trial. Sooner or later the soul enters Gethsemane. I found mine that day, and in the, little state-room the soul was staggered awhile. But it was not for long. The Word brought light. The psalm marked on the fly-leaf of my Bible began, 'I will lift up mine eyes unto the hills' and the promise was, 'Lo, I am with you always.' And then the 46th Psalm—oh, how often it has brought comfort and peace. Begone, unbelief! God in heaven is the keeper of my soul. The glorified Jesus says, 'Lo, I am with you always.'"

After arriving at Formosa, and travelling through the northern part on a tour of inspection, he settled in Tamsui. Respecting that occasion, he says:—"I moved into my new home with all my furniture——two pine boxes. In full possession of this retreat, this is the record entered in my diary under date April 10th, 1872, 'Here I am in this house, having been led all the way from the old homestead in Zona by Jesus, as direct as though my boxes were labelled "Tamsui, Formosa, China." Again I swear allegiance to Thee, O King Jesus, my Captain. So help me, God.'"

II.— *The First Convert.*

"One forenoon a young man, prepossessing in appearance, and of more than ordinary intelligence, called upon me and questioned me

SCRIPTURE TESTIMONY
God's work will not lack God's supply
PHILIPPIANS 4:19

on many subjects. When he was leaving I invited him to return in the evening and have another talk. There was something about the young man that attracted my attention and made me think more about him after he had gone than about any other whom I had met. He was intelligent and respectable; but there was a seriousness, a downrightness, that marked him as superior. I had been pleading with God to give me as the first convert an intelligent and active young man. Long before I had reached Formosa that had been the burden of my prayer. That night when I was alone in my room the thought flashed upon my mind that my prayer was heard, and that this young stranger was the man I had prayed for. So powerfully did the conviction come home to me that, although I had not a little of evidence of his conversion, I slept little that night for very gratitude. In a day or two the young man returned, bringing with him a graduate of some note, who discussed questions of religion with me for some time. They left, but within half an-hour the young man returned. He said, 'I have thought a great deal about these things of late, and I am determined to be a Christian, even though I suffer death for it. The Book you have has the true doctrine, and I should like to study it with you.' I even now recall something of the feelings of that hour —the strange thrill of joy, the hope, perhaps the fear, the gratitude, and the prayer. I look back through these twenty-three years, see the earnest face of that young man, and hear again his words of resolve and conviction. That young man became a Christian, a student, a preacher, and is to-day, after twenty-three years long of trial and testing there, still the chief among the native preachers, the man to whom more than to any other the care of sixty churches in the Mission in North Formosa falls. His name is Giam Chheng Hoa."

III.— *The Painter and his Mother.*

SCRIPTURE TESTIMONY
Believer as former persecutor of the church
ACTS 8:3 · PHILIPPIANS 3:6

"Some time after A. Hoa became a disciple, a painter in Tamsui, named Go Ek Ju, persisted in disturbing our meetings and molesting us.

When I was addressing the people at night, with the door open, he would pass by and throw pebbles inside. His habitual custom was to lie in wait for A. Hoa when on his way home after worship. Then he would jerk Hoa's cue, slap him in the face, and insult him in other ways. We just pleaded with God every day to give the man light from above. One afternoon a medium-sized, thin-faced, pock-marked, intelligent- looking fellow came to me and said, 'I am sorry for my past conduct towards A. Hoa and you, and beg you to forgive me.' It was Go Ek Ju, the painter. He took his stand as a Christian that night, and publicly declared his allegiance to Christ.

"After his conversion he spent every spare hour in study. But his aged mother—how she cried, raged, and threatened when she heard what her only son had done. How true it sometimes is that 'a man's foes shall be they of his own household.' His two sisters sent him word privately to keep away from the house lest something serious should happen. The poor, warm-hearted son was to be pitied, and A. Hoa went with him to his home. They were received with bitterness, for relatives had goaded the mother to desperation. At length I went to the house with him and A. Hoa. Go Ek Ju sat beside me. The mother, who was engaged pounding rice, looked angry and fierce. She gave a few replies to my explanations, then flew into a rage and moved towards her son with a mallet in her uplifted hand. I intercepted her, grasped the mallet, and threw it aside. We walked out, followed by abuse from the infuriated mother. We now prayed for that woman. In a few days one of the daughters was prostrated with a severe illness. Sorcerers, doctors, and idols were consulted in vain, and the poor mother's heart was bleeding. Some one advised European medicines, and I was called in to prescribe. The malarial fever, from which the girl was suffering, soon yielded to the remedies. With the mother's heart now softened and gladdened, there was no difficulty to getting her consent to the son's continuance as a student. Before long, son, mother, and daughter all shared in the hope of the Gospel. It became a Christian household, and all have remained steadfast unto this day. The son has been a preacher for twenty-one years, and the mother a Bible woman for a third of that time."

THE COUNTESS SCHIMMELMAN.

I.—*Her First Answer.*

SCRIPTURE TESTIMONY
Jesus will never send away those who come to Him
JOHN 6:37

The following answer to prayer is recorded by the Countess Schimmelman:—"It was while a mere child that I received my first wonderful answer to prayer, A terrible murder had been committed in Holstein by a farmer of the name of Tim Tode. In the most barbarous manner he had put to death his entire family of seven persons. Twenty stabs were found in the body of his mother. No quarrel had preceded the tragedy, and no motive could be discovered for the crime, except that he was desirous of getting possession of the farm. It was the first time I had heard of a deed so terrible, and yet it pierced me to the heart when I heard that the man was to be executed. My indignation turned to pity. Was this soul to be eternally lost? He denied his guilt, and remained obdurate in his impenitence almost to the last. With all my heart I began to pray for his salvation. When four weeks after this the execution took place, the papers announced that to the astonishment of all the murderer had confessed his guilt, and that in deep penitence for his sin he had come to the Cross of Christ, and found pardon through faith in His blood. My heart was filled with joy when I heard the news, and I knew it was in answer to my prayers."

II.—*"Room Must be found for them!"*

An incident is related by the Countess in connection with her mission work among the unemployed fishermen whom she set to work to carve furniture, afterwards selling it among her own friends. "All went well until my workmen began to sing hymns. The landlord became indignant, and when we returned one morning we found the door locked, and were forbidden to take the furniture we had made. My poor proteges stood around me in the snow, cold and hungry. I was in great distress, and cried with all my heart to God for help. Was it possible that in so large a city no small room could be found in which I could speak to these men of Jesus, and enable them to earn their living? I took a cab, and went at once to the police station. I went straight to the officer in charge, but he did not think he would be justified in interfering. Then, just as a higher officer entered, an old policeman ventured to remark, 'Can you not send one of us to help the lady in the interests of her good work? We have seen what she has been able to do in the streets.' Upon this the higher official ordered him to accompany me. The sight of a policeman was quite enough for our landlord. He at once opened the room and put out the furniture in the street. More he would not do. Our case was now almost as desperate as before, but I continued to cry to God for help. There were souls willing to listen to the Gospel, and to come to Jesus, and *room must be found for them*. Then by a wonderful train of circumstances, God came to our help, and within an hour I was lodged with my band of workmen in first-rate quarters in one of the best streets in Berlin. Mr Schmidt, a kind-hearted landlord, placed at my disposal a large workroom, a cellar, a little parlour for myself, and a shop in which we could sell our furniture."

III.—*Released by Prayer.*

The Countess Schimmelman was at one time forcibly removed by perse-cuting relatives to an asylum, and the rumour that she had gone on a voyage to England or Germany was suspected by friends to be a ruse to conceal some foul play on the part of her enemies. Their suspicions were also aroused by the manner in which her estate was being despoiled by those who, on the ground of her alleged insanity, had had themselves appointed guardians. Inquiries were made, and after five weeks' confinement in such a dreadful place, she was released by the visit of a member of Parliament. The certificate of her supposed madness was annulled, and she was received very cordially by all classes of society. When in that place of "durance vile," in the midst of her deep distress, "I remember," she says, "falling on my knees, and praying with bitter tears: 'Oh God, no one can do anything which Thou dost not permit; and if Satan is now attempting to silence in this prison the lips which have testified of Jesus, let even this tend to the furtherance and welfare of Thy Kingdom. Grant me in this hour my prayer that this attempt of the evil one may be frustrated, and that through me as a humble instrument Thy Gospel may yet be carried to thousands.' In my desperation I used great words, and added, 'Unto distant lands, over half the world, and even to the far away islands of the sea.' I state this to the glory of God, because it has become true." Since that prayer was offered in helplessness and captivity, Countess Schimmelman has travelled over land and sea, and she testifies, "My public meetings have frequently been attended by as many as three thousand persons. These meetings have been richly blessed to many, and I could never have believed it possible that the prayer I offered during the first hour of my imprisonment would be so signally answered."

Countess Schimmelman paid a visit to this country; she drew large crowds, and gained their interest in the work she has so much at heart, and also in herself as one whose faith in God has upheld her through trials so exceptionally severe.

A SWEDISH MISSIONARY'S EXPERIENCES.

Mrs Cooper, Shanghai, writes:—"At our Saturday evening missionary prayer meeting we were privileged to hear from the lips of one of our Swedish brethren some incidents which had taken place in his experience in the north of Shan-si, which illustrate in a wonderful manner what simple trust in the Lord can do."

I.— *The Robbers Scared.*

SCRIPTURE TESTIMONY
Deliverance from enemies and circumstances
LUKE 1:71

"Our brother told us that one time when he, with a native evangelist, was out itinerating, he came to a village where the people seemed very hostile. The landlord of the inn in which he had taken lodgings pleaded with him to move on, as a band of robbers meant to come and destroy his place to get the foreigner's money, and the poor man knew not what to do. 'I will tell you what we will do; we will have a prayer meeting, and pray to God, and *He* will deliver us.' They called all the inmates together, and our brother and his assistant prayed to God for deliverance, and He heard and answered, as the robbers were too scared to attack them. For two weeks they stayed in that place, having a prayer meeting every night, and not a hand was raised against them; but souls were awakened and blessing was the result, and this all through trust in the Lord."

II.—*Stolen Shoes and Cash Prayed Back.*

"They visited another village, and while the missionary was sleeping some one stole his shoes. When he awoke he had no shoes to put on, and none could be bought. He called the friends together to pray for the restoration of his shoes, and while they were praying, first one shoe and then another was thrown through the window, while a voice called out, 'Here, take your shoes and stop praying, as I am afraid your God will beat me.' 'While they are yet speaking I will hear.'

"At another inn he was robbed of all his money and some of his clothing. He told the people of his loss, and said he must get it back, as he had about 200 miles to go ere he could reach the nearest station to get any more. 'Now,' he says, 'my God knows who has done it, and we will ask Him to get it back for me.' So they began praying, and prayed on till some one said, 'Let us search every one in the inn.' So they began searching, and at last it was found sewn up in a man's clothing who had stayed the night there. He said he had tried three or four times to get away, but could not succeed, so he must confess that their God is indeed a great God. All his money and garments were returned, and with a full heart he praised his God for thus honouring simple trust."

III.— *Through Floods.*

"Once while travelling he came to a river which was very much swollen and filled with blocks of broken ice, and yet must be crossed. There was not any bridge or ferry boat to be seen, but the Chinese said they would carry him over if he gave them a lot of silver. He said, 'I have no silver, so cannot give it, only cash.' They refused, therefore, to help; so seeing it must be done, he called upon his God and boldly went into the water, and his assistant followed him. It was hard work, as the water was up to their neck, but they trusted in God and He failed them not, and in safety they reached the other shore, where they praised God with grateful hearts, and were all preserved from cold."

IV.—*At the Lords Bidding.*

"At one time our brother fell off his horse, and, according to Dr Stewart's report, broke his thigh bone. The doctor said he must lie still six months, but in three weeks he heard the Lord saying, 'Why are you lying here? Arise,' and slowly he sat up, then put his feet on the ground, and walked round the room. The Christians ran in when they heard him praising God, and joined in his loud hallelujahs. I wish you could have seen our brother's face when he was telling these stories; it was all aglow with the joy of the Lord, and if you could have heard him shout, 'Ah, yes, simple trust in the Lord can do all things,' it would have caused your heart also to praise and trust the Lord."

MR GRUBB'S TESTIMONY.

I.— *The Soldiers' Meeting.*

In giving a report at the Keswick Convention of his late missionary tour, the Rev. G. C. Grubb related several answers to prayer. He said: — "When we reached Gibraltar a sailor came on board and asked if we would come and hold a meeting that night in the Soldiers' Institute. I said we could not do that, as the steamer was to sail in two hours. 'Well,' said the man, 'I am surprised at that, because we prayed last night, and we all felt in our souls that God had answered our prayer.' 'Then,' said I 'if we go we go, but if we hold the meeting the Lord will have to work a miracle, and I won't be surprised if He does.' At eleven o'clock that day the screw turned, and off went the boat. Where were the soldiers' prayers then? We went on for about a hundred yards, when there was a sudden stoppage. We ran to see what was the matter, and there was a chain cable wound round our propellor. God had stopped the P. and O. boat in His own way, and according to the soldiers' prayers the meeting was held that night."

II.—*"The Lord's Release."*

"Mr Bidlake joined the Mission party in Australia. After some years of wandering from the Lord in a very terrible way, he came back to Him during the Melbourne Mission.

SCRIPTURE TESTIMONY
God provides exactly what is needed
2 CORINTHIANS 8:15 · PHILIPPIANS 4:19

That you may understand what a blessing it was that Mr Bidlake got, let me tell you what an old friend of his, a Roman Catholic, said to him on the Sydney platform. 'Well, Bidlake, I am glad to see you. I never quite believed in the conversion of the Apostle Paul, but since I have seen you I do believe it.' I say no more than that; but I am sure there is one thing he would like me to mention. He said to us when it came home to our mind that God wanted him to join the Mission party, 'I never can do it.' 'Why?' 'Because I am £300 in debt through my betting and other things. God wants me to pay off that debt, and I will have to stop in business for the rest of my life and pay it off.' I said, 'Let us ask the Lord to send £300 to pay your debt. If God wants you for His work He will pay your debt off very soon. I won't have anything to do in this Mission with any man who is in debt.' So we prayed. Some days afterwards a cheque for £50 arrived, and from that day to this we have not been able to find out who sent it. Some time later a cheque arrived for £250; and so the debt was paid. It was addressed to Mr Bidlake, and inside was written, 'The Lord's Release.'"

III.—*£110 Received.*

"At Sydney we were joyfully received. A number of the clergy threw open their churches to us, and their hearts too. The Melbourne people added their prayers to those at Sydney, and there was a flood of blessing sweeping everything before it. I am sure the prayers of Keswick were not behind. God told us to trust Him still more in Sydney, and especially for personal needs. Let me give you an example. Perhaps I ought to tell you we were not always very flush of cash. For instance, at one place we had not enough money to pay for our tickets back to Melbourne. There were seven of us, and it was nearly two hundred miles. We would have been willing to walk, but we did not quite think that was the Lord's will. So we had a prayer meeting.

'O Lord, we have only a few pounds left, so please send us some money.' That afternoon, as Mr Campbell was going along the street, a gentleman touched him and said, 'Give that to Mr Grubb, please.' He looked at it, and it was £10. Next morning brought a letter in which there was a cheque for £100. When I got back to Caulfield I found £35 more. One day we would be down to sixpence, and another day we would be up to £300"

A BAD DEBT MADE GOOD.

SCRIPTURE TESTIMONY
Ask Me anything in My name
MATTHEW 18:19 · JOHN 14:13-14 · JOHN 16:23-24

Rev. George Grubb gives an illustration of trusting the Lord in temporal matters. He says:—"When my dear co-worker, Mr Millard, and I were conducting a mission in Cape Town in the year 1890, two of the chief banks in Cape Town failed, and a large number of people to whom I was preaching on Sunday were beggars on Monday, and the very gentleman in whose house I had been staying lost heavily. He was an earnest Christian man, well known in Cape Town. Some time after that he had to pay a sum of £60 of trust money; he was trustee for some little property, and £60 of this money was due, and he had to send it to England by a certain day. Well, he had not the money to pay it with, so he went to God in prayer, 'Oh, my Heavenly Father, it is not Thy will that any child of Thine should be in debt; Thou hast declared in Thy Holy Book that debt is a sin. Now, O Father, Thou hast never yet allowed me to owe one penny in my life, and I do not believe Thou wilt allow me to do so now; my Father, I ask Thee to send me £60 before such a day comes that I may send it to England.'

"The day came, but no money had been received. Then my friend told me how he prayed to God in these words, 'Father, I am trusting Thee: and Thou hast said that whatsoever I shall ask in the name of Jesus shall be done; now, Father, Thou art able to rain down the money from heaven to me if necessary; I believe that Thou wilt send me that £60 to-day; I do not know how.'

"He went to his office, and one o'clock came, and the mail was to go at two o'clock. No money had come; he went out to his lunch, and he came back about half-past one o'clock, and, looking upon his desk, he saw a cheque lying there for £60 sterling, and said to his clerk, 'How did this cheque come here?' 'Well, sir,' he replied, 'after you went off to luncheon, a gentleman came in and laid that cheque on the counter, and went out again.'

"Mr W. looked at the signature. He did not recognise it; he turned up his books and found that some years ago he had marked off this sum of money as a bad debt that would never be paid. This gentleman lived a long way up the country, and God had made that gentleman remember the old outstanding debt of many years ago, and God had brought him down to Cape Town and lay the cheque of £60 upon the counter, and he went out of the office knowing no more than you did of Mr W.'s need of the money."

REV. WILLIAM BRAMWELL.
The following is taken from the "Life of the Rev. William Bramwell."

I .— "The Earth is the Lords."
On the 28th of May 1798, Mr Bramwell visited Nottingham, and in answer to his inquiry, Mr Tatham informed him that after the most diligent search they had not been able to obtain land for the erection of a new chapel. Mr Bramwell said, "Brother Tatham, let us pray about it." In prayer he said, "The earth is the Lord's, and the fulness thereof, and the cattle also upon a thousand hills, the hearts of all men are in His hands, and he can turn them as the rivers of the south." He then most feelingly described the situation, crying, "Lord, thou seest their necessity, and I believe thou wilt provide a piece of land for them on which to build this chapel." Soon after with increasing faith he said, "Lord, I believe thou wilt provide them a piece of land this day." This he repeated several times, laying particular stress upon this day. Perhaps no one ever entertained a higher opinion of Mr Bramwell's faith and prayer than myself, yet when I called to remembrance the various applications we had made, and the disappointments which had followed, I found it difficult to believe against hope. After breakfast we agreed to search the town for some piece of land,

but I was called off on business, and could not go with the others. I found that Mr Bramwell and Mr Longden had gone to Mr Sherwin's paddock, which he had entirely despaired of obtaining. Mr Longden on his return stated that they had seen some land near the theatre suitable for the purpose. I asked if it belonged to Mr Bellows, because I recollected that he had some ground near the theatre, to which he replied, "I think that is the gentleman's name." I then proposed to wait upon Mr Fellows, and ask if he would sell us a part of his garden as a site for a Methodist Chapel. I did so, and after a short pause that worthy gentleman said, "Agreed." Soon after my return I discovered that the land promised, though very eligible, was not the same as that fixed on by Mr Longden, but Mr Sherwin's paddock had often been refused us, and now through the mistake of the name I went to Mr Fellows, with whom we succeeded. How mysterious are the ways of Providence, that two circumstances apparently so trivial as my absence and Mr Longden's mistake of the name Fellows for Sherwin should put us in possession of the land upon which our chapel was built. Thus Mr Bramwell's prayer of faith was answered, and was a source of grateful praise on the evening of the same day.

II.— *Two Cases of Healing.*

SCRIPTURE TESTIMONY
God bestows gifts and healing through the laying on of hands
MATTHEW 9:18 · MATTHEW 19:13 · MARK 16:17-18 · LUKE 4:40 · ACTS 8:17 · ACTS 9:12 · ACTS 9:17 · ACTS 13:3 · ACTS 19:6 · ACTS 28:8 · I TIMOTHY 4:14 · 2 TIMOTHY 1:6

Several remarkable answers to prayer occurred during Mr Bramwell's labours at Nottingham. Wm. Greensmith, when about nine years old, was afflicted in his eyes, and was unable to bear the light, even with bandages. Mr Bramwell in his regular turn had to preach at the house of his father, where he remained all night. On the following morning, when about to depart, he asked for the afflicted boy, who was called from a dark room. Mr Bramwell then put his hand on his head, and looked upward as in the act of prayer. When Mr Bramwell was gone, the boy, being conscious of some change, pulled off his bandage, looked through the window, and asked if Mr Bramwell was gone. On perceiving that his eyes were healed, the family were astonished, and gave glory to God. The complaint never returned.

Mr John Clarke bears the following testimony:— "I was once attacked by a violent plueritic fever, and all around me despaired of my life. Many kind friends visited me, and supplications were offered to God without ceasing for my recovery. When Mr Bramwell returned home out of the circuit, he immediately called to see me. He thought I bore also the mark of speedy dissolution; and casting on me a look of the greatest sympathy, raised my head on a pillow. He then began to pray to God on my behalf; his faith seemed to gain strength as he proceeded. He continued his intercessions with the greatest fervency, and in an agony asked, in submission to the will of God, that I might be restored. The Lord answered his servant's prayer, for I presently experienced such a secret tranquillity of soul as I am unable to describe. From that time my recovery began, and I was soon restored to health, and able to resume my ordinary occupations."

MR QUARRIER'S RUNAWAY.

Mr Quarrier relates the following:—"One night Mr Adam, of Langside, gave an interesting address at the Wednesday evening meeting on 'Some Answers to Prayer.' In the course of his remarks he mentioned the case of a lad who was a member of our Shoeblack Brigade 30 years ago. He ran off from the Brigade, and after a time of wandering got a situation as herd boy on a farm in the north. He was converted, and being desirous to become a preacher of the Gospel, obtained a better situation, where he was able to earn sufficient to put him through the Aberdeen College, and he is now minister of a church in one of our large towns. We were indeed cheered by the good news regarding this lad, the subject of many prayers, whom we had not heard of for several years, and our hearts went out in praise to the Lord, who, even after many days, enabled us to find fruit on his behalf."

MRS STOTT.

In her account of "Twenty-six Years' Missionary Work in China," Mrs Stott records some striking answers to prayer. She says:—

I.—*"Take this as from Him?*

"When in London I had only just enough money to take me back by rail to Glasgow. Wishing to have a few shillings in my pocket by which to obtain lodgings, I wanted to go by steamer, that being the cheaper way. Friends tried to dissuade me, not knowing my reason. The expenses were figured up, and I found I would save but 4s. 6d., and they urged it was not worth taking so long a journey for that sum. I had been asked to visit a young lady on that day, and was about to write a note to say that, leaving by steamer, I could not keep my engagement, when the thought came to me, Could I not give up that 4s. 6d. for the Lord's sake? Perhaps He had some service for me to do, or I might interest her in China, so I decided to go by the night train and to keep my engagement. We had a time of sweet fellowship together, and, when leaving, she pressed a small packet into my hand, saying, 'Take this as from Him.' When I opened it there was exactly 4s. 6d. inside. Oh, how strengthened and helped I was by that simple act! It seemed as if God had said, 'Do not doubt; I will care for you.'"

II.—*"More than they all."*

"One woman, Ah-Chang-na, a real praying saint, was very poor, yet had a joy in giving to the Lord that surprised us all; for when we began our native women's missionary band, she was one of the most regular contributors. I remember one New Year's time at our native missionary meeting telling the women God would be no man's debtor, and that whenever we from a true heart desired to spread the knowledge of His name and gave what we could ill afford, He would be sure to reward. I looked to this woman for confirmation, and said, 'Ah-Chang-na, you are one of the poorest of us, yet you have given to God this year more than ever before and more than any of the others; will you tell us how God has dealt with you—has it been harder for you to pass this year than formerly?' I asked this in faith, yet trembling, not knowing what the answer would be. With a beaming face she declared before all that at the end of the year, after paying off her little debts, she had one dollar left, and she said, 'Never in my whole life have I had one dollar to begin the New Year with before.' We did praise God for that blessed testimony, and often has it been quoted since."

III.— *"One Soul each Sunday"*

"In the beginning of the year 1886, my husband felt much led to ask God to give him at least one soul each Sunday. Week by week he kept his request before the Lord, pleading there might be no barren week during the year; and at its close we were much interested to find that just fifty-two persons had been added to our church. I remember my husband looking into my face with a sad expression as he said, 'Why did I not ask more? Oh, how we limit God when He might do great things for us, if only we would open our mouths wide unto Him.'"

IV.—*A Truant Son Changed.*

"At a meeting of converts the native pastor said there were passages in Scripture proving that God heard and answered prayer, and asked if they had ever experienced any answers to their prayers. At once a blind man rose and said, 'Three or four years ago, when I was a young Christian, and knew little of God, I was much tried about my son, who had become careless and idle in his habits, had left his work, and nothing I said seemed to influence him. I took the matter to God, told Him I was helpless and ignorant, not knowing how to pray aright. I told Him how disobedient my son was, and asked Him to influence his heart and make him go to work again. My son had gone out in the morning, and I did not know where he had gone to, but just after I had prayed a neighbour came in and told me he had gone to his work. Thus the Lord heard and answered while I was praying.' Was this not a striking example of the truth of the words, 'Before they call I will answer, and while they are yet speaking I will hear?'"

V.— *The Opium-Smoker's Victory.*

SCRIPTURE TESTIMONY
Salvation transforms
2 CORINTHIANS 5:16-17 · GALATIANS 6:15

"The preacher then asked if any one had anything else to say, and another blind man began, 'You all know I was an opium-smoker before I trusted in Jesus. I knew I could not be a follower of Christ and smoke opium. I prayed God to give me strength to break it off. It was a hard struggle, for I had smoked for twelve or fourteen years. The first day in the morning the desire for opium came upon me. I had decided not to take any medicine but to trust in the Lord, so I knelt down and prayed. I told the Lord how bad I felt, and how the desire for opium was tormenting me, and how helpless and weak I was. While I prayed the desire left me, but about mid-day it came back again, and again I resorted to prayer and was relieved. And so for three days, three times a day, the desire returned and was relieved by prayer alone. Then I got the final victory, and have never had any desire for the drug since.'"

VI.—*A Small Deficit.*

"In looking over my accounts at the end of this year 1890, there was a small deficit in almost every branch of our work. I took the matter to the Lord, and the very last steamer of the year brought me gifts from two friends, not only enough, but a balance to begin the new year with, and open an account for the boys we hope to train. 'Bless the Lord, oh my soul,' I can say. 'Goodness and mercy have followed me all the days of my life.'"

VII.—*Redeemed by Prayer.*

After describing the damage done at a riot, Mrs Stott continues:—"But, what was most serious of all, our servant, the son of the house, and another neighbour, were nowhere to be found. They were doubtless taken off by the banditti for the purpose of being held to ransom. . . . We were very anxious as to the safety of our Christian servant. We had received a message that he would be released upon our paying one hundred dollars. Later on the demand became less and less, until it was believed that he would be released on payment of ten dollars, and I was urged by the native Christians to settle the matter thus. I pointed out, however, to them that even the smallest sum must not be given for such a purpose. If we ransomed, we would never be safe, and not only our servants but we ourselves would be liable to capture at any time; we must therefore wait and pray. It seemed hard to keep our brother in bondage when a few dollars might set him free, but the principle involved was too great, and I was firm, although gladly would I have given more to see him once more among us. We frequently met together to pray that our brother might soon be released, that he should not suffer hunger or ill-treatment while in bonds, and that he might have good opportunities of preaching to the robbers. All these requests were granted by our loving Father. One day, just as we had risen from prayer, and I had asked that while we were praying the answer might come, the captive walked in. A stranger to us in the city, with whom our servant had business dealings, heard of his capture, and having a brother in the village where he was bound, interceded with his brother, and, without our knowledge, they redeemed him for two dollars, he having been nearly three weeks in captivity. Oh, how our hearts did rejoice when we heard how they had listened to the Gospel, and treated him kindly, providing sufficient straw to keep him warm. So our prayers were abundantly answered."

VIII.—*A Companion Provided.*

"During the last few weeks of Mr Stott's life he frequently prayed that God would raise up one who might be as a daughter to me, in whom my lonely heart might find comfort, and who would be a real help in the work. When at a previous Keswick Convention, Miss Bardsley was introduced to me as a young lady going out to India in the autumn. How little I then thought she was the one God had appointed. From Scotland I wrote to have my passage taken for November 28th. Friends thought I was too rash in deciding the date of my sailing while as yet no companion had been found; but God says, 'He that believeth shall not make haste,' and He kept me at rest. Returning to London in October, I found there was a party sailing the following week, of whom Miss Bardsley was one. The arrangements had all been made, passages taken, 'Good-byes' said, and it seemed as though it were too late to suggest a change; yet I felt sure she was the one God had chosen for me. On mentioning this to Mr Broomhall, and afterwards to Mr Taylor, the suitability was also apparent to them, and they kindly suggested that she should be kept back, while her place was filled by another; and, what was more remarkable still, upon my asking Miss Bardsley whether she would like to accompany me as a friend and companion, she unhesitatingly replied ' Yes,' and at the same time told me that it was the expressed desire both of her father and mother, who had met me months before. Thus on all sides God's will was manifested. And now for six years she has been all my husband prayed for—a loving, helpful daughter."

RICHARD WEAVER.

We take the following from "Richard Weaver's Life Story ":—

I.— *The Class-Leader's Visit.*

SCRIPTURE TESTIMONY
Don't be anxious, instead make requests known to God
PHILIPPIANS 4:6

"One Saturday night we sat in our little home wondering where the next meal was to come from. I thought of the good home from which I had brought my wife; I thought of our empty cupboard; and I burst out weeping. She jumped up, threw her arms around my neck, and kissing me, said:—

"'The Lord has promised that our bread shall be given, and our water shall be sure; let us kneel down and pray.'

"We knelt down, but I was too much overcome to pray. *She* prayed. It was as though she was talking to some friend in the house. And there *was* such a Friend. Has He not said, 'Where two are gathered together in My name, there am I in the midst?'

"We rose from our knees, and were about to retire to rest. A knock was heard at the door. I opened it. In walked our class-leader's wife with something bulky in her apron. She said—

"'Mrs Weaver, are you in need of anything?' My wife sat down unable to speak, and burst into tears. I spoke for her—

"'Yes, we have not a bit of food in the house, nor money to buy any.'"'Well, here is a loaf and some butter and sugar and tea; and our George has sent you a shilling, and you are to come to our house for dinner to-morrow. We were at prayer, and the master felt impressed that you needed help.'

"The kind sister left. My wife said—

"'Now, Richard, you see that God will answer prayer; let us have faith in Him."

"After thanksgiving we were again retiring - another knock at the door.
"'Who is there?'
"'Open the door,' was the reply.
"I opened it. A hand was put in, and a man's voice said—'Take this from the Lord, He will provide;' and five shillings were placed in my hand. To this day I know not the bearer of those five shillings; but I know the Lord was the sender."

II.—'An Hungered" and Fed front Heaven.

"Shortly after this I returned to Prescot for a little necessary rest. Many were under the impression that by leaving the coal-pit for the platform I had an eye to the bettering of my worldly position. Had that been my motive, I would have been disappointed. It was so far otherwise, that soon after my return to my family there was no food in the house, nor was there any money to buy it. I remember one morning on which we had not broken our fast for thirty-six hours. I did not care for myself; but it was a severe trial to see my wife and two children without food. "I had received an invitation to return to London, but I had no money to pay my fare. On the table were the tea-cups and other crockery; but there was nothing in the way of food. My wife sat with the baby on her knee. I took the Bible and read a portion of God's Word, and then knelt to pray. My little boy came to me, and said—

"'Stop praying, pa. Me so hungry. Give me my breakfast, and pray afterwards. Me so hungry.'

"He went to his mother, and said—-

"'Ma, I wish pa would stop praying, and give me breakfast. Me so hungry.'

"He came again to me and laid his little face to mine. I felt his tears wet my cheek. I shall feel them to my dying day. What could I do but plead with God? There was a knock at the door. I got up from my knees, and opened to the postman. He placed a registered letter in my hand which contained a five pound note from an unknown friend. It meant food for my family and my fare to London.

"I set off with my bag. When I reached Rainhill Station I found the parliamentary train had gone, so I had to take a second-class ticket.

When I entered the compartment I was greeted with a social 'Good morning!' by the gentleman who was already there. He immediately began to talk to me about politics. When I understood I replied; when I did not understand I held my peace. By and by I said to him, 'Let us change the subject.'

"He was willing, and asked what subject I wished to talk about.

"I said, 'God is love.'

"He dropped his paper and pulled off his hat, and said—

"'Do you know anything of the love of God?'

"'A little,' I replied. 'I know that He loves me, and gave His Son for me.'

"He said. 'Thank God!'

"I suggested that we pray in the railway carriage. He agreed. I prayed and he prayed, and I prayed, and then I sang. When I had done singing, he asked my name.

"'Richard Weaver,' I said. In a moment his hand was thrust into his pocket for a well-filled purse, which he offered to me with the words, 'God bless you : this is yours.'

"'Nay,' said I, 'I cannot accept it until I know what it is for.'

"He asked if I remembered preaching in the theatre in Liverpool.

"I said, 'Yes.'

"'Well,' he said, 'I had a son who, through associating with bad companions, had become one of the worst characters in Liverpool. He was drinking and gambling to a fearful extent, and robbing us at home on every hand. He went to hear you preach, and came home a new man in Christ Jesus. He is now the greatest comfort we have got. This purse has been in my pocket for some time as a present to you for what the Lord, through you, has done for our boy.'"

GEORGE MULLER.

The life of Mr George Muller is full of answers to prayer in connection with the Orphanages and the other branches of work in which he engaged. We extract a few from his Annual Reports to show the Lord's faithfulness as proved by Mr Muller:—

I.— *The Railwayman's Savings.*

As the income of late had been little in comparison with the expenses, I besought the Lord particularly that He would be pleased to send us larger donations to meet our

SCRIPTURE TESTIMONY
Giving all one has to live on, and trusting God for provision
MARK 12:41-44 · LUKE 21:1-4

present requirements. Now this morning I received £137 from Scotland from a person who works on the railroad, and who sends his all, which had been laid aside for a time of need. He says—"Dear Mr Muller, it is with much pleasure that my wife and I enclose £137 to you to help on the work of faith and labour of love that our Lord has these many years laid on your heart. And truly, from what we have read of your testimony of simple faith and trust in the living God in fully supplying all your need, we have been led to encourage your faith in God by giving the little we had laid aside for an evil day, and your testimony has been blessed to us in leading us out to a fuller trust in God, who has so richly supplied all our need in the past; and we would not like our Lord to find what belongs to Him lying idly by when He comes."

II.—*Nothing left but Prayer.*

Day after day, and week after week, the income has been very little, about the fourth part of our expenses, so that our balance in hand was all but entirely spent. Under these circumstances nothing remained to be done but more prayer, more exercise of faith, and patiently waiting God's time for help. Thus I gave myself particularly to prayer yesterday, and the two first deliveries brought £104 1s. for the orphans and the other objects. Of this amount £50 came with the following letter—"Dear Mr Muller, I have for years desired to make a gift to the work of the Lord in your hands of £50, and I am enabled this day to do so."

Letter after letter of the first two deliveries contained either no money at all or sums not over 10s., but I continued yet to expect an answer to prayer for a larger sum. I had now come almost to the last letter, when taking up a letter I said in prayer, "Lord, now let me have the answer," and I found in it a cheque for £250—a quite unexpected payment of another part of a legacy paid in 1878, therefore more than seventeen years since. How deeply important is it to go on expecting answers to prayer!

III.—*From New Zealand.*

From New Zealand came the following letter:— "Please find enclosed draft on Bank of England for £50, to be devoted to any portion of the Lord's work which is most in need. The above amount is the joint offering of Mr--- and myself, being portion of profits made by us in the business during the past year. The Lord our Master and Head of our business has again caused us to have a prosperous year, after three years of depression, common to all in our line of business; but through it all our faith has not failed, though the path has often been hedged round with difficulties. If time permitted we could give many examples of the way in which the Lord has most marvellously given us direct answers to prayer, and from sources (wholly unexpected) helped us in times of great financial pressure. In fact, we are every day experiencing His guidance in business matters and protection from worries that harass those who have not learned to cast their burden upon the Lord. It is no broken reed, but a firm foundation we rest upon who trust the Lord Jesus."

IV.—*For the Next Meal.*

SCRIPTURE TESTIMONY
God will provide for our daily needs
MATTHEW 6:11

One day we had four prayer meetings before each meal for the supply of the next, and at 10 p.m., because there was nothing in hand for breakfast next day, I went home, hoping something had come in there; but no, there was no money. I went down between six and seven next morning to share the need with my co-workers, and when not far from the Orphan House I met a gentleman who wished me good morning, and after he had passed came back after me and handed me some gold, and thus we were helped for that day. Another day I was taking my usual morning walk; we were then in great need; I came to a certain turning and said, "Shall I go this way instead of the way I usually go?" I felt I must go the other way, and shortly afterwards I met a gentleman, a member of the Society of Friends, who, after shaking hands, handed me some gold. Now I understood why God inclined me to go home another way. Thus we went on, ever in need, but ever having our needs supplied, month after month, and one year after another.

V.—*Help Comes.*

When the third house was filled, all the money was gone. Then came days that I had been looking for, viz.—days when God would be glorified by answers to prayer in time of need.

This was not the case a few times, or a hundred times. Thousands of times the day commenced with nothing to carry through the day, or nothing in hand from meal to meal, but God invariably helped. My most intimate wealthy friends never had a hint of our need, not one besides those actually engaged in the work, and who united with me in prayer. One day we had three prayer meetings from meal to meal for help, but I had to go home after the last prayer meeting with nothing in hand for the breakfast next morning (and we paid cash on delivery for everything). On reaching home I expected to find something there, but there was nothing. The next morning I went down to the Orphan Houses early to see if anything had come in. When I arrived, my chief helper showed me £3 he had just received, between 6 and 7 a.m. The receipt of this sum in such a time of need was recorded in the next Report, and after the Report had been published, the donor came and said—"On the morning I gave the £3, I was expecting important letters at my counting-house, and went down early in consequence. On my way down it came into my mind, should I not give something for the orphans to-day? but I decided to do so in the evening. Again the thought was pressed on my mind, Why cannot I do so now? Still I went on, but after walking a mile further in the direction of my office, I could not go on, and turned back to walk at once to the Orphan House. When I had walked half a mile back I stopped, and, remembering my important letters, turned again in the direction of the office, but once more I felt I could not go, and then turned and went direct to the Orphan House, and gave the This came before the milkman had arrived, and supplied our needs for the day.

VI.—*Helpers Wanted.*

SCRIPTURE TESTIMONY
God's work will not lack God's supply
PHILIPPIANS 4:19

We have repeatedly had to wait upon God for helpers, situations having become vacant through sickness or otherwise. In these cases we might advertise for candidates; but though we should not consider it wrong to do so, we prefer simply to wait upon God, asking Him to direct the right persons to us, for He knows our need; the work is His, not ours; and He knows who are fit for the work. In all simplicity we ask Him, under such circumstances, that He would be pleased to make known our need, and incline suitable persons to apply, and during the year we were again and again helped in answer to our prayers. In one instance when we needed a laundress, we began to pray on July 15th, 1865, and brought this matter before God day by day, and generally two or three times a day; but no answer seemed to come. In the beginning of October it looked as if the answer were given; but all proved a disappointment. Instead of being discouraged by this, and thinking it useless to continue in prayer, we began afresh and with more earnestness than ever to call upon the Lord; and on October 26th, after we had thus daily waited upon God for three months and eleven days regarding this matter, our prayers were answered.

VII.—*Conversion of Girls.*

Of all the many answers to prayer which we had during the year, the choicest was that it pleased the Lord to work greatly by His Spirit among the girls, especially in two schools at the Orphan Houses, as He had been pleased to do in the previous year among the boys. Without any apparent means, humanly speaking, all at once, God stirred up more than one hundred girls to be greatly in earnest about their souls. We are not surprised at His thus working, for we look for it, and daily pray for it, and generally several times daily; yet when the answers come they are very refreshing to the inner man, and they greatly quicken the divine life, and lead to still further and yet greater trust in God.

DR A. J. GORDON.

I.—*A Student's Deliverance.*

Dr A. J. Gordon relates the following:—"Opening my mail one morning I found a most earnest appeal from a poor student in whom I had for some time taken much interest. He detailed the circumstances by which, in spite of his utmost endeavours, he had been brought into rare straits, debts for board and books severely pressing him, until he was utterly discouraged. He was extremely reluctant to ask aid, and only wrote now, he said, to tell me how earnestly he had besought the Lord for deliverance, and to request my prayers on his behalf. It was only a little sum that he needed to help him out of his difficulties —fifty dollars—but it was a great sum for a poor student, and he was now asking the Lord to send it. Having read his letter with real sympathy, I continued opening my mail, when to my surprise the next letter whose seal I broke was from a wealthy gentle-man, expressing great thankfulness for a service I had rendered him a few days before, and enclosing a cheque for fifty dollars, which he begged me to accept as a token of his gratitude. Instantly I perceived that the poor student's prayers were heard—that the second letter contained the answer to the first; and, endorsing the cheque, I sent it by return mail to the young man, with my congratulations for his speedy deliverance."

II.—*The Lord's Cheque.*

"The noon mail of the same day brought another letter of the same sort from another college. A young coloured man, full of faith and earnest desire to fit himself for useful service in the Lord's work, had made himself known to me some months before; and, as he had, by his earnest piety and diligent scholarship, approved himself to his teacher, I had done what I could to help him. He now wrote, telling a pathetic story of his struggles, how sparingly he had lived, how he had failed in getting help from expected sources, and how now, having reached the end of the term, he was in debt and nothing to pay. He too had called earnestly upon the Lord, but as yet no help had come. To show me how prudently he had lived he enclosed a list of his expenditures, which demonstrated clearly enough how poorly he had fared. Toward night I was at the telegraph office writing a despatch to the poor student to say I would be responsible for one-half of the amount needed, provided he could raise the other half from Mr W. But what his street number was I could not remember; neither could I recall just the amount needed. So I went back to the house to find his letter in order to get the exact address. On my way I called at a certain place to pay a bill—*thirty-seven dollars and fifty cents.* I had written a cheque for the sum, and as I passed it to the book-keeper, he turned to look up the account, and said, 'This bill is paid, sir; you do not owe us anything.' 'Who paid it? ' I enquired. 'I cannot say; only I know that it was settled several weeks ago.' And so saying, he handed back my cheque. I took it, quite surprised to find myself so much better off than I expected, and returned to my house to find the poor student's letter. Referring to it, I found that, in adding up his little list of debts, it came to just *thirtyseven dollars and fifty cents.* The Lord had provided the exact amount, even to the cents. I had only to endorse the Lord's cheque again, and send it forward.

"Mark you, it was not my prayers that were answered, for I had not been moved specially to pray for these young men, not being aware of the necessity. It was not my money; the Lord provided the exact funds in each instance; but I have told you literally what happened. Does not the Lord know how to provide?"

III.—*The Mist Lifted.*

A godly man, the master of an American ship, during one voyage found his vessel bemisted for days, and he became rather anxious respecting her safety. He went down to his cabin and prayed. The thought struck him, if he had with confidence committed his soul to God, he might certainly commit his ship to Him; and so accordingly he gave all into the hands of God, and felt at perfect peace; but still he prayed that if He would be pleased to give a cloudless sky at twelve o'clock, he should like to take an observation to ascertain their real position, and whether they were on the right course. He came on deck at eleven o'clock, with the quadrant under his coat. As it was thick and drizzling, the men looked at him with amazement. He went to his cabin, prayed, and came up. There seemed still to be no hope. Again he went down and prayed, and again he appeared on deck with his quadrant in his hand. It was now ten minutes to twelve o'clock, and still there was not any appearance of a change; but he stood on deck, waiting upon the Lord, when in a few minutes the mist seemed to be folded up and rolled away as by an Omnipotent hand; the sun shone clearly from the blue vault of heaven, and there stood the man of prayer with the quadrant in his hand, but so awestruck did he feel and so dreadful was that place that he could scarcely take advantage of that answer to his prayer. He, however, succeeded, although with trembling hands, and found to his comfort that all was well. But no sooner had he finished taking his observation than the mist rolled back over the heavens, and it began to drizzle as before. This story of prayer was received from the lips of the good Captain Crossby, and he himself was the man who prayed and waited upon his God with the quadrant in his hand.

FROM THE "MEMOIR OF MRS MARY WINSLOW."

I.—*Praying Mothers.*

A number of Christian mothers met weekly for the purpose of special and united prayer for the Divine blessing upon their families. The wrestling intercessions of this band of holy women, of praying mothers — mighty in their weakness — soon brought the blessing for which they pleaded. Over Mrs Winslow's family especially the mercy-cloud gathered, unveiling its heaven-sent treasure. Commencing with herself, the blessing extended to one and another and yet another of her circle, until there was not a room in her house but resounded with the voice of prayer and praise. She thus speaks of this good and wondrous work:—"In the commencement of the year, before a revival was even thought of, the Lord met with my soul after some months of comparative darkness and desertion, during which time I felt like wrestling Israel; for my spirit was in heaviness, and I earnestly sought after my absent Lord. At last He appeared and filled my heart with unspeakable joy. Like Mary, I arose from the sepulchre, and hastened to tell the disciples that the Lord had risen upon me as the Sun of Righteousness. My heart was enlarged, and my mouth was open to speak good of His holy name, not only in my own family, but to others, exhorting them to ask and expect great things, for the Lord was at hand. I entreated them to arise out of the spiritual lethargy they appeared to be in, and Jesus would bless them as He had blessed me.

"In what language can I express my gratitude to God for all His abundant goodness to me and mine? I am at a loss. My cup at times overflows. Praise Him on my behalf, my dear friends, who know the value of this great salvation. My children are now walking in the narrow road, and are united in the tenderest bonds of Christian love. Not one unconverted soul is under my roof. All love the Saviour. My house is a house of prayer."

II.— *The Great Healer.*

SCRIPTURE TESTIMONY

Peaceful resignation to the will of God

MATTHEW 26:36-46 · MARK
14:35-42 · LUKE 22:42

"The Lord sometimes places us in such peculiar circumstances as to compel us to apply to Him for the help we can get nowhere else. At one time I had great trouble in the loss of the use of my limb. I was obliged to be carried about like an infant. Then often I went to the Lord, and earnestly besought Him to restore to me its use. I filled my mouth with arguments, and told Him He had but to speak the word and I should be whole. Still my lameness continued, and I was totally helpless. And now Satan took advantage of this to upbraid me, 'Where is the answer to your prayers? You asked not to be left a burden to yourself or to others—where is now the answer of which you so often boast?' But still I clung to the Lord and believed; bad as my case was, He would heal me. One day these words came powerfully to my mind, 'Ask for submission.' I immediately obeyed the heavenly admonition, and turned my prayer into an earnest petition for this grace. At the very moment it was given. A fortnight after this my medical man called, and seeing me in the drawing-room in my wheelchair, inquired the cause. I told him. He asked to examine the limb, which presented a highly inflamed appearance. He said nothing then, but called the following day. He took my arm, and insisted, against my remonstrance, that I should walk round the room. This I did three times; and from that time the healing process commenced, and continued till I was perfectly restored. Was not this of the Lord? He first gave me submission to His will, then answered my prayer by restoring my limb, and I was no longer a burden."

III.— *The Lord's Care for His Own.*

"I know who commands the winds and the waves, and I know also who has said, 'If ye shall ask anything in My name, it shall be granted you.' I awoke one night,

SCRIPTURE TESTIMONY
Deliverance from enemies and circumstances
LUKE I:7I

and discovered my room was on fire. Three of my children were with me. I had prayed that the Lord would watch over me and mine, and keep us from danger. He heard my petition. I awoke just in time to save myself and family from being burned. It was occasioned by a spark falling from the rushlight upon the dressing-table, and setting fire to the wainscot and the table, which were burning when I awoke. I extinguished the fire, opened the door to let the smoke escape, and retired to bed again, praising the Lord for His goodness to such an unworthy creature."

IV.— *The Minister's Dilemma.*

"Rev. Mr W. called and mentioned that, after an unsuccessful attempt to obtain a curacy, he received a letter from his wife saying she intended to dismiss her servant. Mr W. wrote to say that she had better keep her for the present, as his circumstances were too straitened to pay her the wages due to her. A few days after he returned home, and found his family much tried by the girl, who had refused to remain, and had gone to a neighbour's, alleging as a reason for her leaving that she would not be paid for her services. In addition to this trial, a bill from a tradesman was sent in demanding immediate payment. They had no money. Mr W. felt his character as a minister was at stake in a village where everything was soon known. In this dilemma they knelt down and laid their case before the Lord. In the morning the postman brought a letter. On opening it, it was found to contain a ten-pound note in a blank cover. This paid all demands, and left a surplus on hand. Oh, that men would praise the Lord for His goodness to the children of men."

IV. PRAYERS—VARIOUS

CONSCIENCE MONEY.

AN EVANGELIST writes as follows:—"In the year 1868 I was employed by a Christian merchant to help in his business, and also to engage in evangelistic work. One day a man entered the shop, and after accosting the merchant they both went into the private room. In a little my master returned to sign a paper at his desk, and presently the man was shown out. My employer asked if I had observed the gentleman, and said, 'I will tell you about him tomorrow.' I was in the habit of going to my master's house every morning before business hours to have prayer and a talk about the Lord's work, and the next morning he told me the following incident:—Some twenty years before a farmer in the district had gone to America, owing him about £100 and although quite able to pay the debt, he always refused. The merchant often prayed about the matter, but no answer came, then he promised the Lord that if He would put it into the heart of this man to pay the debt, he would devote the half of the money to the Lord's work. This he pleaded for a considerable time, but still no answer. Then he put all the money at the Lord's disposal, saying it should all be spent in some effort to win souls. Then it was not long before he got his request. The stranger who had called the preceding day was the son of the debtor, and he said that, although his father was still unwilling to pay the amount, the other members of the family wished it settled, and he had called to do so. 'And now,' said the merchant, 'this is the Lord's money; how are we to use it?' Weeks of prayer followed; an evangelist was engaged for some twenty months, labouring in the district, and many were known to be hopefully converted. The delay in getting an answer to his prayer resulted in a greater blessing both to himself and the district. It enabled him to give a much larger sum to the Lord's work, and it secured the services of an evangelist for twenty months instead of ten."

THE LOST £5 NOTE.

A business man went out one evening to collect money for a religious purpose. He made several calls, and was successful in obtaining a considerable sum. On returning home he was greatly concerned to find that he had lost a five-pound note of his own from his coat pocket. It was bad enough to lose the money, but the evil heart suggested that it was pretty severe discipline to pass through when he was engaged in raising money for others. The note, however, was gone, and he could only advertise and offer a reward to the finder. Day after day passed without any sign of the money, and it seemed as if he would never see or hear more of it. His wife, who is a regular reader of Trust, had been much interested in seeing the answers to prayer about money in it, and she thought if others got answers why should not they? She resolved to lay the matter before the Lord, and during Saturday and Sunday she pleaded that He would enable them to recover their loss. On the Monday following, a woman called at their house with the five-pound note, which she had found in a field, very much soiled through exposure to the rain. On her husband's return to his dinner, the first thing he saw on the table was the lost five-pound note. It is needless to say that very hearty thanksgivings arose to God for this gracious answer to prayer, and both husband and wife have been led to a more intimate acquaintance with the Lord as One who is interested in their temporal as well as their spiritual affairs.

A MORE EXCELLENT WAY.

A business man writes:—"A house with whom our firm had done business for some years refused to pay our account.

"I was much surprised at this refusal, for we had sought to oblige them, and it seemed quite unfair.

"What was to be done? Should we put the matter into a lawyer's hand and compel payment?

"There was a more excellent way. I took it to the Lord in prayer, and asked for what I needed— guidance, meekness, wisdom, deliverance. "I saw the customer; he was self-assertive and peremptory in his refusal. I needed meekness, and the Lord gave it, but the interview did not attain any satisfactory result. Afterwards I wrote a letter calmly stating the matter, and suggesting a proposal for final settlement. This soon brought a reply, accepting my proposal, and I rejoiced and praised God for answering my petition.

"And the faithful Promiser showed me how He still answers prayer, and gives guidance, and meekness, and wisdom, and deliverance to those who ask Him."

MISSIONARIES DELIVERED FROM DEATH.

I.—Dr Chamberlain.

Dr Jacob Chamberlain, of the Arcot Mission, India, was once in circumstances of great danger in a walled town in Hyderabad. The natives, enraged at his telling of a

SCRIPTURE TESTIMONY
Gospel is the power of God for salvation
ROMANS 1:16

different God from theirs, bade him leave at once. He replied that he had a message which he must first give, but they declared that if he should say another word he would be instantly killed. He saw them standing with their arms filled with pavingstones, and he heard them say one to another—"You throw the first stone and I will throw the next; " but he lifted his heart to Him who can subdue man's angry passions, and asked their leave to "tell them a story," with the understanding that then, if they pleased, they might stone him. It was the "old, old story," that he told them, beginning with the birth of Jesus. When he spoke of the Cross, and explained that the agony there suffered was for each one of them, they listened with wonder. Surely God was speaking through the words of the missionary. Their anger ceased; their hearts were touched; they threw down their pavingstones. After telling of Christ's resurrection and ascension, and of the glorious offer of salvation for all, Dr Chamberlain said he was done—now they might stone him. But he had nothing now to fear; those men, lately so infuriated, were weeping. They gathered around to buy his books, that they might read for themselves these wonderful things.

II.—*Bishop Patteson.*

Bishop Coleridge Patteson was delivered many times from those who sought to take his life before he suffered martyrdom at their hands. For example, while on a tour he landed on an island, and inquiring where the chief lived, the natives offered to conduct him thither. From their excited words, some of which he caught, and especially from their expressive gestures, he became convinced that they meant to take his life. He could do nothing in defence; God alone could protect him. Wishing to escape for a little from the burning sun, he entered a small hut. There on bended knees he pleaded that God would spare his life, adding, "Thy will be done." Knowing that his own soul was safe, he besought the Lord for the souls of these darkened ones. Then rising he calmly told the natives that he was ready. God heard his prayer, and granted him such peace and serenity of countenance as disarmed his foes. He heard them say—"He does not look like a murderer; he cannot have been a party to our brother's death; therefore we will not harm him." And he received only kindness at their hands.

III.—*Dr Robert Moffat.*

SCRIPTURE TESTIMONY
Willing to die for faith in Christ
ACTS 20:22-24

In labouring among the Bechuanas of South Africa, Robert Moffat at one time had nearly been the victim of their superstition. A terrible drought had continued so long that many cattle died. A renowned rain-maker was sent for, but his sorceries had not had any effect. Then all, sorcerer and people alike, charged their troubles upon Moffat and his associate, Hamilton. They said of these servants of God, "They bowed down their heads and talked as if to something bad in the ground. The clouds were afraid of their chapel bell; it frightened them back." At last a native council was held, and a chief and twelve of his men were sent to them. The chief met Moffat with his spear in his right hand, and declared that the missionaries should be tolerated no longer. "They might leave if they would, but if not they should be put to death." Moffat, looking into the eyes of the savage, calmly said, "We are resolved to abide by our post. You may shed our blood or burn us out. Then shall they who sent us know that we are persecuted indeed." Mrs Moffat stood by with her babe in her arms. Moffat threw open his waistcoat and said, "Now then, if you will, drive your spears to my heart." The Lord again heard prayer; the chief was confounded. He shook his head significantly, and said to his followers, "These men must have ten lives when they are so fearless of death. There must be something in immortality."

THE LOST PURSE.

Seventeen years have passed since the following incident occurred, but the impression it left on my mind has not faded, nor ever will fade, from my memory.

Located, during my College course, within five minutes' walk of an old friend, I often dropped in for a short season of fellowship, after my lessons were ready for next day. So it happened on a certain Saturday afternoon, having no Sunday engagement to carry me into the country, I thought to spend an hour with my friend.

I found him just in a fever of excitement, and elicited the following explanation: He had paid his men in the city, closed his shop, and hurried to the train at Ludgate Hill, with his overcoat on his arm. As he jumped into the train, he thought he heard something drop on the carriage floor; he looked down, but seeing nothing, took no further notice.

On reaching Walworth Road (his destination), he alighted and came in to dinner; and wishing to hand his wife some coin, went to his greatcoat, and then discovered he had lost his purse, containing £20 in gold. He had just made the discovery as I entered.

He was a good man and true; but, Peter-like, very impulsive; hence, when I proposed a word of prayer over the matter, he at once protested, "No, not *now*! There is a time for everything; *this* is the time for *action!*'

"Very well; what are you going to do?"

"I don't know; I cannot make up my mind what is the best to be done."

"*That*, I venture to think, is a sufficient reason in itself for prayer."

"Perhaps; but I don't feel like praying just now. I think I'll go to the Crystal Palace, the destination of the train in which I travelled, and see if honest hands have picked up the purse and handed it in at the terminus; and I'll telegraph to Moorgate, from whence the train started, advising them of my loss."

As soon as he had gone, his good wife suggested that *now* we might have a little prayer together. We knelt and pleaded that God would direct and overrule to the recovery of this purse; and then rose with a calm confidence that all would be well.

Turning to his wife, I said, "I think I will go into the city and see the officials at Moorgate Street."

"What for?" she inquired; "Charles has wired them, and no end can be served by going."

"I cannot tell you why, but I feel it laid on my heart to go."

"Then I will go with you; for I am far too excited to tarry alone just now."

We hurried to Walworth Station, and, taking return tickets for Moorgate, made for the first platform just as a G.N.R. train was signalled. Already the train was in sight; but in our impatience we would not wait, but hurried down the steps again, and up to the centre platform, as we saw a train just stopping there. Rushing to a carriage, we were about to enter, when my friend said, "That is a smoking compartment, we wont get in there and opening the next, *there was the purse just under the seat*; of course we caught at it, much to the surprise of four gentlemen in the carriage, and walked home, gladly forfeiting our tickets.

There are several points to be observed, rendering the finding of this purse remarkable. This train had gone on to the Crystal Palace, stopping at every station *en route*, on a busy Saturday afternoon, with the frequent interchange of passengers, and yet nobody appears to have noticed the purse. Again, had we waited for our train, already in sight, we should have missed the purse, and, had we *aimed* to catch this train on its return from the Palace, the probability is we should have failed; for, most remarkable of all, we found this train was not timed to stop at Walworth; should have run express from Loughboro' Junction to Elephant and Castle; but the traffic being unusually heavy, the signal was against this train at Walworth, and stopped it at the platform just for the half minute, whilst we took from the carriage the missing purse.

When Charles returned, I inquired, "Have you seen or heard anything of the purse"? "No," said he, in a despondent tone, "and do not expect to. The traffic being heavier than usual, and the purse containing hard coin only, the officials hold out little hope of its recovery."

"Is this anything like it"? (holding up the purse). "Where did you find it"? "Where you lost it." And as we explained this remarkable recovery, Charles burst into tears, and exclaimed, "This is the Lord's doings, and it is marvellous in our eyes"!

> "Oh, what peace we often forfeit;
> Oh, what pain we often bear;
> All because we do not carry
> Everything to God in prayer."

John Bunyan.

A BUSINESS TROUBLE.

An agent once got an order for a considerable quantity of goods. As these had to come from South America, the agent wrote to the principals of the firm which he represented, urging them to telegraph to their house abroad to send on the goods, but they refused on account of the high price it would cost, and they wrote instead. The consequence was that it took about sixteen weeks instead of six to bring home the goods. On their arrival they were forwarded to the firm that had ordered them, but were flatly refused as being very much behind time. The agent is a Christian man, and is in the habit of laying everything before the Lord, so he took this matter to the throne of grace, and pleaded for help in his difficulty. He wrote urging the purchasers of the goods to reconsider their decision, but he got a second letter, peremptorily refusing to have anything to do with them. This was a trial of faith, but still the agent kept pleading with the Lord, who has the hearts of all men in His hand, and can turn them whithersoever He will. He wrote a third time, and received a third answer, refusing in as strong terms as before to receive the merchandise; but what was the good man's joy when, in a postscript at its close, he read that rather than inconvenience him they would agree to receive them. Very fervent were the thanksgivings to the Lord for His help in this business matter; and yet this is only one of many deliverances which this Christian man has received in answer to prayer in the course of a long and highly honourable career.

A TERRIBLE DELIVERANCE.

SCRIPTURE TESTIMONY
Deliverance from enemies and circumstances
LUKE 1:71

The following circumstance is related by a United States surgeon:— After the close of the Mexican War, and in the year 1849, a train was sent out from San Antonio to establish military posts on the Upper Rio Grande, particularly at El Paso. I was surgeon of the Quartermaster's department, numbering about four hundred men. While the train was making up, the cholera prevailed in camp for about six weeks, at first with terrible severity. On the 1st of June it had so far subsided that we took up the line of march. After four days out from San Antonio, the health of the men became very good and continued so, with occasional cases of prostration from heat. One evening in July I received a call to see a man who had been taken sick on the march. I found him lying under his waggon. The waggon was loaded with bacon, in bulk about two tons. The heat with the pressure had caused it to drip freely. I asked him to come out from the waggon that I might examine his case and prescribe for him. This he refused to do; but demanded that I should crawl under the waggon to him, which I, of course, would not consent to do. No persuasion would induce him to change his position in the least. Becoming satisfied that he was not much, if at all sick, I left him. His profanity, threats, and imprecations were fearful. His career in the past had not been at all to his credit. He had the reputation of being a thief, a robber, and an assassin. Next morning a teamster came to me and said in a hasty and abrupt manner, "Doctor, Mac. will kill you to-day or to-night. He is full of rage, and mutters terrible threats. He was out very early this morning, and emptied his six-shooter, and reloaded it and put it in first-rate order. When I asked him what that was for, he said he would kill that old doctor to-day or to-night, and I believe he will do it. So I came to warn you, but he must not know that I have seen you." Knowing the man, I realised the danger, and felt I was powerless either to resist or avoid it. I retired within my tent, and closed it up. I prostrated myself before Him who is able to save. I prayed for deliverance from the hands of this cruel and bloodthirsty man. I submitted my cause into the hands of Him who doeth all things well, and prayed for entire submission to His will. My anxiety subsided; my fear was removed, and I commenced the duties of the day with usual cheerfulness.

Soon after this the camp broke up, and we were on the march. I fell back with the officers of the rearguard, and the excitement of the morning was soon forgotten. About ten o'clock a courier came back in haste for me to see a man who had been thrown from his mule and crushed under the wheels of his waggon. He did not know who the man was—he was about half a mile ahead. The thought then occurred to me, I shall probably have to pass Mac.'s team. I will ride square up with the courier, and keep him between myself and the train. When we came to the spot I enquired who the man was, for he was so mutilated I could not recognise him. *It was Mac. God was there.* Awe and terror took hold upon me. I was dumb with amazement.

Mac. had dismounted and walked some fifty rods by the side of his team. Attempting to remount, his mule whirled and pitched; he was thrown upon his back, and his team with fourteen others instantly stampeded. Both the fore and hind wheels on the near side of his waggon passed directly over his face, and crushed every bone in his head. It was a fearful sight; not a feature of the human face could be discerned. When the stampeded teams came in it was found that no other person was injured, nor any damage done. The philosopher may tell us of the reign of law; of coincidences; of circumstances; of the action of natural causes; but, to the Christian, the fact still remains—prayer was answered.

INSANITY PREVENTED.

SCRIPTURE TESTIMONY
Whatever you ask in prayer, in faith, abiding, you will receive
MATTHEW 21:22 · MARK 11:24 · JOHN 15:7 · I JOHN 5:14-15

Some years ago a man of God received the following letter from a lady abroad:—"I should like to interest you in a young lady who has been for a long time suffering from deep melancholy. We have tried many remedies, but without result. She feels her position keenly, and is persuaded that nothing short of a miracle can cure her. She thinks that her disease will soon end in insanity. She does not find pleasure in anything, and even doubts God Himself. She would welcome death, but she fears it, as she has not peace with the Lord. I would specially commend her to your prayers, for I believe in the power of God according to His promise, 'That if two of you shall agree on earth as touching anything that they shall ask, it shall be done for them of My Father which is in heaven.'—Matt, xviii. 19." Earnest prayer was offered up for her recovery, and another letter was received some time afterwards from the same lady, in which she said, "The young lady is cured and is happy, bless God." United prayer has a special promise attached to it. If we would unite oftener with each other, and continue presenting our petitions, we would prove the truth of the promise in its fulfilment.

THE MINISTER'S REMINDER.

A widow had several sons. One of them wished to enter the employment of a certain firm, and as her late husband had very intimate dealings with the firm she thought she would not have any difficulty in the matter. She did not pray about it, as was her wont in her other affairs. When she called she was received very coldly, and was told that there was not a vacancy for her son. She left with a heavy heart, thinking of the ingratitude of men who had received much kindness both from her husband and from herself. On the way home she met her minister, and told him how sad she was. He went into her house with her, and they committed the matter to the Lord in prayer. A fortnight afterwards she received a note from another firm in the same line of business, inquiring if she had a son who wanted a situation. She did not know the principals, but called with her son. She was received with unusual kindness. The manager was called, and told to conduct her son over the works, and to find him a place in any department he chose. He entered their service, and has since got on well in life.

THE PET DOG.

An invalid girl had a pet dog which had been given her by a friend. It was a source of great pleasure, and helped her to pass many a weary hour as she lay on her bed of

SCRIPTURE TESTIMONY
Don't be anxious, instead make requests known to God
PHILIPPIANS 4:6

pain. The dog tax, amounting to seven shillings, was due, but she had no money with which to pay it. Her father feared that they might have to sell the dog, and the little sufferer was greatly distressed at the thought of it. She knew the Lord, and was in the habit of telling Him all her wants and cares, and she resolved to lay her case before Him. She prayed, but day after day passed, and her request remained unanswered. She was not, however, much cast down; "Jesus can send it," she said. The last day for payment came, but still no money. In the evening her father told her that he thought she was not going to get it, as it was almost seven o'clock, the hour for payment. She bade him wait a little, as the post which was nearly due had not yet come in. In a few minutes the postman knocked and handed in a letter. It was quickly opened, and was found to contain seven shillings. The little invalid's heart was full; her father hastened to the office, paid the tax, and the pet dog was left to cheer the young girl as long as she lived.

THE PRAYER OF INTERCESSION.

<table>
<tr><td>SCRIPTURE TESTIMONY</td></tr>
<tr><td>Timely prayer for someone far away</td></tr>
<tr><td>MATTHEW 18:19 · JOHN 4:53</td></tr>
</table>

A series of meetings was arranged to be held in a country town, and several ministers were to take part in them. A Christian lady living at a distance was anxious to attend, and was just leaving when she suddenly became dangerously ill. She lay at the point of death, and her recovery appeared hopeless. When in this weak state Satan tempted her sorely. He told her she had lived for her husband and for this world, and had neglected her own spiritual life, and she was now unfit to die. The arrows wounded her, and she lay greatly troubled in soul, and felt quite unable to plead with God for help. Suddenly the words, "He is our sanctification," came into her mind, and she turned to the tempter and told him Jesus was her sanctification. She then lay in peace, and her heart became filled with comfort. She asked a neighbour who came in at the time to mark down the hour, as she was certain some one was praying for her. The neighbour did so. It was Sabbath morning at nine o'clock. In the country town the ministers and others who were conducting the meetings were gathered together. They had learned of the lady's serious illness, and they agreed to kneel down and pray for her. That was on Sabbath morning at nine o'clock, and while they were yet speaking the Lord heard and answered. When relating this answer to prayer, the lady said it had impressed her with the blessedness of being able to plead for others when they were unable or unwilling to pray for themselves.

A REFORMATORY BOY.

A boy ran away from a reformatory. The superintendent was much troubled about it, but felt he could neither go after him nor inform the police. He was specially busy at the time, and tried to go on with his work, but his heart was ever going out towards the poor runaway, and he was constrained to give himself to prayer for him. For two hours he prayed, and cried "Hear me speedily, O Lord." In about four hours the boy came back of his own accord; and, on being questioned, it was found the desire to return had come upon him at the very time prayer was being offered. Importunate pleadings bring speedy answers.

RECOVERY FROM SICKNESS.

An earnest Christian man, who spent much of his time in the Lord's work, had a little boy who was dangerously ill. He was nursed with tender care, but he still became worse; and one day, after examining him carefully, the doctor told the anxious parents that he could not hold out any hope of recovery. In that sad hour the sorrowing father betook himself to the throne of grace. Medical skill had done its utmost, and had failed; but could not the Lord, who, when on earth, healed all who were sick, and who even called Lazarus back from the silence of the grave— could not that same Jesus speak the word of power and arrest the progress of the disease? He lifted the child from the bed, and, wrapping him carefully in blankets, carried him to another room and laid him on a couch. Kneeling beside him he pleaded with the Lord to restore his son. How long he lay there he could not tell, but he did not rise until he got the assurance that his loved one would not die. He then rose and bore his precious burden back to bed. The disease was checked, strength returned, and the boy was able again to join his playmates in their games.

HOW THE BILL WAS PAID.

A business man who lived a godly life, and who used day by day to lay his concerns before the Lord, found himself one morning quite unable to meet a bill which fell due that day. He was an honourable man, and felt keenly the prospect of being unable to fulfil his obligations. He was also a Christian, and anything that would bring reproach on the name of his Lord was to him a cause of deep concern. He had a lady friend who was a woman of prayer, to whom he confided his trouble, and asked her to pray that the Lord would come to his help in his time of difficulty. Earnest prayer was offered, and the Lord whom he served heard and answered. As the merchant was walking along the street a friend met him, and said, "I hear you are in difficulty just now, and as I happen to have some money by me for which I have no immediate use, you can have the loan of it, if you choose, without interest." The merchant's heart was full as he gladly accepted the generous offer of his friend. His God whom he trusted, and before whom he daily laid his business matters, had not left him in his hour of trial. Blessed are all they who put their trust in Him.

IN PERILS OF ROBBERS.

SCRIPTURE TESTIMONY
Timely prayer for someone far away
MATTHEW 18:19 · JOHN 4:53

A friend who has experienced much of the Lord's goodness during her life writes:—"In the year 1855, I was travelling in Turkey, and was one of a party of nine. We were all mounted on Arab horses. Some parts of the road we had to travel were very narrow and steep. There was only room enough for a horse to pass, and on either side there were deep ravines. It was a perilous journey, and I began to get giddy and was afraid of falling. I closed my eyes, and in my extremity I cried to the Lord for help. Almost immediately one of the party looked towards me, and seeing me trembling and very white, called an Arab to go before and lead my horse. He did so, and I regained confidence, and escaped what to me appeared almost instant death.

"It was late that evening before we arrived at our destination, and it was midnight before I was shown to my room. I passed down a flight of stairs, and then, after descending some stone steps, I went along a dark, dismal passage. A porter led the way, carrying my luggage and a candle. The room seemed comfortable, and I felt thankful that the Lord had brought me so far on my way in safety. By and by a feeling came over me that all was not right. I searched the room, and on examining the window, which was on a level with the path outside, I found it very unsafely fastened, and large enough to admit a person. The door did not have a lock, only a catch which could be easily pushed open. I became very uneasy, and dared not go out into the dark passage. I prayed earnestly to the Lord to protect me, so far from home and in such a place. I could not sleep, and in about an hour I heard some one at the door trying to open it. My heart beat quickly, and I cried to God for protection. I rose, went quickly to the door, and lifted (I know not how) a large chest of drawers and placed them against the door. I piled several articles on the top, so that if they came again and forced the door the noise would attract attention and bring some one to my help. I again prayed, and became calmer and more restful, but still I was unable to sleep. After half an hour the door was again tried, this time with greater force. I felt a choking sensation in my throat, and was unable to cry out, but almost mechanically I struck the wall violently with my hand and made a loud noise. I then heard footsteps running along the passage. I felt that the enemy had fled and would not return, and I lifted up my heart in thanksgiving to the Lord and soon fell asleep. The next year, on my return to England, I met my mother, who was a godly praying woman, who told me she had been much in prayer for me, sometimes for hours, and especially during that week when I was in so great danger. So my dear mother was praying for me in England, I was praying for myself in Turkey, and our loving Father heard and answered both."

BEFORE THEY CALL.

A friend whose whole time is devoted to Christian work said that he lately had a very direct answer to prayer. The only provision he had made for his wife and family in the event of his death was a policy insurance on his life. The time for paying the premium on it was close at hand, and he found he was quite unable to meet it. He did not know how the money was to be got, and he and his wife became anxious about it. He prayed earnestly that the Lord would send help in this time of need. One day shortly before the payment became due he received a letter from a friend in India enclosing the required amount. His friend knew nothing of his special difficulty, but was led by the Lord to send it at the very time it was needed. When we are sorely beset, we cry to our God and He answers us in a special manner and we are filled with praise, but if we were more careful to watch His daily providential dealings with us, we would see that our prayers were being often answered, and not merely on rare occasions.

ONE HUNDRED DOLLARS.

Some time ago, I met in Montreal a French Canadian colporteur, whose work for Christ lay in the Canton Chambly. He wrote me a letter telling me the Lord had laid it on his heart to write to me regarding a load of financial difficulty resting upon him, greatly hindering his work. He asked me to send him one hundred dollars (£21 sterling), which would relieve him of his burden. It seemed a ridiculous letter to come from a stranger to me, whose moneyed influence was nil; but, strange to say, it did not appear ridiculous to me—quite the contrary. I simply took Hezekiah's plan—I "spread the letter before the Lord" (Isaiah xxxvii. 14). A very singular impression took possession of me, viz., to go and ask a gentleman with whom I had a bowing acquaintance for the amount. I did not even know where the gentleman lived; but I had no doubt whatever the impression was of the Lord, and my heart was full of joyful anticipation. When I came down to tea I told my wife. She looked at me anxiously and said, "I think you must be going off your head. The idea to ask a gentleman you don't know—ignorant of even where he lives—for a hundred dollars. I think you need what they say Mr Moody is so richly endowed with—sanctified commonsense. Don't be absurd.' Oh dear, oh dear; all my confidence and trust seemed to slip out at the tips of my fingers, for, judging by sight, I felt she was altogether right; so I returned upstairs and shut the door (Matthew vi. 6), and dropping on my knees, said, "Lord, give me a word to rest my faith on if this matter is of Thee." I opened at Mark xvi. 14, "He upbraided them with their unbelief and hardness of heart because they believed not." That was enough, and I felt inclined, but dared not, to put Psalm xlii. 1 in force, "O clap your hands all ye people; shout unto God with the voice of triumph." I simply did as recorded in those precious verses in 2 Chronicles xxxii. 7-8, "I rested myself on the words of my King then got the city directory to find the gentleman's address, and set out "in full assurance of faith." He was just leaving his house, but turned back. Even then it seemed such a foolish thing to do that I said nothing, but simply handed him the colporteur's letter, which he read, "Ah, I see; he wants one hundred dollars. I will have great pleasure in giving you a cheque for that amount." And he did. "Open thy mouth and I will fill it" (Psalm Ixxxi. 10). "Before they call I will answer, and while they are yet speaking I will hear" (Isaiah Ixv. 24). Hallelujah!

J. L.

MONEY FOR A Y.W.C.A.

In a large city in the west of Scotland the work of the Y.W.C.A. had developed, and it was necessary to get new premises for the boarding-house for millworkers. The "hired house" was not suitable, and the work was being hampered for want of proper accommodation. One of the members of Committee formed a Prayer Union with most of the ladies on the Committee, and made this need a matter of definite prayer. Months passed, and there came to be a distribution of money left by a rich lady for religious and philanthropic work. The trustees voted £1,000 to the Y.W.C.A. for a site, on condition that the money required for the building was secured. The ladies continued to pray. Two months after getting the £1,000 the annual meeting of the Association was held. It was a very large gathering, and the friend who submitted the report stated the need of this special work, and how the money for the site had been secured, and hoped that the Lord might dispose some of those present to give the amount needed for the building (£2, 000). A gentleman who happened to be present, and who had not specially known of the need, and certainly had no intention of giving a subscription, put into the hands of the speaker before he had concluded his address a note to the following effect: "I will gladly give the £2,000 required for the building." The enthusiasm of the audience was unbounsded. It was the Lord's doing, and all in answer to believing, importunate prayer. The Master will never see His children want, if they are doing His work according to His mind.

DR BAEDEKER'S POCKET-BOOK.

In the periodical, *China's Millions*, Miss M. Beschnidt writes from Yang-chau Training Home of a visit paid them by Dr Baedeker:—"We were so glad to have Dr Baedeker with us on a visit. He could only stay two days; but they were days of blessing. One day when all the missionaries in the city were invited to afternoon tea, the Doctor told us about his recent travels and the Lord's wonderful leading. He had gone through Russia and Siberia, visiting the Stundists and other persecuted Christians in their prisons and exile, and had now emerged in China with his faithful Armenian interpreter. I was much struck by an incident which he recounted.

Travelling by a very crowded train one day, he found on arrival at his destination that his pocket-book, containing his passport and the precious document which authorised his entrance into the prisons, besides a large sum of money, was gone. He told Jesus his great trouble, and telegraphed to St Petersburg asking for a renewal, if possible, of the document and passport. The reply that came back was that he should have both, and although he had not mentioned the loss of the money, they added, 'How much money have you lost?' On receipt of his answer they telegraphed again, 'One thousand roubles (the amount lost) on the way to you.' But the best part of it was that the new document gave him more liberty and opened doors he had not had before. Plow like the Lord Jesus! When He takes anything away it is only to give something better in its place."

THE WELL LAHAI-ROI.

Mr Henry Hunt tells, in *China's Millions*, of an answer to prayer in Kan-suh Province:—"Suen-ye, the first member received here, was much exercised in his mind because no good water could be obtained near his own dwelling and those of his neighbours. It was supposed that their situation, which is a few hundred feet above the level of the plain, was unfavourable for a water supply. In past years astrologers had been consulted and wells sunk, but only utter failure resulted, and water had still to be laboriously carried in pails for a distance of about half a mile. Suen-ye called together his relations and friends, and told them he did not now believe in astrology, but trusted in the true God, who could give them a supply of water if they asked Him. He for one would definitely wait upon God for guidance as to where he should dig a well. After some days of thought and prayer, the old man got his workmen, and showed them the exact spot where he believed they would find good water. The well was sunk to a depth of 60 Chinese feet (72 English feet), and sure enough good water flowed forth, and has been enjoyed now for long. The old man was so delighted that he told everyone he met about God's answer to his prayer. It is the custom among the heathen to have an idol shrine over a well. Instead of this Suen-ye wrote the following inscription in Chinese and put it over the well:—'By the Heavenly Father's direction —The Well Lahai-roi—God thinketh upon me.'"

Idols Abolished.

A missionary in China bears testi-mony to the Lord's willingness to hear and answer prayer:— "To-day our hearts are full of praise, for the Lord has again answered prayer.

SCRIPTURE TESTIMONY
Believers exchange supersti-tion for faith in Christ
ACTS 19:18-19

We realise more and more how much the phrase means, 'ye also helping together by prayer.' So large a part of the work in China is done by friends at home on their knees. We prayed specially that the idolatry might be removed from the house of our teacher, Mr Ting; and when Miss Holms went there this morning she found that the incense bowl, candlestick, and all the rest of the things were gone. Mrs Ting said that two days ago her husband had burned his ancestral tablet. Every Chinaman believes that he has three souls. After death one departs to the other world, one lives in the grave, and one in the ancestral tablet. You can understand what it means to burn this sacred thing—braving not only the wrath of the departed, but the much more tangible wrath of the living members of the clan. We believe that this is truly God's work in his soul in answer to prayer."

Home Revisited.

A friend who has had much experience of the Lord's goodness in answer-ing prayer sends the following:—"Ten years ago a great longing took possession of my heart once more to revisit my native land, specially to see an aged sister who had acted both as father and mother to me. But we were very poor, and my prayers in that connection seemed so absurd to my dear wife that she rebuked me, 'it seemed such nonsense.' Well, one day I was called out of the noon prayer meeting, as a gentleman wanted to speak to me. Said he, 'A dreadful thing has happened to our family in London, and I have a cable to come immediately; but I cannot possibly do so. Could you take my place and go?' 'Why,' I said, 'that is the way the Lord is to answer my prayer.' 'Well, you must go right away, and I will defray all expenses.' It was a wonderful two months —'as the days of heaven upon earth.' Without formal introduction I made the personal acquaintance of some of the excellent of the earth, and received a baptism of power and consecration at the holiness meeting of the Salvation Army in Regent Hall that abides on me still.

"Once again the same desire took possession of me, and again the Lord has answered so graciously, for my wife is with me, and our sense of His loving-kindness is new every morning. Oh, how great is His faithfulness. I will not go into detail, but as surely as the manna fell in the wilderness every morning, as surely did God in His providence increase our store, permitting us to escape the great heat of Canada and enjoy 'days of heaven upon the earth' in beloved Scotland. One very blessed day was spent at a small fishing village on the east coast. I had ministered the Gospel to a dear lad in the General Hospital, Montreal, as he passed through the weary stages of typhoid fever. His people lived at Ferryden, and he begged me to visit them. But, oh, such a welcome! They were very poor—only two rooms, and such a number of children. But they would not hear of me going to a hotel. How they managed to put me up was most amusing—I was going to say ridiculous; but the love that overlaid and underlaid it all was very precious. In the evening the dear old godly fisherman father took me to the top of a cliff overlooking the German Ocean, where we sat and talked of the deep things of God, and prayed and sought His face and listened to His voice whom we loved. It reminded me of the scene described by Longfellow—

> 'I lay upon the headland height and listened
> To the incessant sobbing of the sea
>   In caverns under me,
> And watched the waves that tossed and fled and glistened,
> Until the rolling meadows of amethyst
>   Melted away in mist.'

Yes, that was one of the 'days of heaven upon the earth.'

"I had another very blessed time when starting for a climb up a lofty mountain to spend a day alone. I have long since passed my threescore years and ten, yet possess what the Americans call vim and snap in no mean degree, so the lofty heights of the mountain range were reached in due time. I sank into a bank of heather in full bloom, and lay looking into the lovely blue sky for over an hour. When the marvellous landscape at my feet was surveyed through the opera glass, I thought of Moses on Mount Nebo, at the top of Pisgah, and repeated the lines, so full of spiritual significance—

'The Lord of all the vast domain has promised it to me,
The length and breadth of all the plain as far as faith can see.'

"There are seasons in the soul's spiritual experience too sacred to put into writing—suffice it to say that as I lay before God, or knelt singing, till the echoes resounded far and near, Herbert Booth's chorus—

'Oh, 'tis coming; oh, 'tis coming-the power of the Holy Ghost,'

the glory of God fell upon me, and such 'a day of heaven upon the earth' visited me, as indeed made 'heaven nearer and Christ dearer than yesterday to me,' and I sang with intensity of meaning as never before the doxology, 'Glory be to the Father.'"

J. L.

A PASSAGE SECURED.

The following is taken from the Reaper:—"In the month of February 1890, the writer arrived at Gibraltar on a Monday night bound on a mission in the Lord's service down the coast of Morocco. The last steamer likely to proceed in that direction for some time to come had sailed on the day previous. Friends in Gibraltar who knew that my time was very precious, and that considerable disappointment would ensue if any serious delay occurred, held a prayer meeting that Sabbath evening, asking God to bring back that steamer, or in some other way to arrange that His work and servant should not be delayed. On Tuesday morning a call was made at the office of the Company to which the steamer belonged with the view of finding out if it would be possible to overtake the vessel at Tangier by crossing in the local steamer. The answer was that there was no hope of this. Just then, however, a cablegram was handed in, and as the agent opened the message he gave an exclamation of astonishment. The cablegram intimated that the 'Fez' would return to Gibraltar at noon of that day. How this should be he could not tell. There was no business for the steamer, and such an event was wholly unprecedented. Believing that the Lord's hand was in the matter, we quietly prepared to join the steamer on her return. In due course the steamer arrived as intimated, and then we discovered that the manager of the Company, who had been enjoying a holiday in Morocco, wanted to catch the homeward-bound P. and O. steamer calling at Gibraltar that day. As something interfered to prevent the little local steamer crossing the straits he had to bring back his own steamer to get the connection. Thus, altogether unwittingly, he was made directly the means of fulfilling God's purpose and answering the prayers of His people. In stepping on board we could not but recognise the direct intervention of God, and give Him thanks accordingly. But, as the sequel will show, we were afterwards constrained to intensify that thanksgiving. After a nine days' passage we duly reached Mogador. There the business of the Mission occupied about a fortnight, and during all that time a steamer had not arrived, but on the very first day after I was free to return, a steamer from the Canaries, bound up the coast, called in at Mogador. Gladly availing myself of this opportunity I went on board, and after three days' sail up the coast, we met the first steamer coming down that I could have got had it not been for this special Divine interposition."

THE MISSIONARY'S MEDICINE MONEY.

Mr Hearn, medical missionary in connection with the Bethel Santhal Mission, says: — "There has been a great deal of sickness in the district throughout the wet season, principally fevers; and we have been able thus to visit many houses, healing the sick. One night a short time ago I was called up at midnight to go to a village two miles distant to see the head-man's son, who, they said, had been ill several days, and had suddenly become worse. I reproved them for not coming before, offered them medicine, and was about returning indoors, not caring to walk four miles in the dark (with snakes, &c., crawling about the roads everywhere) only, as I expected, to see the child die; for I felt I would likely be too late to do anything for him. However, they prostrated themselves at my feet, and implored me to accompany them, and at the same time placed ten rupees before me for my acceptance. This did not encourage me at all, for a heathen Bengalese is not usually inclined to part with his money unless sorely pressed, and unpleasant thoughts crossed my mind as to the possibility of their having associates lying in wait, and that the ten rupees were simply a bait thrown out with the hope of entering the house in my absence and obtaining much more than they gave. So I returned indoors and spoke with Mrs Hearn about it, and silently prayed to the Lord for guidance, when suddenly I remembered what the burden of my prayer had been ere retiring to rest that evening. I had just got some medicines, &c., from Calcutta, and had prayed for money to pay for them, as I had none. At once all doubts vanished as I realised that the Lord was answering my prayer by sending this rich man to me, so, taking a lantern and a few school lads with me for company, I went with the sick lad's brothers. On returning to the village an hour or two afterwards I was more than ever convinced that it was an answer to prayer, for the lad was very slightly ill; indeed, he jumped up from his bed to greet me when I entered, and altogether it looked as if the Lord had given these rich people a good fright to supply His servant's need."

THE TRAIN DELAYED.

A remarkable answer to prayer is thus told by the editor of *The Watchman and Reflector*. — "Not long ago an engineer brought his train to a stand at a little Massachusetts village, where the passengers had five minutes for lunch. A lady came along the platform and said, 'The conductor tells me the train at the junction in P--- leaves fifteen minutes before our arrival. It is Saturday night, and that is the last train. I have a very sick child in the car, and no money for a hotel, and none for a private conveyance for the long, long journey into the country. What shall I do?' 'Well,' said the engineer, 'I wish I could tell you.' 'Would it be possible for you to hurry a little?' said the anxious, tearful mother. 'No, madam, I have the time-table, and the rules say I must run by it.' She turned sorrowfully away; presently she returned and said, 'Are you a Christian?' 'I trust I am,' was the reply. 'Will you pray with me that the Lord may in some way delay the train at the Junction?' 'Why, yes, I will pray with you, but I have not much faith.' Just then the conductor cried, 'All aboard.' The poor woman hurried back to her sick and deformed child, and away went the train climbing the grade. 'Somehow,' says the engineer, 'everything worked like a charm. As I prayed I couldn't help letting my engine out just a little. We hardly stopped at the first station, people got on and off with wonderful alacrity, the conductor's lantern was in the air in half a minute, and then away again. Once over the summit it was dreadfully easy to give her a little more, and then a little more as I prayed, till she seemed to shoot through the air like an arrow. Somehow I couldn't hold her, knowing we had the road, so we dashed up to the junction six minutes ahead of time.' There stood the train, and the conductor with his lantern on his arm. 'Well,' said he, 'can you tell me what I'm waiting here for? Somehow I felt I must wait your coming to-night, but I don't know why.' 'I guess,' said his brother conductor, 'it is for this woman with her sick and deformed child, dreadfully anxious to get home this Saturday night.' But the man on the engine and the grateful mother think they can tell why the train waited. God held it to answer their prayers."

HOW THE BOOKS SOLD.

A colporteur in the Wabash valley became quite discouraged, and was almost ready to give up his work on account of the smallness of his sales. On every side his ears were filled with complaints of "hard times." The wheat crop had partially failed two years in succession, the Californian emigration and railroad speculation had almost drained the country of money. Frequently he would be told that if he could come after harvest they would buy his books, but that it was impossible to do so then. His sales were daily decreasing, and he became more and more disheartened, until one night after a laborious day's effort he found he had *only sold twenty-five cents worth*. He felt he could not go on this way any longer. He was wasting his strength and time, and the money of the Society. On considering the state of his heart, he realised that it had gradually and almost unconsciously grown cold and indifferent towards Christ. He felt that he had not prayed as he ought to have done, especially he had neglected each morning, and on his approach to each dwelling, *to pray that then and there God would guide him* and own and bless his efforts to sell books. He saw that probably here was at least a part of the cause why his sales had become so small. Early the next morning, before any of the family were up, he went to the adjoining woods, where he had a long and precious time of communion with God. There he anew dedicated himself and his all to the service of Christ. There, as under the eye of the Master, he reviewed the time he had laboured as a colporteur, and prayed forgiveness for the past and grace for the future. Then he told the Saviour all about his work, and asked Him to go with him that day, preparing the way and enabling him to succeed in the work on which he had entered. The result was what might have been expected. He went forth a new man; his heart was interested more deeply in the truths he was circulating—they were more precious to his own soul, and he could recommend his books in a way he could not do when his heart was cold and prayerless. *That first day he sold more books than during the whole week before.* In one instance he sold several dollars' worth in a family where, as he was afterwards told by godly men in the neighbourhood, the father was most bitterly opposed to everything connected with true religion. God had prepared that man's heart, so that he was ready to purchase quite a library for his family. And in many families that met him that day with the usual salutation "no money," he succeeded in disposing of more than one volume by sale. As he went from family to family, lifting up his heart in prayer to God for success in the particular object of his visit, God heard his prayers, and blessed his efforts. And so, he testifies, it had been ever since; whenever he had been prayerful—*prayerful for this particular object*, and then had diligently and faithfully done his best, he had invariably succeeded in doing even more than he expected.

THE SOLDIERS' HOME.

Mrs Todd Osborne, so well known for her work among the soldiers, relates the following answer to prayer: The deep need of a Home for Maryhill, Glasgow, was borne in upon my spirit in September 1876. I had been holding a weekly meeting in the Barracks, and as I passed up and down the road, I saw that for the soldiers temptations abounded on every side—so many public-houses lay between them and the town, and the little Home in London Street was so far away. They did not need to tell me it was hard to do right; I saw it for myself, and I longed to help them. One day the Staff Officer of Pensioners came to see me, and asked me kindly if anything troubled me. I told him that for three days it had been my prayer, day and night, that the Lord would give me the house at the corner, that I was distressed at the thought of a public-house so near the gate.

"What would you do with it if you had it?" he asked.

"Make it into a Soldiers' Reading and Refreshment Room," I said.

"But you have one already."

"Yes, but Maryhill is more than three miles away, and after the men have been working all day they are too tired to come so far."

"How would it do for my wife and I to go with you and see this place?" he said. "Could you go with us?" I said as far as I knew I could.

On the following Monday we drove up, and after looking at both houses, one at one side and another at the other side of the gate, the Major asked, "If you were taking one of these houses, which would you take?"

"The one nearest Glasgow."

"Why?"

"Because the soldiers would naturally turn down that way when they leave the Barracks, and having to pass the door might come in."

"You are right," he said, "and if you can get the house for £40 a year I will pay the first year's rent."

How glad I was that night, but next day the landlord told me he could not let it for less than £60 a year. I told him I could only give £40, and at last he agreed to let it at £45.

But furniture was needed. In a little notebook I have I find, "Sept. 9th, 1876, Asked the Lord to give me furniture for the shop on the Maryhill Road."

One day the gentleman whom Mrs Allan had entrusted with the furnishing of the little Home in London Street called and asked me what I was going to do with the shop I had taken. I told him I was going to furnish it as the first British Workman Public House in the Gallowgate was, and use it for a refreshment and reading room.

"Have you got any furniture for it?" he said.

"No," I replied.

"Where are you going to get it?"

"The Lord will give it," I answered.

"If some one was willing to furnish it and wait for the money, would you take it?"

"No."

"Why?"

"Because the Bible says, 'Owe no man anything, but to love one another.'"

"Then I will do it," he said, and left me.

I scarcely took it in for very joy. Wonderful it was that this house was to be a place to win souls to God, instead of being a trap to curse the souls and bodies of men. God answered prayer for many things that were needed, and one after another they came. I remember I had set my heart on a bright coal stove, and the kind friend had spoken of giving us a gas stove. I did not like to say that I wanted a Smith & Wellstood cooking stove with an open front to make the place look warm and bright, but I told my God, and one day having to go to Smith & Wellstood's on private matters, one of the firm asked me about the Homes, and offering to help me, I told him we needed a stove, and he sent one up, and with it a bright copper boiler.

On the 10th December 1876, our Home was opened with a tea meeting. 26th Cameronians, 78th Highlanders, and Engineers were there. God began to bless. A Christian of the 26th, Captain Beers Beers, conducted a weekly Bible class. We had a prayer meeting, and every Sunday evening a gospel meeting, attended by civilians as well as soldiers. Through the preaching of the Word many were led out of darkness into light, and from the power of Satan unto God. The hall was crowded to overflowing on Sunday nights, and the coffee bar, if not a financial, was a spiritual success.

ATTACKED BY PIRATES.

Some few years ago an East Indian trader was attacked while cruising in the Indian Ocean by a piratical schooner; and the attack being sudden and unlooked for, the merchantman fell an easy prey into the hands of the pirates. The captain and several of the crew were slain during the conflict, and the rest, being gagged and heavily ironed, were laid in the pirates' boats for removal to their own vessel; and then the murderous gang proceeded to the ship's cabin, intending there to complete the work of destruction, and see of what treasures they could possess themselves. As they descended the companionway they heard a soft voice evidently engaged in supplication; and the chief, directing his followers to halt at the entrance, went noiselessly forward to ascertain whence the voice proceeded. Bending low to avoid observation, he peered into a door that stood ajar, and there knelt a fair, young woman, with a young boy at her side, one arm clasped caressingly round the little child, and the other raised in earnest supplication. "O God of all mercy," said the beseeching voice, "save the life of my child, if such be Thy holy will; but rather let him perish now by the assassin's knife than fall a living prey into such hands, to be trained up to a life of sin and infamy. Let him die now, if such be Thy decree; but, oh, let him not live to dishonour Thee and perish at last eternally!" The voice ceased, choked with tears of agony; and there stood the pirate, transfixed to the spot by the tumult of his own emotions. In imagination he was again a child; his own pious mother's prayers and instructions, for long years forgotten, rose before him, and God's Spirit sent such an arrow of conviction to his heart that, instead of carrying out his murderous designs, he sank upon his knees and cried out for mercy. After assuring the lady that no harm should be done her, he hastened to the deck, unbound the captive crew, and restoring them to their ship again, returned with his men to their own. Shortly afterwards he surrendered himself to the British East Indian Government; but so great was the remorse he suffered for his past crimes that before his trial came on he was attacked with fever that in a few days proved fatal. Before his death he made a full confession of the crimes of his past life; and he expired humbly trusting in Jesus for mercy and acceptance with Him. Thus were his pious mother's prayers answered at last, and her erring child saved, as we may trust, even at the eleventh hour. What a heritage for good are the prayers of a Christian mother!—*Word and Work.*

RESCUED FROM SHIPWRECK.

A remarkable illustration of God's mysterious way is found in connection with the rescue of some of the passengers of the ill-fated French steamship "Ville de Havre," which was sunk by a collision with the

SCRIPTURE TESTIMONY
Death for the believer is to be with Christ
PHILIPPIANS 1:21-23 · I THESSALONIANS 4:13

"Loch Earn," November 22nd, 1873, on her voyage from New York to France. After the sinking of the "Ville de Havre" with about two hundred of her passengers, the rest were taken up by the "Loch Earn," from which the most of them were afterwards transferred to the "Trimountain." Others remained on board the "Loch Earn," where, in consequence of its disabled condition, they seemed in imminent danger of being lost.

On the 11th of December, while Mr D. L. Moody was conducting a noonday prayer meeting in Edinburgh, Rev. Dr Andrew Thomson read a letter from a Christian lady, the mother of one of those imperilled passengers, which contained the following account:— "After the 'Trimountain' left them, and they had examined their ship, many a heart failed, and they feared they would never see land again. They could not navigate the vessel, and were left to the mercy of the wind and waves, or rather to the care of Him who ruleth the wind and waves. Vain was the help of man. The wind drove them out of the course of ships northward. Two ministers were left on board the 'Loch Earn.' One of these, a Mr Cook, a truly good man, did all he could to encourage their hearts. Every day at noon he gathered them together and earnestly by prayer strove to lead them to the Saviour; and this he continued to do till they reached England. The day before they were rescued they knew that very shortly the ship must go down. The wind had changed, bringing them nearer the track of ships, but they had little hope of being saved. Mr Cook told them of his hope—that death to him would be eternal life; and he urgently entreated them to put their trust in Him who was 'mighty to save.' At the same time he told them he did not have any doubt they would be rescued, and that even then a vessel was speeding to save them; that God had answered their prayers; that next day as morning dawned they would see her. That night was one of great anxiety.

"As morning dawned every eye was strained to see the promised ship. There truly she was, and the 'British Queen' bore down upon them. You may think with what thankful hearts they left the 'Loch Earn.' One thing is remarkable. The officer in charge on board the 'British Queen' had a most unaccountable feeling that there was something for him to do, and three times during the night he changed the course of the vessel, bearing northward. He told the watch to keep a sharp lookout for a ship, and immediately on sighting the 'Loch Earn,' bore down upon her. At first he thought she had been abandoned, as she lay helpless in the trough of the sea, but soon they saw her signal of distress. It seems to me a remarkable instance of faith on the one side and a guiding Providence on the other. After they were taken on board the pilot-boat that brought them into Plymouth, at noon, when they for the last time joined together in prayer, Mr Cook read to them the account of Paul's shipwreck, showing the similarity of their experience. 'What made that captain change his course against his will but the ever-present Spirit of God?'"

THE MISTAKE FOUND.

Some time ago the cashier of a business house found on balancing the firm's books for the year a considerable deficiency. His employer having every confidence in him, told him it must be some clerical error, and not to trouble over it. This did not satisfy the cashier, however, who felt that everything must come out correct and satisfactory. He made several cursory attempts to find out the mistake, but, failing to do so, resolved to go over and check each item. For this purpose he could only spare the Wednesday evenings, the nights of the weekly prayer meeting, and he said when telling it, "my heart sank within me as I thought how many meetings I might miss before I could get back again. I prayed very earnestly that the mistake might be found out, and that I might be saved the sorrow of having to forsake the prayer meeting. Well, on settling down to go over all the transactions, I found the mistake the first night. I was not only glad, but felt that God had heard and answered my prayer."

FOR DEAR HOME.

A Norwegian barque lay in port. The cook, who was also steward, was a bright and humble Christian man of three years' standing. The first time I saw him he was considerably troubled. When he joined the ship he had engaged for two years.

The vessel had been away eighteen months, and now he was wishing to visit his home (he had a wife and two children), especially as he happened now to be near to it. If the ship left this country with a cargo again it might be nearly two years before she returned, and it made him sick at heart to think of the long separation.

Some of the men who were paid off went home, and this made him feel all the more anxious to go too. He went to the captain and asked a holiday, saying he would be back in a fortnight, but the captain would not allow him away. He then offered to get another man to take his place, but the captain would not consent to this. Then he offered to let the captain keep some of his wages if he would let him go, but he would not do this either. Then said he, "I thought I would not get home, and I prayed that I might be kept from doing wrong, and that the way might be opened up for me to get home, although I did not see how it could be.

One morning at breakfast I heard the captain say that the ship was going home in ballast to load a cargo for Melbourne, and I knew that God had graciously answered my cry, and that in a short time I should get home without any trouble or expense."

PRAY AND WORK.

A certain ship was overtaken in a severe and prolonged storm at sea. She had a noble Christian man for a captain, and as good a sailor as ever trod the quarter-deck, and he had under him an able and obedient crew. But they could not save the ship; she was too badly strained; her leaks were too great for the pumps; she must go to the bottom. The captain committed them all to the care of the God in whom he put his trust, and they made ready to take to their boats. Just then a sail was descried, and by signals of distress drawn to their relief. All on board were taken off safely and put on the ship, soon after which they saw their own ship go down. Now comes the peculiar part. This ship was soon overtaken by a dreadful storm, was cast on her beam-ends, and everything seemed to be lost. The passengers were praying, and many of the old seamen were calling on God to save them from the great deep. The captain of the ship had done his best, but could not right the vessel, and all was given up. The captain whose ship was lost then asked if he might take his crew and try to right the vessel. "Take them and do what you can," was the reply. He called to his men and told them they must save that ship. He inspired them with confidence, for they knew he was a true man of God. They executed his orders with alacrity and care. They cut away the mast, and cleared away the rigging, and brought all the force they could to right the vessel. God prospered the effort. The ship righted. They got the pumps at work, rigged a sail, and were finally all saved. It seemed as if it was necessary to put the captain of the first ship and crew on the second ship that they might save it and those on board when the terrible storm came.

Now it was particularly noticed in connection with this deliverance that the captain of the lost vessel did not make any ado in prayer or in calling on God while the storm was raging; and knowing that he was a Christian man, they asked him the reason of this. He answered them that *he did his praying in fair weather.* "And then," said he, "when the storm comes I work." He did not distrust God then anymore than in fair weather; but he knew that God requires man to do all he can to save himself, and praying might lose him his ship, when his own efforts must save it.

GUIDANCE GIVEN.

When labouring as an evangelist, I was seized with influenza on one occasion which sent me home, and kept me there for some time. I recovered, and started another mission. The meetings were very large and hot, and I had a relapse, and after this second attack my body became weak, and I could not work without perspiring very badly, and feeling the danger of going into strange beds. I knew I was the Lord's, and had the right to tell Him of my difficulty, and to look to Him for deliverance, or an opening in a way that would be more suitable. I made it a definite matter of prayer day after day, and asked the Lord to lead me. Nothing was clear to me, no way or plan, no work or opening, nor had I mentioned the matter to any one. All I did was to pray. After four days waiting on the Lord, a letter came asking me if I had any desire to become a missionary in connection with a large mission hall. I feared to respond too quickly lest I should step out of the will of the Lord, or it should not be for His glory. I went to the gentleman at once, and said to him that I could not say yes, but would like him to give me two or three days more to make it a definite matter of prayer. We agreed both to pray that if it were not the Lord's will, He would interpose some difficulty that would indicate to us that He was blocking the way, or that we would somehow have a clear indication to this effect. At the end of three days as agreed, I met my friend at his mission hall, and said to him—"Well, I have prayed, and there is no difficulty in the way, and nothing that will hinder me from responding; have you anything?" He said that he had prayed, and no difficulty had come in the way, and nothing had appeared to him to hinder me accepting his offer. There and then we agreed upon it. I was to enter on my work at the hall on a certain day, and he was to introduce me as his helper and co-worker. On the night of that day he lay down, and in a few days was with the Lord, and I have been filling his place ever since, with much blessing attending the work.

R. L.

A LAWSUIT.

In one of the northern cities of America a trial at law took place between a Christian and an infidel. The latter had sued the former for a heavy sum, falsely alleging his

> SCRIPTURE TESTIMONY
>
> *Deliverance from enemies and circumstances*
>
> LUKE 1:71

promise to pay it for some stock which he claimed to have sold him. The Christian admitted an offer of the stock, but protested that so far from promising the sum demanded he had steadily refused to make any trade whatever with the plaintiff. Each of the parties to the suit had a friend who fully corroborated their assertions. Thus the case went before the jury for decision.

The charge of the Judge was stern and significant. It was a grave and most painful task which devolved upon him to instruct the jurors that one of the parties before them must be guilty of deliberate and wilful perjury. Their statements were wholly irreconcilable with each other, and that either was innocently mistaken in his assertions was impossible. "Your verdict, gentlemen," he said, in conclusion, "must decide upon which side this awful and heaven-daring iniquity belongs. The God of truth help you to find the truth, that the innocent suffer not." It was late in the day when the Judge's charge was given, and the finding of the jury was to be announced next morning. The plaintiff went carelessly from the court arm in arm with his wicked associate whom he had bribed to swear falsely on his behalf. The defendant and his friend walked away together in painful silence. When the Christian reached his home he told his family of the Judge's solemn charge, and of the grave responsibility which rested upon the jurors. "They are to decide which of us has perjured ourselves on this trial," he said, "and how terrible a thing for me if they should be mistaken in their judgment. There is so little of anything tangible for their decision to rest upon that it seems to me as if a breath might blow it any way. They cannot see our hearts, and I feel as if only God could enable them to discern the truth. Let us spend the evening in prayer that He may give them a clear vision."

The twelve jurymen ate their supper in perplexed silence, and were shut in their room for deliberation and consultation. "I never sat in such a case before," said the foreman. "The plaintiff and defendant have sworn point blank against each other, and how we are to find the truth I cannot see. I should not like to make a mistake in the matter; it would be a sad affair to convict an honest man of perjury." Again there was silence among them as if each was weighing the case in his own mind. "*For myself* I feel as if the truth should be with the defendant. I am constrained to think he is an honest man. What say you, gentlemen?" *Every hand was raised in affirmation of his opinion.* They were fully persuaded of its truth, and gave a unanimous verdict accordingly. Thus the Christian ruffian was rightfully acquitted, and gave thanks to God, with a new and stronger confidence in the power of prayer. "Call upon Me in the day of trouble; I will deliver thee, and thou shalt glorify me," saith the Lord.

AFTER FOURTEEN YEARS!

At the precise time in missions to Tahiti, when the labours of fourteen years seemed wholly in vain, when the tireless toil, faithful witness, and unsparing self-denial

SCRIPTURE TESTIMONY
Spiritual burden for a lost people group to be saved
ROMANS 9:1-3

of the early missionaries seemed like blows of a feather against a wall of adamant, when as yet not a single convert had rewarded all this long labour, and abominable idolatry and desolation seemed to reign, one of the clearest signs and greatest wonders of God's power was seen in the South Seas. The Directors of the London Missionary Society seriously proposed abandoning this fruitless field. But there were a few who felt that this was the very hour when God was about to rebuke unbelief and reward faith in His promise and fidelity to duty. Dr Haweis backed up his solemn remonstrance against the withdrawal of missionaries from the field by another donation of £200, and Matthew Wilks, the pastor of John Williams, said, "I will sell my clothes from my back rather than give up this work." And instead of abandoning the mission, it was urged that a special season of united prayer be appointed that the Lord of the Harvest would give fruit from this long seedsowing. The proposal prevailed; letters of hope and encouragement were sent to the disheartened toilers at Tahiti; and the friends of missions confessing the unbelief that had made God's mighty works impossible, implored God to make bare His arm.

Now mark the coincidence. Two vessels started, unknown to each other, from opposite ports—one from Tahiti, bound for London, and the other from the Thames, bound for Tahiti—and crossed each other's track in mid-ocean. That from the South Seas bore the letters from the missionaries, announcing a work of God so mighty that idolatry was entirely overthrown; and the same ship bore also the very idols which a converted people had surrendered to the missionaries. That other vessel from London carried to the missionaries the letters of encouragement that bade them hold on to God, and gave pledges of increased prayerfulness and more earnest support. Here was not only an answer to prayer of the most wonderful sort, but the promise was literally fulfilled, "Before they call I will answer, and while they are yet speaking I will hear."—*The New Acts of the Apostles.*

THE RETURNED LETTER.

A few years ago I was elected an elder in a Presbyterian church. The minister waited upon me, and said he would be pleased if I would agree to accept the office. I had been an elder in a congregation to which I previously belonged, but had resigned. I was very reluctant to again enter on the duties, as the whole of my time was already taken up with the Lord's work, and I was very far from being in robust health. I, however, told the minister that if he could convince me or show me it was the Lord's will that I should accept, I would do it. He replied he could not do that. An old friend with whom I had served as an elder in another congregation was at this time also elected to office in this church, to which we had both in the providence of God attached ourselves. He had agreed to accept the eldership, and was anxious that I should do so also. He called several times and talked the matter over, but I could not see my way to accept. I thought and prayed over the matter, and decided to decline. I wrote a letter to that effect, but before posting it I laid it before the Lord, and prayed that, although I had declined, if it were His will that I should accept, I would still do so. I said, "Lord, if Thou dost want me to accept, send back my letter." A day or two after I had done so my friend again called, and walking across the room, without a word on the subject, simply said, "There's your letter," and handed it to me. We talked a minute or two on some general subject, and he left. Shortly after he again called, and began this time to urge me to accept office, when I at once told him that the Lord had settled the matter for me. At the next Communion we both stood together round the sacred elements, and in a more marked manner than at any previous Communion season I felt the Lord's presence, which I accepted as a further confirmation of His approval.

One or two points in the prayer and answer are noticeable. First—I prayed that if the Lord wished me to accept, the letter should be sent back. The usual custom when anyone declines office is for the minister or a deputation to wait upon him. Such a deputation I should have been prepared to meet, but it was not sent. Second—I addressed my letter to the minister, and either he or the Session Clerk should naturally have answered it; but in this case it was returned to me by one who was not at the time even a member of Session. Third—I asked that my letter might be returned—no more, no less; and it was returned exactly as I sent it, even unaddressed to me, and without note or comment.

J. H. S.

"MY MOTHER'S BEEN PRAYING."

In February 1861 a terrible gale raged along the coast of England. In Hartlepool Bay it wrecked eighty-one vessels. While the storm was at its height, the "Rising Sun," a stout brig, struck on Longrear Rock, a reef extending a mile from one side of the bay. She sank, leaving only her topmasts above the foaming waves.

The shore lifeboats were away rescuing other wrecked crews. The only means of saving the men clinging to the swaying masts was the rocket apparatus. Before it could be adjusted one mast fell. Just as the rocket, bearing the life-line, went whizzing through the air, the other mast toppled over.

Sadly the rocket men began to draw in their line, when suddenly they felt that something was attached to it, and in a few minutes hauled on to the beach the apparently lifeless body of a sailor boy. Trained and tender hands were promptly at work, and in a short time he became conscious.

With wild amazement he gazed around on the crowd of kind and sympathizing friends. They raised him to his feet. He looked up into the weatherbeaten face of the old fisherman near him, and asked, "Where am I?" "Thou art here, my lad." "Where's the cap'n?" "Drowned, my lad." "The mate, then?" "He's drowned, too." "The crew?" "They are lost, my lad; thou art the only one saved."

The boy stood overwhelmed for a few moments; then he raised both his hands and cried in a loud voice, "My mother's been praying for me! My mother's been praying for me!"

And then he dropped on his knees on the wet sand and hid his sobbing face in his hands.

The little fellow was taken to a house near by, and in a few days was sent home to his mother's cottage in Northumberland.

HONOURED OF THE LORD.

Christian young men who act as salesmen in the shops of licensed grocers are sorely tried. They may have entered such employment unwittingly, and have only found out when it is too late that they could not maintain their spiritual life and at the same time sell strong drink to the poor creatures who were being ruined by it. A young man whom I knew very well, and who served in such a shop, told me how keenly he felt his position. When forced to sell drink to women or children he was often moved to tears, and had to go behind the whisky barrel to hide his emotion. He was greatly distressed, and began to pray earnestly that the Lord would help him to get another situation where drink was not sold. He was a decided Christian, and was actively engaged in the Lord's work, and he felt that a crisis had come in his life, and that at all hazards he must get out of his present situation. His prayers were heard. He learned that a situation in another shop where drink was not sold was vacant, and he was successful in getting it. Shortly afterwards he was enabled to commence business on his own account, and prospered. He was full of praise to the Lord, who had delivered him, and he was able to carry on his much-loved Christian work with a clear conscience.

J. H. S.

INDEX

PRAYER FOR TEMPORAL NEEDS

PRAYER FOR SPIRITUAL BLESSINGS

PRAYERS—VARIOUS

SCRIPTURE TESTIMONY INDEX

In the face of financial uncertainty, a believer's unwavering trust in God's promise becomes evident as anonymous donations arrive when needed most. This faith is further exemplified as the believer, despite personal need, generously shares the received blessings with others, demonstrating a profound belief in the reciprocity of divine provision.

Amidst financial uncertainty, Lawson's reliance on divine guidance is evident as the burden of unpaid bills looms. Trusting in the Lord, he finds unexpected relief through a deceased acquaintance's posthumous generosity, highlighting the profound and unexpected ways in which divine care can be manifested.

Blind Aggie Graham, in her memoir, illustrates the spiritual message of trust and reliance on God's provision through her experiences of praying for new slippers and witnessing their timely arrival despite her dire circumstances, emphasizing the power of faith and divine intervention in meeting her needs.

God will provide for our daily needs.. 5

Matthew 6:11

In the midst of prolonged ill-health, a couple facing financial struggles turned to the Lord for help. Despite their dire circumstances, God provided relief through unexpected sources, exemplifying the faith-driven resilience that allowed them to overcome adversity and emerge with grateful hearts for the divine intervention in their time of need.

God communicating during prayer.. 6

Acts 11:5 · Acts 13:2-3

In a remarkable tale of answered prayer, a man lost a significant donation intended for a mission. Turning to the Lord for guidance, he was led to search in an unlikely place—the dust-bin—where, miraculously, he found the misplaced notes, reaffirming the power of faith and divine intervention in even the smallest details of life.

God will provide for our daily needs.. 7

Matthew 6:11

A widowed mother faced with the daunting task of providing for her large family found herself in need of passing an exam in a distant city to secure employment. With only a few pence to her name, she embarked on the journey with her child, relying solely on God for assistance. A "chance" encounter with a unbelieving acquaintance resulted in unexpected financial support, enabling her to travel, pass the exam, and secure a livelihood for her family.

God's work will not lack God's supply...................................... 10

Philippians 4:19

Miss Abbot, of the American Board of Missions in Bombay, recounts how amidst financial and personnel challenges, they experienced the fulfillment of God's promises. Despite their depleted resources and the departure of a colleague, they found divine provision in unexpected ways: through a substantial financial gift, timely assistance for the boys' clothing needs, and the generosity of friends offering to help meet other pressing needs. These instances reaffirmed their belief that the Lord cares for His work, providing for their needs and guiding them through trials, even when their prayers for additional laborers seemingly went unanswered.

God using an inner voice to communicate 11

John 14:26 · Acts 10:19-20 · Acts 11:12

A tragic incident led to the untimely death of an elder, leaving behind a grieving widow and children in dire need. Prompted by a strong impression from the Lord, a young woman named Miss M. felt compelled to offer assistance but was unsure whom to help. Through prayer, she was led to the widow's door, where she found the family in desperate circumstances, having exhausted their resources after the elder's passing. Recognizing the divine hand at work, Miss M. provided much-needed provisions, bringing relief and gratitude to the widow, who recognized God's provision through her timely visit.

The sheep know and hear His voice 18

John 10:3-4 · John 10:16

In a poignant example of divine guidance and generosity, a young man, prompted by an inner voice, gave a shilling to Mrs. H., a woman who had overcome a life of drunkenness through conversion to Christ. Despite not knowing how to approach her, he followed the prompting and tapped her on the shoulder, offering the money. She, having spent her last shilling on Gospel literature to distribute, received the unexpected gift with gratitude, seeing it as a prompt answer to her prayer.

God answers prayer 19

Luke 18:7 · John 15:7 · Acts 12:5 · James 5:15

In a remarkable display of divine providence, a Christian minister in Northern Indiana faced financial distress when his quarterly allowance was withheld. Unbeknownst to him, his plight was highlighted in a missionary paper read by a lady in Massachusetts. Moved by compassion and guided by what she believed to be a divine prompting, she sent $25 to aid the anonymous minister. Through the swift action of Rev. Dr. H, the donation reached its intended recipient, who expressed profound gratitude for the timely assistance, seeing it as a direct answer to his prayers.

God answers prayer... 23

Luke 18:7 · John 15:7 · Acts 12:5 · James 5:15

In a heartwarming tale, a struggling shoemaker's family, facing empty hands and an unpaid wage, turned to prayer for their daily bread. As they prayed, a kind neighbor arrived with a loaf of bread, and later, another neighbor provided additional provisions, highlighting the transformative power of faith and divine intervention.

Don't be anxious, instead make requests known to God.............. 24

Philippians 4:6

In response to a scarcity crisis at a leper asylum in India, the Missionary Pence Association faced financial constraints. Despite having no funds for extra assistance, they fervently prayed for help at their monthly meeting. Just eight days later, after a dedicated day of fasting and prayer by the lepers themselves, the association received £100 and could joyfully send a telegram stating, "Admit lepers, help coming." The subsequent public confession of faith and baptisms among the lepers reflected the profound impact of their collective prayer and the timely divine provision.

God provides exactly what is needed...................................... 26

2 Corinthians 8:15 · Philippians 4:19

Despite plans to travel to Gibraltar to negotiate the purchase of cottages, a missionary in North Africa felt compelled by prayer to stay, leading to a chance encounter with the absentee landlord at the steamer landing. Through providential events and the unexpected generosity of fellow missionaries and a native teacher, the missionary obtained the full purchase amount in time, highlighting the power of prayer and divine intervention in meeting pressing needs.

God provides exactly what is needed.. 28

2 Corinthians 8:15 · Philippians 4:19

Daniel Loest, a Christian businessman deep in debt, surrendered his financial struggles to God, trusting in the promise of divine deliverance in times of trouble. In a testament to God's faithfulness, Daniel Loest experienced a remarkable deliverance in a way that could only be attributed to the intervention of the Lord.

God provides exactly what is needed.. 33

2 Corinthians 8:15 · Philippians 4:19

Facing financial uncertainty due to the lack of appropriation for Bible women, the co-laborer considered dismissing them, but they insisted on continuing their God-called mission to teach salvation. Despite not knowing where their daily bread would come from, they persevered. Eventually, a timely provision came through a roll of banknotes, exactly covering their needs until the end of November, illustrating their unwavering faith and trust in God's provision.

Ask Me anything in My name... 38

Matthew 18:19 · John 14:13-14 · John 16:23-24

Since Mr. Kearn learned of the power in the name of Jesus, he prayed in no other name but that name alone, and was blessed to have his prayers answered by the Lord Jesus Christ.

**Don't be anxious, make requests known to God, and
He will give peace**... 39

Philippians 4:6-7

In a New England snowstorm, an elderly Christian woman and her daughters found themselves in dire need of food and fuel, without means to procure sustenance. Undeterred, the mother, trusting in God's providence, reassured her daughters, "Don't worry; the Lord will provide." As the storm raged on, their distress grew, but the mother maintained her faith. In a remarkable turn of events, a neighbor, guided by divine inspiration, braved the storm to bring precisely what was needed—wood and flour.

God answers prayer.. 42

Luke 18:7 · John 15:7 · Acts 12:5 · James 5:15

In answer to the fervent prayers of a group of missionaries after learning about a child's dangerous condition, the dying child was restored to health, to the glory of God.

The sheep know and hear His voice.. 44

John 10:3-4 · John 10:16

In a time of desperate need, George B., a godly miner facing financial distress due to illness in his family, found himself with only fourpence in the house. Despairing and unsure where to turn, he remembered God's promise that no righteous man would beg for bread. Kneeling beside his sick wife, he earnestly prayed for help. That very night, his father and a friend separately visited, each feeling an unexplained sense of George's need. His father left a half-sovereign, and the friend brought a sum collected from fellow teachers in a Sunday School, providing an almost instant answer to his heartfelt prayer.

God answers prayer.. 46

Luke 18:7 · John 15:7 · Acts 12:5 · James 5:15

In dire straits with only fourpence and six mouths to feed, a poor widow along the banks of the Tweed refrained from seeking help, trusting God to provide. Her tearful prayer during a time of hunger was answered unexpectedly when her daughter discovered a stranded salmon in a pool of water left by the thaw, delivering a timely provision, teaching her the importance of prayer and recognizing God's hand in daily sustenance.

Our Father in heaven gives good things................................ 48

Matthew 7:9-11

In the depths of winter, facing dire poverty with inadequate provisions, a minister's wife and her family endured hardships, their faith tested to the limit, until a seemingly miraculous delivery of a generous box of provisions brought them overwhelming relief and renewed faith in God's providence and care, reminding them of the power of prayer and the unfailing support of their community and their unwavering trust in divine guidance.

The prayer of a person in right relationship with God is effective .. 56

James 5:16-18

Facing financial distress after a poor fishing season, a fisherman's son-in-law, a devout Parish Clerk, earnestly prayed for help during family worship. Miraculously, the next day, the distressed fisherman found five guineas while digging for bait, providing him the means to settle debts and obtain essential provisions, serving as a tangible testament to the efficacy of earnest and righteous prayer.

Holy Spirit convicts people of their sin 59

John 16:8

A troubled and ungodly husband, resistant to religious conversations, faced a transformative moment when he stumbled upon a tract titled "One shall be taken and the other left." The personal impact of these words, coupled with fervent prayers from his godly wife and their minister, led to a profound conviction of sin. Overwhelmed with remorse, he attended church, where the same text was preached, solidifying his decision to accept God's salvation. The once resistant husband underwent a remarkable transformation, dedicating his life to working zealously for the salvation of the youth, a testament to the power of prayer and divine intervention.

The blood of Jesus cleanses us from all sin 63

1 John 1:7

A dedicated evangelist, troubled by his wife's indifference to Gospel work, prayed for her conversion for years. When she fell seriously ill and was near death, she whispered a comforting message about the cleansing power of blood. As he prayed during her passing, he experienced a clear vision of the heavens opening, confirming that his prayers had been answered, and his wife had entered glory. The impact of this revelation stayed with him for years.

All great movements of God are birthed in prayer...................... 65

Acts 1:14 · Acts 4:31

In a rural area, two young women formed a prayer partnership, meeting weekly for two years to intercede for spiritual blessings in their community. When an evangelist finally visited the region, their persistent prayers bore fruit as numerous conversions occurred during successful services, underscoring the importance of small prayer groups in sparking revivals.

The believer is to be persistent in prayer 66

Luke 11:5-10

A man in a country village prayed for an evangelist from a specific Mission, and after his death, an evangelist from that Mission arrived, leading to successful meetings and conversions in the village. The evangelist coincidentally stayed in the room of the deceased man's sister, emphasizing the impact of persistent prayer.

No longer I who live, but Christ who lives in me...................... 69

Galatians 2:20

James Brainerd Taylor, at the age of fifteen, underwent a profound spiritual experience on April 23, 1822, while visiting Haddam, Connecticut. Longing for a deeper connection with God, he earnestly prayed for the Holy Spirit to fill him, to eradicate worldly desires, and to prepare him for his future as a minister. In a moment of surrender, he felt a profound sense of peace and love, experiencing a transformative encounter with Christ that led him to dedicate his life wholly to God's service.

Holy Spirit directs believers in ministry 71

Matthew 10:19-20 · Acts 8:29 · Acts 13:2 · Acts 15:28 · Acts 16:6-10 · Acts 20:22 · Romans 8:14

A preacher, on the brink of delivering a sermon, delayed his appearance, insisting that he had "Some One" with him in his room, whom he begged to accompany him. This persistent request for the Holy Spirit's presence preceded a powerful ministry session, sparking a long period of spiritual revival, underscoring the importance of seeking divine guidance and relying on the Holy Spirit rather than human methods to foster genuine spiritual awakening.

Luke 18:7 · John 15:7 · Acts 12:5 · James 5:15

Two Chinese Christians, Mr. Uang and Mr. U., faced initial challenges in a small town while spreading the Gospel, but after fervent fasting and prayer, they witnessed miraculous conversions, including a family healed by prayer and others being delivered from opium addiction. Despite trials and superstitions, their persistence in faith led to multiple families embracing Christianity, highlighting the transformative power of prayer and unwavering dedication to their mission.

Luke 11:5-10

An agent of the London City Mission faced hostility while trying to discuss spiritual matters with a non-Christian in a wheelwright's shop. Despite the initial resistance and even a threat of violence, persistent prayers for three weeks led to a transformative encounter, and the once resistant individual became a humble and devoted Christian.

James 4:8-10 · James 5:16 · 1 John 1:9

A distressed man, feeling spiritually bankrupt, approached a busy banker seeking help. Instead of financial aid, the man confessed his neglect of family prayer and departure from church attendance, leading to a loss of peace and rest. Encouraged by the banker, he recommitted to prayer, finding renewed joy and harmony in his family as they walked together toward spiritual renewal.

Luke 11:5-10

A hardened unbeliever in Edinburgh scoffed at prayer and faith, but persistent prayer planted a seed that bloomed into a remarkable conversion, bringing him and sixteen others to Christ.

1 Timothy 2:1-4

It took ten years but a believer's persistent prayer for the salvation of his friend was answered. In a letter from the one for whom he daily petitioned heaven, he received the good news of his friend's conversion.

Romans 9:1-3

Consumed by a fiery desire for souls, missionary David Brainerd embarked on a day of fasting and prayer. His heart overflowed with anguish, sweating through tears despite the cool wind, as he wrestled with God for the salvation of multitudes.

Acts 9:4-7

G.V. Wigram's once-distant faith found profound revelation through a powerful spiritual presence. Awakened by a love that condemned darkness yet embraced him wholly, he found his next morning marked by a single, life-changing desire: "Get a Bible."

John 3:16

In a touching encounter, a young man, initially unsure about salvation, found peace and joy in faith after persistent prayer and guidance. Despite his physical decline, his newfound faith brought him comfort and assurance until his last breath, demonstrating the transformative power of trust in Christ.

2 Corinthians 5:16-17 · Galatians 6:15

In a dark period of his life marked by severe intemperance, a man found redemption through a fervent, two-hour prayer session in a barn. He emerged transformed, free from the grip of addiction, testifying to the power of sincere prayer and a renewed commitment to a life devoted to Christ.

Matthew 18:19 · John 14:13-14 · John 16:23-24

John Wesley's life was profoundly characterized by prayer, with a daily habit of two hours dedicated to private prayer. Instances from his journal highlight the significant role prayer played in his life, such as influencing the weather during preaching or bringing healing to the sick. Wesley attributed the resolution of various challenges, from weather hindrances to sickness, to the power of prayer, illustrating the centrality of prayer in his leadership.

Romans 8:28

James Gilmour's diary highlights answered prayers, showing his reliance on God's guidance. From finding a companion for his journey to Russia to challenges in securing a language teacher, Gilmour recognized God's hand in his path. The overall lesson is one of trust in God's ways, as delays and disappointments turned out to be providential, preventing harm, and providing unexpected opportunities.

Acts 11:11

Answering a call to treat soldiers with bullet wounds, James Gilmour faced a challenging bone injury. Lacking medical knowledge and resources, he turned to prayer. An unexpected encounter with an elderly man with visible bones led to a solution, showcasing the startling ways prayers can be answered in dire situations.

Acts 1:14

The Metropolitan Tabernacle witnessed the power of persistent prayer when Pastor Charles H. Spurgeon fell gravely ill in 1892. Despite medical prognoses, congregants united in daily prayer for his recovery, holding meetings twice a day for twenty-one weeks. The Tabernacle exemplifies a house of prayer, with prayer meetings preceding and following preaching, demonstrating the transformative impact of prayer in church work and ministry success.

God's work will not lack God's supply 102

Philippians 4:19

Dr. Cullis experienced numerous answers to prayer in obtaining resources for the Consumptives' Home. One day, two ladies revealed that an anonymous friend had committed to furnishing the new house entirely. Dr. Cullis expressed profound gratitude, recognizing it as a direct response to his prayers for means to furnish the home.

Deliverance from enemies and circumstances 105

Luke 1:71

Rev. J. Hudson Taylor recounts a perilous situation during a voyage to China when their ship, endangered by a strong current and drifting towards cannibal-inhabited shores, seemed helpless. As a last resort, four Christians on board, including the captain, engaged in fervent prayer, asking the Lord for a breeze to avert the danger. Miraculously, the wind arrived swiftly, saving them from the perilous reefs and potential threat from the nearby cannibals.

All great movements of God are birthed in prayer 106

Acts 1:14 · Acts 4:31

At a meeting of the Glasgow Y.M.C.A., Mr. Moody recounted an experience in London where, despite initial indifference from the congregation, a powerful spiritual awakening occurred after his preaching. Hundreds responded to the call to become Christians, leading to a significant revival in the church. This remarkable turn of events was attributed to the earnest prayers of a bedridden member of the church, demonstrating the profound impact of prayer even from those who may feel physically limited in their abilities to serve.

God's work will not lack God's supply 110

Philippians 4:19

Pastors Fliedner, Gossner, and Harms, highlighted by Dr. A. J. Gordon, exemplify the powerful impact of prayer on missions. They attribute their remarkable achievements, including supporting missionaries and establishing institutions, to a deep reliance on prayer for financial sustenance. Their lives serve as modern illustrations of God's provision, echoing the disciples' experience of lacking nothing when sent without resources.

Nothing can separate us from the love of God.......................... 114

Romans 8:31-39

In 1869, facing severe persecutions in Constantinople after converting to Christianity, Mr. Bassin's relatives and friends bribed the Russian Consul to unlawfully seize and send him to Russia. Despite dark moments, fervent prayers led to his deliverance, and while contemplating casting himself into the sea, the timely remembrance of Romans 8:35-39 strengthened him, reminding him of the love of Christ that nothing can separate us from.

Whatever you ask in prayer, in faith, abiding, you will receive.... 113

Matthew 21:22 · Mark 11:24 · John 15:7 · 1 John 5:14-15

Despite facing illegal conscription into the Russian army after his conversion, Rev. Bassin's fervent prayers to be relieved from wielding a rifle were answered unexpectedly. Instead of being compelled to shed blood, he was appointed as a clerk and later pursued a career as a Medical Officer, becoming a healer of the wounded. The outcome exceeded his initial request, demonstrating the remarkable ways in which prayers can be answered.

God's work will not lack God's supply.................................... 120

Philippians 4:19

Facing the financial burden of the Pastors' College, Mr. Spurgeon, with his income strained, came to his last pound. Desperate for funds, he prayed about it and, upon opening his letters, discovered a banker's letter informing him that an unknown lady had left £200 for the education of young men, providing a miraculous answer to his financial need.

God provides exactly what is needed...................................... 122

2 Corinthians 8:15 · Philippians 4:19

Mrs. Hudson Taylor felt called to leave her family and travel to Shansi to help with relief work during a famine in 1878, despite concerns from friends. She prayed for a sign from God before embarking on the journey, asking for funds for her outfit and a specific gift of £50 for another purpose. A gentleman unexpectedly provided the exact amount needed for her outfit, and soon after, she received a separate £50 donation, confirming her decision to go on the mission.

God's work will not lack God's supply..................................... 123

Philippians 4:19

Mr. Hudson Taylor recounts a story about how he and Mr. Jones, running an organization that feeds the poor, were left with no money but trusted in God to provide. They were amazed when a bill arrived earlier than expected, giving them the needed funds to continue their work and feed the poor. Through their faith and reliance on God's provision, they continued to help those in need and saw how their needs and the needs of others were met miraculously.

Whatever you ask in prayer, in faith, abiding, you will receive.... 129

Matthew 21:22 · Mark 11:24 · John 15:7 · 1 John 5:14-15

Mrs. Smith, facing financial challenges, prayed to the Lord for help in buying shoes before her mission trip to Salem. The Lord answered her prayer through the unexpected gift of five dollars from Father B., allowing her to purchase the much-needed shoes and reaffirming her faith in divine providence.

Ask Me anything in My name 130

Matthew 18:19 · John 14:13-14 · John 16:23-24

Mrs. Smith prayed for the wind to stop blowing so people could hear her message in Salem. Her prayer was answered when the wind suddenly ceased, allowing her to hold a successful church service where a revival broke out over a twenty-mile radius.

John 14:26 · Acts 10:19-20 · Acts 11:12

Mrs. Smith wanted to go to the camp-meeting in Knoxville, but she needed $50 for the trip. A lady, following the Lord's guidance, gave Mrs. Smith the money, allowing her to attend the camp-meeting.

Matthew 6:25-34 · 1 Peter 5:6-7

Amanda Smith was in Africa trying to help native boys. She had been relying on her friends in America to send her money, but God helped her realize she needed to put her trust in Him instead. Once she changed her mindset and let go of her reliance on America, she received unexpected financial support from friends in Ireland and India, and even a small donation from America.

Philippians 4:19

Mrs. Spurgeon, after speaking out against fundraising events for God's work, found herself facing a financial crisis for her Book Fund. Trusting in God and sharing her story, she received unexpected donations just in time, proving that in times of need, God can provide abundantly. Mrs. Spurgeon's experience serves as a testament to the power of prayer and reliance on God's faithfulness, encouraging others to also depend on God in times of financial need.

Philippians 4:19

C. T. Lipshytz, a missionary, shares the amazing way their prayers of over two years were answered when a gentleman provided a new, better location for their mission work, 33 Finsbury Square, rent and taxes, and furnishing, for seven whole years.

Philippians 4:19

Dr. Barnardo, facing a financial crisis with a mortgage deadline looming, received a miraculous blessing when Colonel's friend delivered a packet with £650 inside, raised from a bazaar in India. This unexpected gift not only covered the mortgage but also provided extra funds, reinforcing Dr. Barnardo's faith and trust in divine providence in times of need.

God answers prayer... 139

Luke 18:7 · John 15:7 · Acts 12:5 · James 5:15

Dr. Barnardo doubted if his idea of putting orphan children in cottage homes was the right path. Through prayer and divine intervention, a man named AE— D— offered to fund the first cottage, fulfilling Dr. Barnardo's mission and providing a miraculous answer to his prayers.

God answers prayer... 144

Luke 18:7 · John 15:7 · Acts 12:5 · James 5:15

A farmer and his wife, facing a dire situation with no bread for their daily needs, were brought unexpected help when a man named Johnston, moved by a sudden change of heart, repaid a long-standing debt. Through fervent prayer and unwavering faith, the wife saw a sign of hope in the form of Johnston approaching their home, demonstrating that sometimes tangible answers can strengthen weak faith in the face of trials.

I can do all things through him who strengthens me................. 143

Philippians 4:13

A woman, mentioned in Mrs. Shipton's book, was miraculously healed from an incurable disease after receiving a promise of healing while on her way to preach the Gospel to a new clergyman, enabling her to undertake tasks that were previously impossible. The healing was offered spontaneously by the Great Healer as a sign of approval for her mission, marking a significant turning point in her life and granting her the ability to carry out her ordained service.

Reading and studying essential for believers.......................... 145

Acts 17:10-12 · Acts 18:24-28 · 2 Timothy 2:15

Major Malan, with three Kaffir brethren, embarked on a mission to establish a station among the Galeka Kaffirs near the Bashee River. Through prayer and divine guidance from the Bible, they found reassurance and direction, ultimately witnessing the Lord's intervention as Kreli and his chiefs easily agreed to the chosen station in one day.

James 5:17

In his book, "South African Missions," Major Malan recounts a tale where he prayed for God to stop a storm so he could continue his journey in spreading the Gospel. When the storm ceased after his prayer, he believed, and rightly so, that it was a direct answer to his plea.

Matthew 18:19 · John 14:13-14 · John 16:23-24

A Christian worker in London prayed to be able to fulfill his speaking engagements before being needed by his ailing mother. He was able to finish his commitments before being summoned to his mother's side, where he arrived in time to share special moments with her before her passing. Through his faith, his prayer was answered, showing that prioritizing God's work can lead to answered prayers and peace in trying times.

James 5:17

In the midst of drought and famine, William Brewster and the other pilgrims humbly prayed and fasted for eight hours, pleading with God for relief. Their prayers were answered when rain started falling, reviving their crops and lifting their spirits, leading them to give thanks publicly for God's gracious provision.

Hebrews 13:5

The Rev. Mackay was faced with loneliness and fear while embarking on a journey far from home as a missionary to Formosa in 1872, but in God's word he found great comfort. Despite moments of doubt and challenges, he found strength in the promise "Lo, I am with you always" and reaffirmed his commitment to Jesus as his captain upon reaching his new home.

God's work will not lack God's supply 153

Philippians 4:19

Giam Chheng Hoa, a young man of intelligence and seriousness, became the first convert of the missionary who had prayed for an intelligent and active young man. His conversion marked by resolve and conviction led him to become a prominent Christian preacher in North Formosa, overseeing the care of sixty churches in the mission.

Believer as former persecutor of the church 154

Acts 8:3 · Philippians 3:6

Go Ek Ju, a painter in Tamsui, used to bother A. Hoa until he converted to Christianity. Despite facing opposition from his mother and sisters, Go Ek Ju's family eventually embraced Christianity, with the son becoming a preacher and the mother a Bible woman.

Jesus will never send away those who come to Him 156

John 6:37

Countess Schimmelman tells of praying for a man named Tim Tode who had brutally murdered his family. Despite his denial, she prayed for his repentance and found joy when he eventually confessed and sought forgiveness through faith in Christ. This experience showed the power of prayer and the possibility of redemption even in the most tragic circumstances.

Deliverance from enemies and circumstances 158

Luke 1:71

During itinerant work, an evangelist and his brother encountered a potentially dangerous situation where robbers planned to attack them for their money. Despite being warned by the innkeeper, the group decided to pray to God for protection, resulting in the robbers becoming too afraid to carry out their plan and blessing the village instead.

Trusting in the Lord's intervention, they stayed in the village for two weeks, holding nightly prayer meetings that led to spiritual awakening and positive outcomes.

2 Corinthians 8:15 · Philippians 4:19

After years of straying from the Lord, Mr. Bidlake found redemption during the Melbourne Mission in Australia. Through divine intervention and the support of friends, he was able to pay off his £300 debt and join the Mission party, culminating in a mysterious and generous donation marked "The Lord's Release."

Matthew 18:19 · John 14:13-14 · John 16:23-24

Rev. George Grubb recounts a story where his friend, Mr. Millard, prayed for £60 to pay a debt on time. Despite not having the money, a mysterious cheque for that exact amount appeared on his desk, resolving the issue miraculously. Through faith and prayer, the debts were settled without any penny owed, demonstrating the power of trust in divine providence.

Matthew 9:18 · Matthew 19:13 · Mark 16:17-18 · Luke 4:40 · Acts 8:17 · Acts 9:12 · Acts 9:17 · Acts 13:3 · Acts 19:6 · Acts 28:8 · 1 Timothy 4:14 · 2 Timothy 1:6

William Greensmith, a boy with eye trouble that made him sensitive to light, was miraculously healed after a prayer by Mr. Bramwell during a visit to his father's house in Nottingham. John Clarke, who was near death with a severe fever, was also prayed for by Mr. Bramwell with great fervency and faith, leading to his sudden recovery and restoration to health.

2 Corinthians 5:16-17 · Galatians 6:15

A former opium-smoker testifies about his struggle to quit using prayer for strength, sharing how he overcame the addiction with God's help gradually. Through persistent prayer, he was able to gain victory over his opium addiction and never felt the desire for the drug again.

Philippians 4:6

Richard Weaver and his wife were facing hunger and poverty, but when they prayed for help, their class-leader's wife arrived with food and money, bringing them comfort and assurance that God answers prayers. Through the kindness of the class-leader's wife and an anonymous donation, their faith was strengthened, and they continued to trust in God's provision.

Mark 12:41-44 · Luke 21:1-4

Mr. Muller, prayed for financial help and received £137 from a railroad worker in Scotland who had saved the money for a time of need. The donor expressed joy in supporting the work of faith and shared that Mr. Muller's testimony had inspired their own trust in God's provision.

Matthew 6:11

George Muller and his co-workers were struggling to find food for their next meal but were miraculously helped by a kind gentleman who provided them with gold. This pattern of trust and provision continued over time, with their needs always being met in unexpected ways.

Philippians 4:19

George Muller and his co-workers prayed consistently for helpers, trusting that God would send the right people to help them rather than advertising for candidates. After praying daily for over three months for a laundress, their prayers were finally answered on October 26, 1865, showing God's commitment to supplying the needs of His work.

Matthew 26:36-46 · Mark 14:35-42 · Luke 22:42

Mary Winslow, in a time of great suffering and disability, prayed fervently for healing but heard a message to ask for submission instead. Upon doing so, her health greatly improved, leading her medical man to witness her miraculous recovery. Through submission to the Lord's will, Mary was healed and no longer burdened by her disability.

Deliverance from enemies and circumstances............................ 181

Luke 1:71

Mary Winslow shares how the Lord protected her family when a fire broke out in their room at night, allowing her to wake up in time and save herself and her children.

Gospel is the power of God for salvation 185

Romans 1:16

Dr. Jacob Chamberlain faced danger in Hyderabad when the enraged locals threatened to stone him for preaching about a different God. Instead of fleeing, he told them the story of Jesus with such power that they were moved to tears and bought his books to learn more about Christianity.

Willing to die for faith in Christ... 186

Acts 20:22-24

Robert Moffat and his associate Hamilton faced persecution and threats of death from the Bechuana people, who blamed them for a drought that killed many cattle. Despite the dangers they faced, Moffat bravely declared their resolve to stay and continue their work, showing remarkable courage and faith in the face of adversity. The chief, impressed by their fearless dedication, ultimately acknowledged the missionaries' conviction and the power of their beliefs regarding immortality.

Deliverance from enemies and circumstances............................ 190

Luke 1:71

In 1849, during a military expedition along the Rio Grande, a surgeon had a close call with a dangerous man named Mac. Despite threats on his life, the surgeon prayed for protection and found himself miraculously saved when Mac tragically died from an accident under his own wagon's wheels while trying to mount his mule. The surgeon, filled with awe, saw this as a direct answer to his prayer for deliverance.

Whatever you ask in prayer, in faith, abiding, you will receive.... 192

Matthew 21:22 · Mark 11:24 · John 15:7 · 1 John 5:14-15

A woman asked a man of God to pray for a young lady suffering from deep melancholy who was on the brink of insanity. After united prayer, the young lady was miraculously cured and found happiness again, demonstrating the power of faith and prayer.

Don't be anxious, instead make requests known to God 193

Philippians 4:6

An invalid girl's pet dog faced the threat of being sold due to an unpaid tax, causing distress to the girl. Despite unanswered prayers, a letter arrived at the last minute with the exact amount needed to save the pet, bringing joy and relief to the girl and her father, allowing the dog to stay with them.

Timely prayer for someone far away...................................... 194

Matthew 18:19 · John 4:53

A woman fell ill and felt unworthy to pray for herself, but remembered that Jesus was her sanctification, finding peace and comfort. Meanwhile, a group of ministers in a country town prayed for her as she lay at the point of death, and their prayers were answered quickly, teaching the woman the power of interceding for others in need.

Timely prayer for someone far away...................................... 196

Matthew 18:19 · John 4:53

A woman traveling in Turkey with a group of friends faced danger on a narrow, steep path and in a poorly secured room, but prayed for protection and was saved from potential harm. Through the combined prayers of the woman and her godly mother in England, they both felt God's presence and protection in their separate locations, demonstrating the power of prayer in times of peril.

Believers exchange superstition for faith in Christ......................201

Acts 19:18-19

A missionary in China shares a tale of prayers being answered by God, as the household of a teacher, Mr. Ting, against all odds removed idolatrous items and even burned an ancestral tablet, a sacred item in their culture.

Death for the believer is to be with Christ................................211

Philippians 1:21-23 · 1 Thessalonians 4:13

As the French steamship "Ville de Havre" sank, some passengers were rescued by the "Loch Earn" but faced imminent danger due to the ship's disabled condition. Mr. Cook, a minister onboard, led them in prayer and reassured them of rescue, which came unexpectedly when the "British Queen" changed course and saved them, demonstrating faith and divine providence.

Deliverance from enemies and circumstances...........................215

Luke 1:71

In a trial between a Christian and an unbeliever over a false accusation of debt, the jury struggled to determine the truth due to conflicting testimonies. Through prayer and deliberation, the jury unanimously found the Christian to be honest and acquitted him, reaffirming the power of prayer in seeking justice.

Spiritual burden for a lost people group to be saved 217

Romans 9:1-3

During a difficult time in the mission to Tahiti, the London Missionary Society considered giving up due to lack of converts. However, Dr. Haweis and Matthew Wilks advocated strongly for continuing the mission, leading to a special season of prayer that resulted in significant success, with news of a powerful work of God reaching the missionaries from both London and Tahiti in a remarkable coincidence. Prayer and faith were rewarded with the conversion of the people and the overthrow of idolatry in Tahiti, proving that perseverance and trust in God's promise can bring about miraculous outcomes.

Walking Together Press is a non-profit publishing company devoted to supporting grassroots libraries in Africa through global book sales and through providing free library editions.

To read our story, to see our catalog, and to learn more about how you can help us in our mission, visit our website at:

walkingtogether.press